Pelican Books
Pelican Geography and Environmental Studies
Editor: Peter Hall

Geology and Scenery in Ireland

After graduating in Geography at Reading University in 1952,
John Whittow studied landform evolution in North Wales, for
which he was awarded a Ph.D. in 1957. He has held university
teaching posts in Ireland, East Africa and Australia and has also
been a Research Associate at the University of California, Los
Angeles. He has contributed to *Collier's Encyclopedia*, *The Grolier
Book of Knowledge* and *Encyclopaedia Brittanica*. At present he is
Senior Lecturer in Geography at the University of Reading.
He is co-editor of *Essays in Geography for Austin Miller* (1965)
and co-author of the revised edition of A. E. Trueman,
Geology and Scenery in England and Wales, (Pelican Books, 1971).
A Fellow of the Royal Geographical Society, he is at present
Chairman of the Landscape Research Group, U.K.
John Whittow is married, with one daughter.

GEOLOGY AND SCENERY
IN IRELAND

J. B. WHITTOW

PENGUIN BOOKS

Penguin Books Ltd, Harmondsworth,
Middlesex, England
Penguin Books Inc., 7110 Ambassador Road,
Baltimore, Maryland 21207, U.S.A.
Penguin Books Australia Ltd, Ringwood,
Victoria, Australia
Penguin Books Canada Ltd,
41 Steelcase Road West, Markham, Ontario, Canada
Penguin Books (N.Z.) Ltd,
182–190 Wairau Road, Auckland 10, New Zealand

First published 1974

Made and printed in Great Britain by
Richard Clay (The Chaucer Press) Ltd, Bungay, Suffolk

To Diane

Contents

Acknowledgements

The publishers wish to thank the following for permission to use their photographs: Bord Fáilte for plates 10, 15, 16, 19, 20, 22, 27, 29, 30, 33 and 34: copyright reserved; Aerofilms Ltd for plates 1, 2, 3, 6, 7 and 25: copyright reserved; Dr J. K. St Joseph, Cambridge University Collection for plates 4, 5, 8, 11, 12, 13, 14, 17, 18, 21, 31, 32, 37 and 38: copyright reserved; Mr R. B. Parry for plate 28; the author supplied plates 9, 23, 24, 26, 35 and 36.

The map on the back cover together with figures 11, 26, 28, 29, 30 and 33 are based on the Ordnance Survey by permission of the Government of the Republic of Ireland (Permit No. 1994). Figures 3, 4, 15, 16, 21, 25 and 36 are based on maps in publications by the late Professor J. K. Charlesworth and are reproduced by permission of Mrs Charlesworth. Figures 12 and 14 are based on diagrams drawn by Professor E. E. Evans and are included with his permission. Figures 37, 38, 39 and 45 are reproduced by permission of the Director of the Royal Irish Academy. Dr M. M. Sweeting kindly gave permission to reproduce figure 24 and Mr F. M. Synge kindly agreed for figure 43 to be included. Associated Book Publishers Ltd gave their permission to include figures 19 and 35 from: T. W. Freeman, *Ireland, A general and regional geography*, 1972; as did Longman Group Ltd for the inclusion of figure 17 adapted from A. R. Orme, *The World's Landscapes, 4 – Ireland*, 1970.

Acknowledgement is gratefully given to Mrs M. Rolley for her help with typing the manuscript and to Mrs K. King who drew the majority of the diagrams.

List of Plates

List of Text Figures

Preface

Some thirty-five years ago Sir Arthur Trueman wrote a book which described and explained the *Geology and Scenery in England and Wales* and this has become something of a classic in its field. In 1970, after having completed (with a colleague, Dr John Hardy) a thorough revision of Sir Arthur Trueman's text (Penguin Books, 1971), I recognized the need for companion volumes on the scenery of Ireland and of Scotland in order to complete a survey of the British Isles. This book – *Geology and Scenery in Ireland* – is intended to go some way towards achieving this end. In the same way that the earlier volume was designed to appeal to interested laymen as well as to students in schools, training colleges and those beginning at university, this volume has been written with the same type of readers in mind.

In recent years there has been a marked growth in outdoor pursuits, linked partly with the increase in leisure time and partly with the greater mobility encouraged by the growing numbers of car owners. Associated with these there has been a reawakening of interest in the countryside together with a greater sense of inquiry as the horizons of the urban dweller have been widened. It is hoped that in this book many of the queries concerning landscape evolution will be answered and that Irish scenery will appear more interesting to the numerous tourists who visit Ireland, primarily to enjoy its unspoiled rural charm. Almost untouched by the Industrial Revolution, Ireland retains landscapes which have all but disappeared in Britain. Its townscapes too have remained largely unaltered for centuries and in the present volume an attempt has been made to describe and explain the character and layout of the larger towns in terms of their building-stones and their adaptation to the local topography.

The geology of Ireland has many affinities with that of highland Britain and frequent comparisons are made with the scenery of these areas. There are many facets of the English scene, however, which are missing in Ireland, partly due to the dearth of rocks younger than the Carboniferous. The lack of major mineral resources, especially the Coal Measures, has also deprived the Irish landscape of the widespread industrialization so characteristic of the British coalfields. Above all, the effects of the Ice Age are more marked in Ireland than in Britain, so much so that Irish terminology has been adopted internationally to describe certain of the glacial and glacio-fluvial landforms. It certainly appears to be true that climatic differences on either shore of the Irish Sea have helped to create landforms of marked contrast, not least in terms of their stature. Finally, the cultural and economic differences have produced landscapes unique in the British Isles. This is especially true the farther west one travels, into the realms of Atlantic Ireland.

I have not attempted to write a textbook of geological principles or a geological history of Ireland, for there are existing works which cover these aspects quite thoroughly. Thus, there is only a short introduction to the basic concepts of rock formation, stratigraphy and the geological time-scale, whilst the few technical terms which are included in the text are explained more precisely in the glossary. Although those with some geological knowledge may prefer to turn randomly to the regions which they know the best, it would be advantageous for the layman to read systematically from the beginning, since many of the more important concepts of landform genesis are introduced in the earlier chapters.

November 1972

J.B.W.

1. The Anatomy of Landscape

Owing to its geographical location to the west of Britain it is not surprising that Ireland exhibits close geological and scenic relationships with Scotland and Wales but has less similarity with the geology and scenery of England, especially that of eastern and southern England. It will be shown in subsequent chapters, therefore, that many of the Irish structures can be traced across the intervening waters of the North Channel and the Irish Sea to link with their counterparts in Scotland and Wales. Even a cursory glance at the geological map will demonstrate to the reader how the lines along which many of the Irish rocks are orientated exhibit two major trends. In the northern two-thirds of the island the rock alignment is generally from north-east to south-west, whilst in the southern third, in the province of Munster, the trend is approximately east to west. The first of these trends is the one which dominates much of highland Britain and since it is most characteristic in Scotland it has been called the Caledonian trend. The east–west trend, on the other hand, can be found elsewhere only in South Wales, North Devon and the Bristol area and is in reality part of an arcuate line which in Kerry and West Cork runs in a south-westerly direction and which near Bristol has swung round to a south-easterly bearing. This is termed the Armorican trend because farther south it can be traced in the older rocks of Brittany (formerly Armorica).

Both of these trend lines represent bygone periods of mountain building during which times the existing sedimentary rocks were folded and subsequently uplifted to form high ranges of fold mountains. Because the pressures responsible for the folding came from a different direction on each of the two occasions, the rocks have aligned themselves generally at right angles to these pressures, so producing the contrasting 'grain' of the Caledonian and Armorican tracts of country described above. Lengthy periods of denudation have subsequently reduced the ancient fold mountain ranges to the hills of the present landscape but they have been unable to obliterate completely these major geological structures which now give distinctive trends to various regions of Ireland (figure 1). It is important to note, however, that not all the Irish rocks exhibit these structures. Thus, in order to explain, for example, the geological layout of central Ireland or the general disposition of the rocks of Mayo, one must look at the historical geology of Ireland, for only then can the major periods of deposition, folding and uplift be related to the geological succession.* Figure 2 illustrates the various rock formations which are found in the British Isles, grouped according to their age, with the oldest at the foot of the table. Many of the rocks referred to in the adjoining table are sedimentary rocks, formed either as marine deposits of lime-stone, gravel, sand or mud on the sea-floor, or as continental deposits of similar sediments formed in lakes, rivers or on the land-surface itself. Geologists have subdivided the eras into a number of periods, the relation-ships of which were initially worked out by an intensive study of fossil assemblages contained within the sedimentary rocks. It was known that organisms, both plant and animal, evolved over a period of time and by examining these sequential changes in the fossil remains it became possible to establish a chronological succession for those sedimentary rocks. The simple law of superposition, i.e. oldest rocks at the bottom and newest at the top, may have seemed at first sight to provide sufficient evidence on which to base a straightforward geological succession. It was not long, however, before studies of fossils suggested that in regions which had experienced severe folding the succession may have been turned completely upside down, as in some of the 'nappe' structures of the Alps. A further complication of the law of superposition was also found wher-ever severe thrust-faulting had affected the rocks. In these cases tangential pressures may have caused enormous slices of the upper crustal rocks to have fractured and been carried forward across adjoining immobile rocks, with the final result that older rocks are now left on top of newer rocks, although divided from them by a thrust fault. Such a situation is some-times found within the Devonian and Carboniferous rocks of Munster since they have been subjected to the severe pressures of Armorican folding and faulting.

* The reader is referred to the various works of Professor J. K. Charlesworth who has dealt adequately with these aspects of the historical geology.

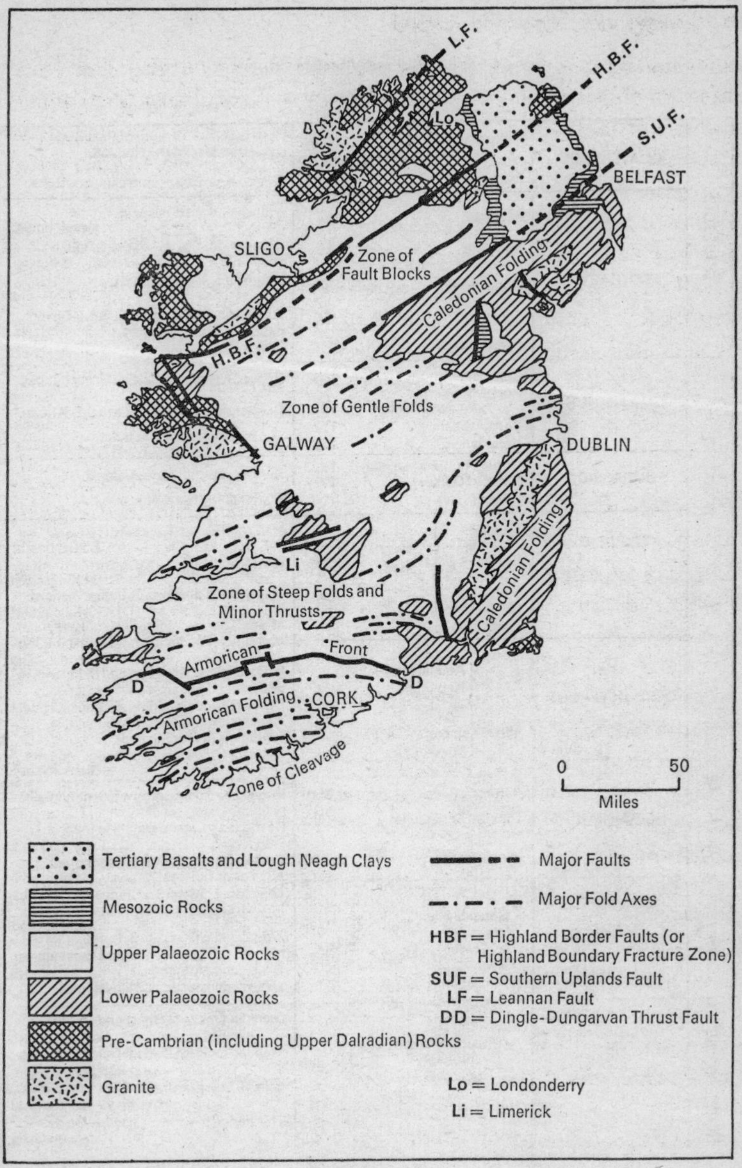
L.F.
H.B.F.
S.U.F.
Lo
BELFAST
SLIGO
Zone of Fault Blocks
Caledonian Folding
H.B.F.
Zone of Gentle Folds
GALWAY
DUBLIN
Li
Caledonian Folding
Zone of Steep Folds and Minor Thrusts
Armorican
Front
D
D
Armorican Folding
CORK
Zone of Cleavage
0
50
Miles
Tertiary Basalts and Lough Neagh Clays
Mesozoic Rocks
Upper Palaeozoic Rocks
Lower Palaeozoic Rocks
Pre-Cambrian (including Upper Dalradian) Rocks
Granite
Major Faults
Major Fold Axes
HBF = Highland Border Faults (or Highland Boundary Fracture Zone)
SUF = Southern Uplands Fault
LF = Leannan Fault
DD = Dingle-Dungarvan Thrust Fault
Lo = Londonderry
Li = Limerick

Fig. 1. *The Structural Geology of Ireland.*

			Absolute Time-scale (BP = Before Present)	Events in Ireland
CAINOZOIC	QUATERNARY	Holocene	12,000 BP Millions BP	Post-Glacial. Growth of Peat Bogs. Appearance of Man in Ireland.
		Pleistocene	c. 1.5	The Ice Age. Deposition of glacial drifts.
	TERTIARY	Pliocene	c. 7	Widespread erosion and drainage development.
		Miocene	26	Widespread uplift. Possible folding in Munster.
		Oligocene	38	Lough Neagh clays. Ballymacadam clays, Tipperary.
		Eocene	54	Vulcanicity in N.E. Ireland. Intrusion of plutonics of the Mournes, Carlingford and Slieve Gullion.
		Palaeocene	65	
MESOZOIC	CRETACEOUS	Chalk	100	Upper Chalk of N.E. Ireland. Tiny outcrop near Killarney.
		Upper Greensand and Gault	105	Thin sandstones and marls in S.E. Antrim.
		Lower Greensand	112	} Not represented in Ireland.
		Wealden	136	
	JURASSIC	Upper (Portlandian etc.)	162	} Not represented in Ireland.
		Middle (Oolites)	172	
		Lower (Lias)	195	Shales and clays in N.E. Ireland.
	TRIASSIC	Keuper		Marls and sandstones in N.E. Ireland. Salt deposits.
		Bunter } New Red Sandstone	225	Marls, sandstones, gypsum in Antrim and at Kingscourt.
PALAEOZOIC	PERMIAN	including Magnesian Limestone	280	Magnesian limestone at Cultra, marls at Kingscourt. Mineralization. Armorican or Hercynian orogeny – a period of mountain-building and folding.
	CARBONIFEROUS	Upper { Ammanian / Namurian	325	Major coal measures formed in Ireland. Widespread grit and shale formation. Ballycastle coals and sandstones. Limerick vulcanicity. Widespread limestone formation (including reefs).
		Lower { Visean / Tournaisian	345	'Carboniferous slates' of South Munster (Culm facies).
	DEVONIAN	Kiltorcan Beds	c. 350	Widespread deposition of 'continental' conglomerates, sandstones and flagstones. No marine deposits known in Ireland.
		Old Red Sandstone	c. 370	Vulcanicity at Killarney, Cushendall and Curlew Mts. Intrusion of major granite plutons of Donegal, Galway, Newry and Leinster. Mineralization. Caledonian orogeny – a period of mountain-building and folding.
		Dingle Beds	c. 390	
	SILURIAN		440	
	ORDOVICIAN	Generally referred to as Lower Palaeozoic	500	Ordovician vulcanicity in Connacht, Tyrone and East Leinster.
	CAMBRIAN		570	Widespread formation of grits, sandstones, shales, mudstones and limestones.
PROTEROZOIC	PRE-CAMBRIAN OR ARCHAEAN	including Dalradian (Upper Dalradian is probably of Lower Palaeozoic Age)	Pre-600	Dalradian rocks of Ulster and Connacht – highly metamorphosed and folded. Moinian rocks of Donegal and Connacht. Torridonian of Scotland unrepresented in Ireland. Lewisian igneous rocks of Donegal, Connacht and Wexford. This period may have lasted some 3,000 million years.

Fig. 2. *Table of Geological Succession.*

So far we have concerned ourselves only with explanations concerning the order in which the layered or sedimentary rocks were laid down, but an examination of figure 2 will show that there are two other types of rocks included within the geological succession, the igneous and the metamorphic rocks. The formation of the igneous or 'fire-formed' rocks, which are created from different varieties of formerly molten material, will be described in detail in chapter two, but it is important to notice at this juncture that because of the genetic difference between sedimentary and igneous rocks the latter do not contain fossils and must therefore be dated in other ways. The order of formation of igneous rocks and their relationship with the surrounding sedimentary rocks have, until recent years, been the only methods available to determine their relative ages, but today radiometric dating, based on studies of the decay of radioactive minerals within the rocks, has given a fairly sound basis for the determination of absolute dating. Thus, the absolute time-scale shown in figure 2 has been based largely on radiometric dating and, providing that the datable rocks, most of which are igneous, can be related to the succession, then the approximate age and length of the geological periods can be established.

Metamorphic rocks, the detailed characteristics of which will be described in subsequent chapters, especially chapter five, differ in their mode of formation from both sedimentary and igneous rocks. The majority of metamorphic rocks were formerly rocks of sedimentary origin that have experienced either prolonged regional pressures or metamorphism by contact with hot molten material from magmatic sources. In either case the detailed character of the minerals and the particles which make up the sedimentary rocks has been radically altered and the rocks converted to metasediments. In some cases the finer-grained rocks have been given a slatey cleavage which cuts across the former layering or bedding planes of the sediments. Generally speaking the changes wrought by intense regional pressures were more widespread than those caused by contact or thermal metamorphism which were localized to the immediate vicinity of the igneous material. Thermal metamorphism on a much larger scale is best seen in the metamorphic aureoles which surround the enormous granitic intrusions of Donegal, the Mournes and Leinster, described in chapters five, eight and seventeen respectively.

Although the complete geological succession for the British Isles is included in figure 2 it will soon become clear that several of the periods are unrepresented in Ireland. In a few cases it seems probable that the sedimentary rocks were never laid down but in other cases there is evidence to suggest that some of the later rocks have been destroyed by subsequent denudation. A tiny patch of Cretaceous Chalk near Killarney and some Tertiary clays in Tipperary suggest, for example, that Mesozoic and early Tertiary rocks may once have extended over much of Ireland. Where certain rock formations or geological periods are missing the gap in the field record is known as an unconformity, with newer rocks in some cases resting unconformably on rocks considerably older, since the rocks of intermediate age may have been worn away or never deposited. This is particularly true of the Mesozoic rocks in Ireland and if we were to speculate on the major scenic differences between England and Ireland it would probably be to the Mesozoic era that we should turn to seek an explanation. Two of the most characteristic features of the English landscape are the rolling Chalk downs and the great Cotswold stone belt with its beautiful honey-coloured villages. The dearth of Chalk has robbed the Irish scene of its scarplands, its flint-faced cottages and its dazzling white sea cliffs; the lack of the Jurassic freestones, such as the Portland stone and the Bath stone, has stifled Irish vernacular architecture. Furthermore, as if it were not enough to lose most of its Palaeozoic Coal Measures by denudation, the valuable Jurassic ironstones too are missing in Ireland.

Except for the volcanic upheaval in north-east Ireland and the deposition of the Lough Neagh Clays there is an enormous gap in the geological record in the 100 million years which have elapsed since the deposition of the Lower Chalk. One can only assume that during most of this time the Irish land-surface was being denuded by a variety of agents. Running water must have been the most important, although mechanical weathering and deep chemical weathering (especially by solution of the calcareous rocks) must also have played important parts. The intermittent tectonic uplift and the lengthy periods of downwearing must have been recurrent themes during Tertiary times, when the Irish river systems established themselves on the slowly evolving land-surface. Finally, it may seem surprising that the shortest of the geological eras, the Quaternary (*c.* 1·5 million years), had the most profound effect on the Irish landscape. Glacial erosion radically altered the highland scenery whilst the ice-sheets transported countless millions of tons of eroded material to the lowlands where it forms the ubiquitous glacial drifts. It must be remembered, however, that despite their widespread distribution these glacial drifts and their overlying post-glacial peats are but a thin veneer when compared with the many thousands of feet of solid rocks which they bury.

The foregoing account of the major geological and geomorphological factors responsible for the shaping of the Irish landforms does not quite complete the record. The scenery of today consists not only of these basic forms but also of the thin but fundamental mantle created by Man, which has changed the land-surface into a landscape. Landscape (or scenery) combines the topographic forms with all the complex mosaics created by human endeavour and is in reality an expression of the total environment. Landscape is, of course, dynamic; it changes through time, sometimes slowly, sometimes rapidly; it changes through natural forces and by human activities. In the following chapters we shall look at various examples of Irish scenery in an attempt to explain the changes which have finally created the countryside of Ireland that we see today.

2. The Antrim Plateau

Most visitors to Belfast arrive either by sea or by air and in both cases they would be impressed by the line of steep hills which overlook the city from the west (figure 12). From Black Mountain at the south-western end to Cave Hill in the north the crest of the hills runs for six miles with scarcely a break, save where the road to the airport climbs steeply over the skyline. This line of hills, which rises to a series of cliffs more than 1,500 feet above the city, is in fact an escarpment, forming the south-eastern edge of the Antrim Plateau. If one were to climb the steep slopes of Cave Hill itself, it would be possible to see that these cliffs were made of black rock layers, weathering to a rusty brown where exposed to the elements. At first the rocks might be mistaken for bedded sedimentary rocks but closer inspection would reveal that they are solidified lava flows, composed of an igneous rock termed basalt. The cliffs from here to Black Mountain happen to result from the thickest known single flow (150 feet), although more commonly, in other sections of the Antrim Plateau margin, series of thinner flows (individually only 20–30 feet thick) are found, but these have succeeded in building up an enormous thickness of lava.

The basaltic province of north-east Ireland occupies an area of some 1,500 square miles and is the largest and most continuous fragment of these rocks to be seen anywhere in the British Isles (figure 3). Similar lava flows can be seen in north-west Scotland, especially in Skye and Mull, and together these parts of the British Isles are often referred to by geologists as the Tertiary Igneous Province for it is known that the volcanic activity took place in early Tertiary times. Basaltic lava cliffs, similar to those in Antrim, can also be seen in the Faroes, Iceland and Greenland and modern lavas, on a much smaller scale, are occasionally forming today in association with the Icelandic volcanoes. It has been suggested that the Irish lavas were once part of the vast Brito–Greenlandic

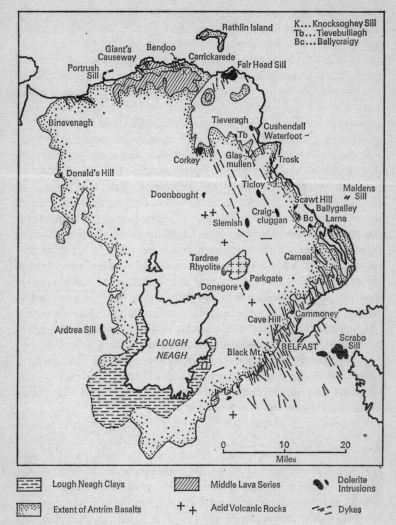

Fig. 3. *The distribution of the Tertiary igneous rocks in north-east Ireland (after J. K. Charlesworth et al.).*

Province and that large areas have been destroyed by subsequent denudation and others increasingly isolated after Continental Drift had
opened up the Atlantic Ocean to its present width.

There is little doubt that in Ireland itself the lavas formerly extended
much greater distances than their present-day limits, for basaltic outliers
can be found at Poyntz Pass and Markethill in County Armagh and at
1,500 feet on the flanks of Slieve Gallion, west of Lough Neagh; all of
these were once part of the main lava plains but have been cut off by
erosion from the main basalt outcrop. It must not be thought, therefore,
that the present steep cliff edges, which flank the basalt plateau on all
sides, represent the terminal limits of the lava flows, for these are scarps
produced by subsequent uplift and denudation of the lava plains. The
escarpments have gradually been worn back by millions of years of
weathering and erosion since the lavas were first poured out from numerous crustal fissures in Eocene times. Consequently small outliers such as
those mentioned above represent unconsumed relics of a former continuous basaltic cover which may have extended scores of miles beyond
the present limits. Calculations have shown that in this same period of
time the surface of the lavas in east Antrim may have been lowered by
erosion by as much as 1,500 feet. Nevertheless, this still leaves an extraordinary mass of lavas at the centre of the basaltic province, for a borehole
near Lough Neagh has revealed a thickness approaching 2,600 feet.

Topographically speaking, only the country east of the Bann Valley is
referred to as the Antrim Plateau, so we shall concern ourselves solely
with this tract in the present chapter. The remainder of the basaltic
province of Ulster will be described in chapter three.

North Antrim

It would be most convenient to begin any description of the igneous
rocks of Ulster in the holiday resort of Portrush on the north coast of
Antrim, for not only is it a splendid centre for exploration of the basaltic
landforms of this region but it is also the site at which a storm of geological
controversy raged at the beginning of the nineteenth century. Here on
the foreshore some flaggy outcrops of grey rock contain fossil ammonites.
The rock is in fact part of the Lias Clay, one of the lowest sedimentary
rocks formed in Jurassic times, although its extremely hard texture would

not suggest a clay to a non-geologist. Since it was formed as a marine mud with its included organisms it has not only become solidified by the weight of overlying sediments but it has also been baked by the close proximity of a much later invasion of molten lava of Eocene age. Such a change in character is known as metamorphism (see glossary).

At the end of the eighteenth century a school of geologists had developed at the University of Freiburg in Germany under Professor Werner and it was their considered opinion that all rocks, including those we now call igneous (fire-formed), could be explained by formation in water. Although they would admit that some contemporaneous lavas, as seen at Vesuvius, were of volcanic origin, they insisted that basalts and other crystalline rocks found elsewhere were chemical precipitates from water, usually sea water. These scholars were termed 'Neptunists', whose views were opposed by the so-called 'Vulcanists' (or 'Plutonists') who believed in the formation of igneous rocks from magmatic sources, a belief now utterly vindicated. Since Neptunism linked closely with the Old Testament description of the Flood, however, the early opponents of the Neptunist doctrines were regarded as nothing less than heretics. It is now known that the true character of the sedimentary Lias Clay outcrop at Portrush must have been completely altered by the heat of the lava flow which had forced its way along the bedding planes of the rock to give it the flinty, basalt-like appearance of a metamorphic rock. But because of its included fossils the Neptunists believed that here they had incontrovertible proof of the aqueous origin of basalt (or dolerite) and it was not until 1835 that the true nature of the doleritic intrusion between the bedding planes of the altered Portrush Lias Clay was established. Such a sheet-like mass of igneous rock forced in between beds of sedimentary rocks is now termed a sill (see p. 280), but it is easy to imagine the confusion that must have arisen when such phenomena were first discovered.

A short drive eastwards from Portrush, through the towns of Bush Mills and Ballycastle, brings us to the north-east corner of Ireland where a bastion of the Antrim Plateau forms a magnificent headland known as Fair Head. Although we have left the plateau basalt country the precipitous cliffs which face out across the North Channel to Scotland are composed of igneous rock in another sheet-like mass similar to that seen at Portrush, but this time some 200–250 feet thick. This is the well-known Fair Head Sill, almost as renowned as the Whin Sill of northern England.

It is composed mainly of olivine-rich dolerite with large crystals of augite and plagioclase clearly discernible in the rock. The cliffs are seamed with deep fissures where joint planes have been picked out by weathering, and these tend only to magnify the verticality of the scene for the rock itself has cooled in the form of gigantic columns, many tumbled portions of which lie in the form of a massive screen at the cliff foot (plate 1). At nearby Farrangandhu the lateral extent of the thick igneous rock can be seen to split into three or four separate masses which interdigitate with the bedded layers of sedimentary Carboniferous shales and sandstones, thus demonstrating that the dolerite was injected as a sill at a later date.

Fair Head is an intriguing place, not only as a viewpoint across to the black and white (basalt and chalk) cliffs of Rathlin Island and across the often turbulent sea to the Mull of Kintyre in Scotland, but also because of the heathery windswept summit with its three small, hidden loughs. One of these, Lough Na Cranagh, is named from the well-preserved crannog in its centre, an artificial feature, stone-wall girt, constructed as a defensive settlement in Neolithic times. Although it is isolated and grass-grown today it is interesting to speculate on the small group of the earliest Irish settlers who must have occupied this coastal hill, making use of the hard stone from the nearby igneous rocks for their rudimentary tools.

It is perhaps fitting that the pleasant little town of Ballycastle, nestling in its bay between Fair Head and the conspicuous hill of Knocklayd (1,695 feet), should have been the home of one of Ireland's most eminent geologists, Professor J. K. Charlesworth. For here is a region of geological treasures, all within walking distance of the town. The coastline is made up of steep sea cliffs, resulting mainly from the resistance to erosion of the igneous rocks, but Ballycastle has grown up at the confluence of three small rivers which drain the plateau that rises to the south. Ballycastle was once a small coal-mining centre and at first such a fact would probably excite no comment, for it has been noted how the Fair Head Sill was intruded into horizontally bedded layers of Carboniferous rocks. In England and Wales we have come to accept the knowledge that all coalfields are found in Carboniferous rocks, generally in the Coal Measures which were deposited after the formation of the Carboniferous Limestone and the Millstone Grit. At Ballycastle, however, we have to amend our ideas for here the coal seams occur within the Carboniferous Limestone Series, together with beds of sandstone and ironstone. Most of the seams are very thin and the coal of poor quality, so that today mining has virtu-ally ceased. It is surprising to find that Ballycastle is essentially a holiday resort untrammelled with the ribbon-built miners' dwellings, colliery clutter and mineral lines so characteristic of the British coalfields. It was fortunate that the decline of the coal trade coincided with the discovery of the town as a watering-place and there seems little doubt that the geological character of the district contributed to the attractiveness of Ballycastle as a tourist centre, not least for its proximity to the Giant's Causeway. But before describing this most famous and spectacular of Irish igneous landforms it would be useful to review the igneous record of the region.

The Tertiary igneous activity of Ireland can be divided into five main episodes: first, there came the outpouring of the basalt lavas as the land of Ulster became fissured and cracked by fault lines, allowing the magma to be extruded quietly and without much apparent violence, since volcanic tuffs and ashes, which are generally associated with explosive activity, are rare. In many places in north-east Ireland the lavas flowed out over a landscape of Cretaceous Chalk, and occasionally charred re-mains are found of a fossil vegetation which flourished on this former land-surface. The junction between the black basalt and the white chalk is often marked by a narrow band of bright red soil, stained from the same iron compounds in the basalt which cause its freshly broken black crystal-line surface to weather into a rust-coloured mass.

After the formation of the hundreds of feet of basaltic lavas, which were later to be uplifted and eroded into the tableland of the Antrim Plateau, there followed a short period of explosive activity during which the volcanic vents were created (figure 3). As volcanic gases at depth built up enormous pressures, so areas of weakness allowed their escape through the crust at points where volcanic pipes or necks can now be seen in the landscape. The vents were drilled through the crust in the same way that contemporary volcanoes, such as Etna or Stromboli, throw out their ash, dust and lava to build their volcanic cones and craters. The less consoli-dated Irish cones, however, have long since been weathered away and only the plug of lava which cooled slowly in the vent, generally in the form of a hard dolerite, remains to form a conspicuous steep-sided hill in an otherwise rolling plateau landscape. Where cooling was rapid the rocks exhibit a small or finely crystalline structure, as noted in the basalt lava flows. If, on the other hand, the cooling was slow, as in the rocks which cool at depth (hence the term plutonic rocks), then the crystals are generally large or coarse, as in the granites.

The third episode is thought to mark the declining phase of volcanic activity in Ireland, for this is the period of sill formation. When the magma had insufficient energy to penetrate what must now have been a prodigious thickness of lava flows, it flowed underground along the bedding planes of the sedimentary rocks as we have already seen at Portrush and the Fair Head Sill. Consequently, the magma cooled rather more slowly and although it retained the chemical composition of the surface basalts its crystal structure differs from these in its somewhat coarser texture.

The penultimate episode in the Tertiary igneous history of Ireland need not detain us long at this juncture, for the intrusion of the plutonic rocks will be examined in detail in chapter eight. The magmatic chambers which supplied the lavas responsible for the great variety of the landforms in north-east Ireland are not exposed in Antrim. One must look farther south, to the Mournes and the mountains of Carlingford.

Finally, the Ulster landscape is seamed with hundreds of narrow linear igneous outcrops known as dykes. Since these are seen to cut quite indiscriminately through all but the Lough Neagh Clays (chapter three), amongst the Ulster rocks, be they sedimentary, igneous or metamorphic, one can conclude that the dyke 'swarms' were the final chapter in the history of volcanic activity in the British Isles. In Scotland, the width of the Tertiary dykes is fairly uniform, being of the order of 10 feet. In Ireland there is less uniformity, with dykes varying in width from a few inches to tens of feet. The dykes are characterized by a finely crystalline structure, which suggests that they cooled rapidly as they were forced vertically upwards from the magma chamber through thousands of feet of overlying crust. The dyke swarms can generally be traced to a handful of major plutonic centres, so that it is common to talk of the Mourne swarm, for example. The high temperatures of the lava within the dykes caused considerable baking of the rocks through which they passed and this is particularly marked where the Chalk has been changed into a crystalline limestone, or marble, by contact metamorphism. Sometimes this metamorphosed rock may be so tough that it will resist denudation more effectively than the dyke itself, so that the line of the dyke may be marked by a linear trench in the landscape. More often, however, the dyke itself is harder than the surrounding rocks and stands up from the surface like a man-made wall. A particularly striking example of such a dyke can be seen in Ballycastle Bay, east of the golf links, where the North Star Dyke projects like an artificial breakwater into the sea.

Before leaving Ballycastle it would be interesting to note that the dome-shaped hill of Knocklayd (1,695 feet), the forestry plantations of which now reach halfway up its slopes, was the scene of an amusing hoax in the late eighteenth century. Accounts appeared in the Irish press about a volcanic eruption on its summit, reputedly associated with a stream of lava which engulfed several settlements. It is now known that such a volcanic outburst did not take place and that a combination of the earliest accounts concerning the volcanic origin of the basalts of Knocklayd, together with a possible catastrophic bog-burst (see p. 40) on its steep slopes, may have been responsible for such a fascinating tale. No volcanic activity has occurred in the British Isles for millions of years, so it is pointless to look for such features as craters in the landscape.

From the south-west slopes of Knocklayd a low ridge runs westwards past Armoy towards Ballymoney, and a glance at the drainage pattern of this area reveals that the courses of both the river Bush and the Breckagh Burn have been affected by this ridge. It represents a terminal moraine, not of a local Irish ice-cap but of an ice-sheet which extended this far south from a very late re-advance of Scottish ice (figure 5). Thus the so-called North Antrim Re-advance ice destroyed the landforms created by earlier Irish glacial advances and left a new spread of Scottish erratics in this north-eastern corner of Ireland. It is now possible to explain the curious courses of the streams mentioned above, for the Bush river must once have entered the sea at Ballycastle before being deflected westwards by the ice-sheet in question. Although not as spectacular as the sudden direction change of the Bush at Armoy, the drainage east of Ballymoney also exhibits the marked change of course resulting from glacial interference.

A picturesque coast road runs westwards out of Ballycastle towards Bush Mills and near the village of Ballintoy stands the fascinating sea-stack of Carrick-a-Rede. Between the mainland cliffs and the stack is a 20-yard chasm spanned by a rope bridge suspended alarmingly some 70 feet above the tide which rips through the gap. The rock formation is of particular interest, for here is the nearest approach that one can discover in Ulster to the landforms of a volcanic crater which formerly stood at this site; the sea has broken through the vent walls to expose the volcanic stratigraphy in the sea cliffs (figure 4). On the path from the road to the stack it is possible to examine a volcanic ash bed which encloses broken pieces of chalk, flint, and wisps of Lias Clay which became detached from

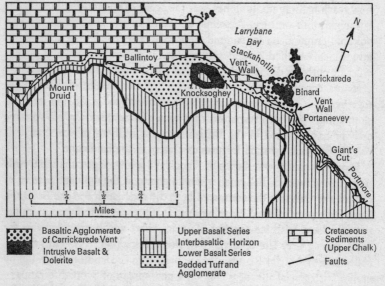

Fig. 4. *The geology of Carrick-a-Rede, North Antrim (after S. I. Tomkieff).*

the walls of the vent when the volcano burst through the crust in Tertiary times. In the sea cliffs themselves may be seen a volcanic agglomerate of basaltic blocks, volcanic bombs and tuffs which must have been thrown high into the air before falling back into the vent.

One may still be pondering the tumultuous events which characterized the geological history of this part of Ireland and speculating on the wonders of the Giant's Causeway, when suddenly the coast road at Ballintoy opens a vista to the west which seems wholly foreign to Ireland. Patches of downland, sloping seawards to dazzling white cliffs of Chalk, and the beautiful curve of the strand and sand dunes of White Park Bay could almost be a corner of south-east England. Numerous remains of Neolithic and Bronze Age occupation have made this a happy hunting-ground for archaeologists, because the ready supply of flint for tool-making helped to support a relatively large prehistoric population in this delightful spot. There are few places where the Chalk emerges from beneath the basalt for so great an extent and it provides a welcome interlude of pastoral countryside before one moves on to the majestic wilderness of the Causeway itself.

The Giant's Causeway

The rock formations which stand on the coast some two miles north of Bush Mills are not only Ireland's most famous geological heritage but rank amongst the world's leading scenic landforms (plate 2).

To take the track down the cliffs to the sea is an experience unique in the British Isles. Despite its solemn dignity, Fingal's Cave on Staffa pales into insignificance against the grandeur of the Causeway. It is little wonder that its earliest chroniclers established the legend of Finn Mac-Cool, the Irish giant who is reputed to have built the Causeway to link up with Scotland, for the architectural character of the rocks is such that it is difficult to conceive how nature could have fashioned such a phenomenon. Nevertheless, in 1694, a speaker dutifully informed the Royal Society that it could not be man-made owing to the lack of mortar between the columns!

There are three major topographic divisions: the Little Causeway, the Honeycomb Causeway, and the Grand Causeway, and as one wanders across the thousands of hexagonal basalt columns, with the sea often thundering against their fretted edges, the mind at last begins to grasp the significance of the Tertiary volcanic record in Ireland. It is here for all to see, layer upon layer of basaltic lavas, stepped upwards in the cliffs of the Amphitheatre to well over 500 feet, the Lower and Middle Basalts separated by the bright red streak of the Interbasaltic Bed.

The fluted basalt columns form the majority of the more fancifully-named features, the Giant's Chair, the Organ, the Fan, etc., and amongst these it is easy to examine the columnar structure of the basalt which resulted from its differential cooling. The columns are always arranged at right angles to the cooling surface and, since in the majority of cases this was horizontal, the columns are vertical. If, however, as at the Grand Causeway, the lava had occupied an existing valley then in some sections the columns are tilted obliquely, sometimes nearer to a horizontal than to a vertical plane. As the outpourings of the first volcanic phase came to an end there appears to have been a lengthy interval during which the lava surface was weathered sufficiently enough to produce a soil. Since the climate at the time was similar to that of the present-day Tropics we find that the soil on the deeply weathered surface of the Lower Basalts is a laterite, similar to the red soils of India, East Africa or Brazil. The deep weathering induced by the tropical sun and rain led to a concentration of residual iron hydroxide and aluminium hydroxide. Weathering of the basaltic columns often resulted in the destruction of all but the unconsumed core so that many of these black core-stones now remain in a bright-red lateritic matrix, giving rise to the local description of 'giant's eyes'. Sufficient iron is present in the Interbasaltic Bed to warrant extraction, so that in some parts of Antrim, although not at the Causeway, it has been extensively worked. Most of this Antrim iron ore was shipped to Cumberland from Red Bay or from Belfast, although working has now ceased. Also of some importance in former years was the aluminium hydroxide, or bauxite, often mined with the iron ores and, after treatment at Larne, transported to the smelters in Scotland. A third economic mineral found in the Interbasaltic Bed, and occasionally between the individual lava flows themselves (especially above the Organ), is lignite, a type of brown coal formed from plant remains, and once mined at Ballintoy. From a scientific viewpoint it is the plant remains of the Inter-basaltic Bed which are most significant for the light they throw on the environment of that period of Tertiary time. Carbonized tree trunks, leaf beds and twigs demonstrate that pine, oak, sequoia and eucalyptus flourished at this period, possibly during late Eocene times.

A resumption of volcanic activity saw the formation of the Middle Basalts and these fresh lavas would soon have buried the organic and weathered layers described above. The lava flows of the Middle Basalts are more strikingly columnar than those of the Lower, and make up the high amphitheatres of the Causeway. So striking are their similarities to classical buildings that Professor S. I. Tomkieff has borrowed architectural terms for their description: the lowest layer of the flow with its regular hexagonal columns is termed the colonnade, the middle layer of narrow, starchy columns is the entablature, while the uppermost thin grey slaggy top could be likened to the pediment. It is necessary to understand how such differences occurred in each lava flow, and as we might expect they are concerned with the different rates of cooling. The thin slaggy crust cooled rapidly to give an almost structureless mass; the middle part of the flow cooled less quickly so that it was able to develop a columnar structure. But it was a structure less regularly disposed than that of the lowest layer of the lava which cooled at an even slower rate and with a more uniform contraction pattern. It was the latter, therefore, which led to the formation of the most spectacular hexagonal columns, regularly spaced and left as pillars when isolated by weathering (plate 2).

The Hills and the Glens of Antrim

South of Fair Head a narrow and ill-frequented road leads past Murlough Bay and Torr Head to Cushendun. It is a perplexing journey, for in the space of ten miles we pass through as wide a variety of landscapes as it is possible to meet anywhere in Ireland in so short a distance. From the rocky treeless plateau formed by the Fair Head Sill, the country suddenly changes into a narrow belt of open chalk downland which in turn descends steeply northwards to the pleasantly wooded slopes of Murlough Bay. Here the coastal slopes are fashioned from a landslip complex of Triassic rocks, Chalk and basalt, although the picturesque whitewashed farmhouses are often built from blocks of Dalradian schist, a metamorphic rock of mainly pre-Cambrian age which occurs widely in this north-east corner of Antrim. As if the stratigraphical complexity were not puzzling enough, our journey takes us past a small plutonic intrusion before leaving us at the pretty village of Cushendun contemplating the spectacular sea-caves carved in Old Red Sandstone conglomerate.

To explain the apparent lack of order in the rock formations hereabouts it is necessary to know something of the rock structures which existed not only before the Tertiary volcanic episode but also before the Mesozoic rocks (Trias, Lias and Chalk) were deposited. A glance at a geological map of the British Isles will show that a series of major fractures or faults run from north-east to south-west in central Scotland. Two of these, the Highland Border Fault in the north and the Southern Uplands Fault in the south, are of the utmost importance for between them they enclose the Midland Valley of Scotland which is a rifted structure of Carboniferous and Old Red Sandstone rocks faulted down between flanking masses of older rocks which stand at higher elevations.

The geographical proximity of Ulster and Scotland is mirrored in their geological relationships for the two major faults can be traced southwestwards into Ireland, the Highland Border Fault coming onshore at Cushendun and the Southern Uplands Fault probably beneath Belfast Lough (see chapter seven). Thus the structures of the rifted Midland Valley of Scotland are repeated in Antrim although the topographic expression is different owing to the subsequent geological history of north-east Ireland. In place of the Midland Valley the hills of Antrim present a bold scarp front of lava-capped Mesozoic rocks to the North Channel. There is one exception, however, for here in north-east Antrim, in the area under discussion, these cover rocks have been almost stripped away by denudation to reveal the ancient structures of the basement rocks. It is now possible to see that the Old Red Sandstone at Cushendun has been preserved by downfaulting in the rift structure which is buried elsewhere in Antrim. In fact the northern mass of the rift valley shoulder flanking the Highland Border Fault is made up here of hard Dalradian schists which form the sea cliffs between Torr Head and Cushendun, and also the plateau country drained by the Glendun River. It is to the few surviving outliers of chalk and basalt, which formerly covered the whole of this ancient rock surface, that we owe much of the geological and scenic variety of the area. The schist areas are generally peat-covered, owing to the acid soils and poor drainage on these plateau tops, so the scene is often a dreary one of undulating heather moors broken only by the green expanse of the coniferous Ballypatrick Forest. On the small chalk outcrops and on the sandstones south of Glendun, however, the soils are generally lighter and less acid so that improved land with mixed farming becomes more characteristic.

The Antrim Plateau, composed almost entirely of basalts, stretches some 50 miles from here to Belfast and nowhere are the peat-covered uplands less than ten miles wide. In general the land stands more than 1,000 feet above sea level and were it not for the intervention of the deeply dissected glens this would be a drab and monotonous peat-covered landscape totally devoid of natural tree growth. Old surfaces of erosion have been recognized on these uplands where denudational processes have removed vast quantities of basalt before the onset of the Ice Age. The most marked of these upland surfaces of denudation, sometimes termed peneplains (see p. 109), is that which lies between 1,000 and 1,250 feet. A few undestroyed residuals stand above this level; in the south Agnew's Hill (1,563 feet) and Slemish (1,437 feet) while farther north Slieveanorra (1,676 feet), Slievenanee (1,782 feet) and Trostan (1,817 feet) form the highest summits of Antrim. They are thought to be remnants of a higher land-surface now destroyed by the rivers which fashioned the 1,000–1,250 feet surface, although Slemish has survived by virtue of its harder rocks. Slemish is a good example of a volcanic neck, with the huge plug of intruded rock rising dramatically above the smooth lava plateau east of Ballymena. Other volcanic necks play a prominent part in the diversification of the plateau landscape, for generally they introduce steeper slopes and more dramatic outlines. One of the best known is that of Tieveragh, which has a dolerite plug that forms a conspicuous hill overlooking the town of Cushendall. The vent of Scawt Hill, four miles south of Glenarm, is not so spectacular since it occurs in the face of the basalt escarpment. The Chalk at Ballygalley Head has been metamorphosed into marble by a volcanic neck, but one of the most interesting of the volcanic plugs is that at Tievebulliagh, west of Cushendall. Here the olivine-dolerite has cut through the Interbasaltic Bed, altering the lateritic material into an extremely hard, speckled metamorphic rock termed porcellanite. Such rock was in great demand by early man and a Neolithic axe-factory which developed here supplied both Britain and Ireland, judging by the widespread distribution of Tievebulliagh stone axes.

The Glens of Antrim bite deeply into the plateau all along its eastern margin. Each of the major settlements along the coast is located where the glens reach the sea, since there is virtually no coastal plain north of Larne. Glenariff, in the north, is the widest and most attractive, for its sides drop steeply from the plateau edge at 1,000 feet to the flat valley floor (plate 3). Because of the steep cliffs at the head of the glen, streams which rise on the plateau create picturesque waterfalls where they plunge into the valley, those of the Mare's Fall and the Fall of the Hooves in the so-called Fairy Glen being the best known. Glenariff is partly aligned along faults which have aided the river in its downcutting through the basalt capping. Triassic sandstones, Jurassic clay and Chalk form the middle and low slopes below the basalt cliffs, although it must be remembered that the slopes are often plastered with glacial drift, screes from the cliffs and patches of peat. This mixture sometimes forms a highly unstable mass subject to major slides, flows and slips on these steep slopes.

There is a long history of slope instability along the Antrim coast owing to a combination of tectonic and erosional factors. In the first instance the margins of both the basalt and the underlying Mesozoic rocks have been faulted down towards the sea along a series of parallel north–south faults associated with the formation of the rifted North Channel, probably in late Tertiary times. This is known as step-faulting, where each successive fault block on the seaward side drops lower than its neighbouring block on the landward side. During the Ice Age the plateau edge was again subject to major landslips which involved the displacement and rotational movement of blocks in a zone varying in width from a few yards up to two miles. Recent authors believe that the slumping was partly a result of undercutting of the plateau edge by a northward-moving Irish ice-sheet. As the ice melted the pressure was released and the support withdrawn, thus causing the oversteepened cliffs to collapse, leaving a jumble of small fault scarps, back-tilted slopes and enclosed hollows. Even in post-glacial times there is evidence of considerable mass-movement, ranging from rockfalls (probably due to freeze–thaw activity), through debris flows (movement of till and scree mixtures), to mudflows and bog-bursts, the latter being the most sudden and sometimes catastrophic. In Glendun, for example, there are scars of two recent bog-bursts where the peat, acting as an immense sponge during a period of prolonged rainfall, became over-saturated and flowed downhill. Mudflows are less dangerous owing to their slower movement, but they often pose considerable long-term threats to the Antrim coast road. They are always associated with steeply dipping outcrops of Liassic clays and shales because of the presence in these of the mineral, montmorillonite. The expansion properties of this particular mineral, when water is added, are remarkably great so that swelling and subsequent downslope movement results, sometimes at the rate of five inches per day.

The landscape of the Glens of Antrim has been enhanced by the way in which farmers have enclosed the fields, and from any viewpoint on the plateau edge the geometric outlines and harlequin colours of the fields on the slopes and valley floor illustrate the fascinating relationships between land use and topography. Here are excellent examples of the

Ulster striped or 'ladder' farms, with each holding rising from the marshy riverside meadows, through the arable land of the better drained slopes, sometimes to the deciduous woodland on the screes beneath the cliffs, sometimes to the rough grazing associated with the cliffs themselves. In most cases a stone wall terminates the upper limit of the holding at some 600 feet to 800 feet, whilst the stone-built farms, often dazzling white against the green backdrop of the hillslope, appear as beads on a necklace along the narrow road which flanks the valley floor (plate 3).

Before we leave the superbly engineered Antrim coast road, constructed during the nineteenth century along the difficult scarp-foot terrain of landslips, coastal cliffs and raised beach fragments, we must turn for a moment to an examination of sea-level changes in north-east Ireland for there is abundant evidence of Man's early settlement along these strandlines. It will be shown in more detail in later chapters how sea level fluctuated considerably along the coasts of Ulster during late-glacial and post-glacial times, due partly to tectonic movement and partly to worldwide changes in ocean levels. But at this time we need concern ourselves only with the post-glacial sea level, the raised beach of which is particularly well seen near Larne, Glenarm and Cushendun. Although it has been loosely termed the '25-foot beach' the height range of the 'raised' post-glacial sand and shingle deposits at these sites is between twenty and thirty feet above sea level. Excavation by Professor H. L. Movius, particularly at Larne, has revealed a multitude of stone implements in the beaches, together with some of the earliest evidence of fishing. The majority of scrapers, adzes, awls, blades and spear-heads were constructed from the ready-made supply of flint pebbles in the beaches and so remarkable is the collection of Mesolithic tools that a distinctive early Irish culture, termed Larnian, has been recognized. The rising post-glacial sea level, responding to the enormous quantities of water released from melting ice-sheets, ultimately drowned these coastal campsites, forcing the Mesolithic inhabitants to move inland where they were faced with marshes and forests in which they failed to improve on their simple hunting and food-collecting habits. Thus their impact on the landscape of Ireland was minimal and it was left to the invasion of the Neolithic farmers several hundred years later to begin the gradual change in the Irish landscape, a change which gathered momentum as the population grew in the succeeding centuries.

3. Lough Neagh and the Bann Lowlands

Despite its claim to be the largest sheet of fresh water in the British Isles (155 square miles) Lough Neagh makes curiously little impact on the traveller; its very size, its lack of major islands and woodlands, its fairly regular shape and, above all, the low elevation of the surrounding terrain combine to lessen its attraction from a scenic point of view. Nowhere are hills mirrored in its waters. Nevertheless, it may be regarded by some as an idyllic place, unencumbered by towns, industry or tourism, with the swans and other aquatic creatures the sole inhabitants of most of its wide, flat, lonely shores. Only in Antrim Bay, at its north-east corner, are the shores lined with the woodland which is so typical of the larger Irish loughs.

Lough Neagh

Although local legends would have us believe otherwise, the formation of the lake is associated with the gradual sinking of the central portion of the basaltic lava plateau of Ulster. It has already been seen in the previous chapter how the eastern margins of the lava plateau in Antrim were faulted down in a series of steps towards the North Channel in post-Eocene times. The enormous weight of the lavas and the evacuation of molten material at depth may have caused a similar thing to happen near the centre of the basalt country and it has been suggested that two major parallel north–south faults have allowed the basalt floor beneath the lake area and the lower Bann valley to be gently lowered to a general level more than 2,000 feet below the surrounding basalt plateaux. It has further been suggested that the faulting was probably of the same age as that which formed the rift of the North Channel and caused a break-up of the Brito–Greenlandic Province. Be that as it may, there is little doubt

that a basin was already in existence in the Lough Neagh area by Oligocene times for there is evidence that a much larger lake occupied the
region during that period.

A subsidence of the magnitude described above would have brought
the basalt surface down to about 1,200 feet below present sea level, but
since the present lake shores stand at 50 feet above sea level it follows
that a considerable amount of infilling has taken place since early Tertiary
times. A series of boreholes (largely to ascertain the underground extent
of the Coalisland coalfield) has given us a clear picture of the sediments
which now occupy the basin. The majority of these are relatively unconsolidated gravels, sands and clays, most of which have been termed
the Lough Neagh Clays, whose age has puzzled scientists for many
years although Oligocene seems to be the most acceptable date of formation. Since it has been shown how these lake clays cover an area of about
200 square miles there is no doubt that the lake's former extent was
greater than at present, mainly in the Moy region of the Blackwater
valley, south-west of Lough Neagh's present shores. The clays are pale
in colour owing to the presence of minerals of the kaolin group, while
white and grey beds of sand and pebbles comprise the lower part of the
formation. Chemical analysis has shown that much of the sediment was
derived from the south, probably from the decomposed acid granites of
the Mournes and Newry. In the upper layers the gravels contain basalt,
flint, Carboniferous Limestone and some gritstone and quartzite which
suggests that the rivers which brought them into the Lough Neagh
basin came mainly from the tilted margins of the downwarped plateau,
infilling its central depression until the lake became quite shallow;
over most of its area Lough Neagh is now only 40 to 50 feet in
depth.

For centuries country folk have discovered pieces of silicified wood
(fossil wood) scattered on the surrounding lowlands, no doubt dispersed
by ice-sheets from an undiscovered source within the Lough Neagh
Clays. This flinty material was, until recently, sold as sharpening stones
in the streets of Belfast, although the petrifying qualities attributed to the
modern lake waters were totally unjustified, since the wood is probably
of Oligocene age. Beds of lignite are also known to occur within the clays
but generally at such depth that they would be uneconomic to work.
Occasionally the lignites are accompanied by layers of large ironstone

nodules which, when exposed in the soil, are the 'petrified potatoes' of local folklore.

It was seen in the previous chapter how hard rocks, generally of volcanic origin, played the greatest part in shaping the landforms of the Antrim Plateau. In the Lough Neagh and Bann Lowlands, however, these hard rocks are buried at considerable depth, and play little direct part in landscape formation of this tract. The relatively soft Lough Neagh Clays and the thick Quaternary drifts, both Pleistocene and Holocene, make the greatest impact on the scenery of this region through their effect on the soils, vegetation and land use. Thus small changes in soil acidity, in drainage characteristics and in slope form can mean major differences in land use.

The shores of Lough Neagh are badly drained, on the whole, having suffered in the past from the maintenance of the artificially high water level by the weirs at the outflow, in the interests of the fisheries. The lack of natural drainage on the heavy clay soils of the western shores of the lake is reflected in the small percentage of improved land in this part of County Tyrone; small holdings of five to ten acres can still be found here, remarkably low by Northern Ireland standards where most farms are between 50 and 100 acres. Near to Washing Bay, for example, farm mechanization is almost absent so that donkeys and spade work are common, bringing to the north-east of Ireland features more readily found in the landscapes of the western seaboard. Similarly, the houses here, occasionally built of mud and usually thatched are still found in irregular clusters or 'clachans', a settlement pattern of great antiquity which will be more fully discussed in chapter five. It is not surprising to discover, therefore, that this isolated corner of Lough Neagh, known as the Montiaghs, is peopled by settlers from Connacht who moved here more than a century and a half ago. Although the dampness of the Lough Neagh Clays generally results in low fertility it has been found that with adequate drainage they provide reasonably good grassland and, where they are mixed with local peat, good cropland. Thus the southern shores of the lake, where the Upper Bann has built a delta into the lough, exhibit a remarkable variety of landscape depending on the extent to which man has modified the clay soils. Where the land has remained undrained there are true fenlands, where the marsh harrier was formerly common and where reeds were once cut for local thatching (in contrast to the more usual use of straw). During the late 1930s it was pointed out by Professor A. G. Tansley that the Lough Neagh fens were probably the most extensive unspoiled fenlands in the entire British Isles owing to the lack of reclamation. Today, however, there are patches of improved land scattered amongst the marshes, with fields of oats and potatoes interspersed with plots of permanent grassland. On the black peaty areas yet another scene prevails, for these rich soils are heavily spade-cultivated on tiny plots, with bush fruits and vegetables predominant since the soil will not support tree crops.

A further change has been wrought in the landscape by the motorway which now crosses the southern lake shores. Between this and the town of Portadown the countryside changes once more, for here is the 'garden of Ulster', the orchards becoming more extensive as one moves up from the Lough Neagh Clays on to the hillocks of the drumlin country where the soil is somewhat lighter in texture on the better drained slopes.

The drumlin hills have played an important part in the location and form of urban settlement in this part of County Armagh (plate 4). The parish church, being the only building of any size, is usually built on the crest of the hill and dominates the urban scene; the main street often runs steeply up the flank of the drumlin so that the houses climb as if in supplication, to give a scene of interest and picturesque silhouette, as at Killylea, Richhill and Tynan. (For an explanation of drumlin formation see p. 48.)

Apple orchards are most characteristic in this 25-square-mile area, where some two-thirds of Northern Ireland's fruit trees are found. It is an area of Ireland which reminds one at once of an English landscape, and the beautiful pink-washed Georgian mansion of Ardress does nothing to dispel this comparison. It is not surprising to learn, therefore, that the degree of concentration of orchards here in County Armagh owes more to history than to the physical environment, for other parts of Ulster, such as north Down and the Foyle lowlands offer equally sheltered terrain and similar soils. It seems that a number of English families who settled here in the seventeenth and eighteenth centuries came from the fruit-growing area of Warwickshire and they continued the tradition of planting an orchard as the necessary adjunct of every dwelling. The ranks of trees in blossom and the thick-set damson hedges, whilst forming a scene of great beauty, are alien to Ireland, creating an English 'veneer' in the landscape as artificial as the massive square church in nearby Kilmore village which, remarkably, encloses within its fabric an almost perfect round tower of great antiquity.

The eastern shores of Lough Neagh also are characterized by a wide stretch of the waterlogged Lough Neagh Clays, so that 90% of the area has been left under grassland; with its rush-grown fields and its high untrimmed hedges the area displays a forlorn and unkempt appearance only broken by the beautiful wooded grounds of Antrim Castle. South of here on the lakeside, overwhelming the former village of Aldergrove, is Belfast's civil airport which, together with two former military airfields, occupies some of the flattest land within the province, for in most other parts of the Lough Neagh lowlands drumlins and mounds of glacial sands and gravels give a very accidented relief, especially in the Kells Water and Six Mile Water valleys of west Antrim where the glacial mounds are set very close together. Before we leave the lake shores, however, it would be instructive to notice the workings which can be seen from the main road where the Bann leaves Lough Neagh at Toome Bridge. Both here and downstream to Lough Beg a curious scene may be witnessed, for what appear to be lumps of white peat are being cut and dried like turf on the surface of the bog. The deposit is in fact a diatomaceous earth, composed almost entirely of the flinty skeletons of millions of diatoms or microscopic freshwater algae. The white layer, some three to six feet in thickness, occurs between layers of peat, and since numerous flint implements of Neolithic type have been identified from the diatom bed we know that both this and the peat layers have formed entirely in the postglacial period, although no such diatom accumulations are forming in the lake at present. This diatomite is termed the Bann Clay, which is used mainly in the manufacture of insulating bricks, refractory blocks and pottery.

The Bann Lowlands

It is necessary to turn once more to a general view of the landforms and drainage of the basaltic province, for on the northern shores of Lough Neagh we are faced with an apparent anomaly. The river Bann drains northwards from the lake at Toome Bridge, yet only five miles to the east the river Main empties southwards into the lake near Randalstown.

There is little doubt that the parallel but opposing courses of these two river valleys, despite their thick infilling of glacial material, are in part structurally controlled. Between them the narrow upland of Long Mountain delimits the two drainage basins and provides the only stretch of rocky, gorse-dotted moorland in the whole region from Lough Neagh to the sea. Long Mountain is a horst-like feature left standing between two parallel faults while the flanking tracts of country were lowered to a greater extent.

If we examine the drainage pattern of the Lough Neagh lowlands we see that eight major rivers drain into Lough Neagh, but only one, the Lower Bann, flows out. The rivers run down from the tilted shoulders of the basalt plateaux, which fringe the lake on almost all sides. This inflowing radial drainage is unusual in the British Isles and is contrary to the more familiar concept of outflowing radial streams that we can witness in such places as the Lake District of northern England. While the latter is a response to a domed uplift, the Lough Neagh drainage has resulted from a centralized sinking of the lava plateaux as described above. This must have initiated an impounded water body soon after Eocene times, judging by the Lough Neagh Clays, and as such makes Lough Neagh the oldest surviving lake in the British Isles, although it must temporarily have disappeared during parts of the Ice Age. Nevertheless, the lake has not always emptied to the north, for during the later Pleistocene there is evidence to show that the Lower Bann drainage was blocked near Coleraine by a Scottish ice advance, described in chapter two (figure 5). Unable to escape northwards the greatly swollen lake waters finally overflowed to the south following the line of a valley aligned along a major fault which can be traced through Newry to Carlingford Lough, a route later to be followed by the Newry canal, the earliest major inland navigation project in the British Isles (1730–42).

Glacial Lough Neagh is thought to have been so extensive that a long narrow arm of it is believed to have extended northwards into the Lower Bann valley to the Ballymoney–Coleraine moraine. Today, extensive stretches of marshy alluvium and peat mark this former lake extension, although more noticeable in the Bann and Main lowlands are the numerous hillocks composed of glacial drift which flank and often enclose the marshy hollows. It is possible to distinguish two types of glacial mound: the first is a landform very common in Ireland, the drumlin; in fact its

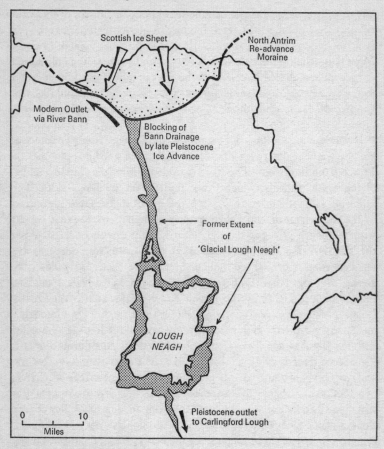

Fig. 5. *Glacial Lough Neagh.*

name is of Irish derivation. Although this is by no means the best area in which to study a drumlin landscape it is convenient to describe such a landform at this juncture. There is no clear agreement about their mode of formation but most would admit that these low whale-back hills of boulder clay (with or without a core of solid rock) have been fashioned by moulding beneath an ice-sheet. Because of this the drumlin 'swarm' generally adopts the major orientation of the former ice movement with all the long axes of the mounds giving a marked 'grain' to the country as they reflect this ice direction. In the Bann lowlands the drumlins, with their accompanying marshy hollows and peaty flats, have had a very marked effect on the road pattern, the field shapes and the farm location (figure 6). Frequently a field boundary encloses the improved land on the steeper slopes of the drumlin, dividing it from the ill-drained flat bogland above which it rises. Generally the farm is perched on the crest

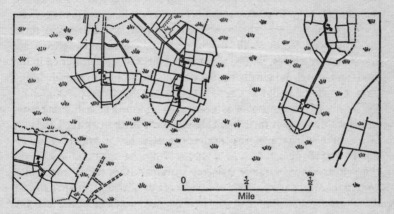

Fig. 6. *Settlement pattern in drumlin terrain (after J. M. Graham). An example from south-west of Lough Neagh where the drumlins rise from flat bogland.*

of the mound, the long axis of which is marked by an access road or field boundary which only heightens the impression of a dorsal fin on this whale-backed landform. Reclamation of the marshy inter-drumlin hollows is a lengthy and expensive business in this moist climate so that many have been left as rush-grown low-quality grazing lands. The colour in this type of landscape is therefore a sombre one, with the dominant burnt umber of the peat bogs and the dark green of the marshy hollows occasionally broken with splashes of emerald green fields and the odd brilliant white farm cottages with their rusty-red outbuilding roofs.

The second type of glacial mound differs from the drumlin in both shape and composition. Less regular in form, sometimes a conical hill, other times a narrow sinuous ridge, these sand and gravel features, although equally a product of a former ice-sheet, were formed in different ways. They are generally referred to as glacio-fluvial landforms, created during the melting phase of an ice-sheet by vast quantities of water coursing beneath and around the masses of decaying ice. Thus while the drumlins were formed by active ice, the majority of the glacio-fluvial landforms are thought to be the product of stagnant ice and as such are often collectively described as 'dead ice' topography. The conical hills, referred to as kames, are tumultuous sand and gravel features which are thought by many to represent former crevasse fillings in the ice-sheet. Sometimes they enclose hollows which lack drainage outlets and these are either occupied by small lakes or peaty sediments. Such features are known as kettle holes, formed when large blocks of ice, left buried in the sands and gravels, gradually melted causing the ground to subside in the form of enclosed hollows.

The linear ridges, known as eskers, were formed in a different way, and since they attain their finest development in the Central Lowlands of Ireland it would be more convenient to describe their mode of formation in chapter nine.

In areas where large ephemeral marginal lakes were impounded around the stagnant ice a succession of more extensive flat-topped former deltas and terraces may have survived the disappearance of the lake and because of their free-draining sandy soils these features are of great agricultural value in a region of generally impeded drainage. But many of the glacio-fluvial landforms exhibit steep slopes (greater than 1 in 4) and are therefore unsuitable for ploughing. Much of the terrain, although free-draining, is therefore left under permanent grassland and the steeper slopes quickly revert to a tangle of bracken, gorse and bramble. It is often a convenient way to distinguish a sand and gravel mound from a hill of boulder clay by looking for the conspicuous splash of yellow gorse (locally called whins) against the mottled greens of the sandy slopes. Until you have been to Ireland in early summer it is impossible to conceive how this prickly growth can light up a countryside with its brilliant colour. Hedges of gorse are commonplace in many farmsteads not only as shelter for the livestock, but also as a source of kindling wood and not least for the interesting Irish custom of providing a means for drying washing.

It would be impossible to leave the landscape of the Bann lowlands without a mention of flax-growing and the linen industry, an occupation which gave early prosperity to such towns as Ballymena with its fine Linen Hall. The valleys of the Main and Bann stand out as the major flax-growing area of Ireland and some of the farms still grow flax on the better drained basaltic soils. But flax-growing has almost ceased today and since most of the raw material is now imported, the former flax fields, which were so much a part of the scene (and indeed the smell) in this corner of Ulster, have reverted to grassland where cattle now graze peacefully in the river meadows. These meadows were also used as 'bleach-greens' until recent years, for the linen bleaching works were located in the countryside on river banks because of the need for water power and for large areas of land for the bleach-greens themselves.

Linen spinning and weaving grew up on the family farm and the small farmer-weaver tradition was as strong in the Bann valley as it was in the Yorkshire dales. As in Yorkshire, however, the cottage industry became gradually centralized in the urban settlements where all the major factories are now found. Only at Banbridge on the Upper Bann do the bleach-greens survive on the river banks.

Apart from the churches, banks and municipal offices most of the buildings in the market towns of north-east Ireland have been faced with stucco. Where this is gaily painted in a multitude of pastel shades the streets display a character which reminds one of sunnier climates. But it also makes it difficult for the traveller to discover any great individuality in the towns for the differences in building materials are generally hidden from view. Where the stucco is missing, however, and where the backs of the houses can be seen, we find that most of the buildings in the Bann valley are either of brick or dark basalt blocks. The village of Gracehill in County Antrim is an exception to the general colour-washing and stucco techniques, for here more than a century ago a central European community settled and built their houses of sombre black basalt.

Before the thirteenth-century Anglo-Norman invasion there were virtually no towns in Ireland and even the famous conqueror de Courcy extended his territories in Ulster no further west than the Lower Bann. It is known that no Norman towns were established west of Coleraine and it is probable that the rivers and marshes on the claylands of the Lough Neagh–Bann lowlands proved a serious obstacle to westward expansion in the north of Ireland. There is considerable evidence to show that these areas were also thickly forested, so that most non-military buildings other than churches were probably constructed of timber frames with wattle and mud infillings and would have been roofed with thatch. But nothing of the domestic architecture has survived from this period. Again, during the period of the Plantation in the seventeenth century, the great majority of the planned towns in these clay lowlands had houses built with half-timbered construction, judging by the illustrated town-plans of Magherafelt and Moneymore which have survived. We learn that in 1613 the planned town of Coleraine was taking shape near the mouth of the Bann and that houses of oak or birch timbering with slate roofs and brick chimney stacks were being rapidly constructed, and that some of the timber frames were being imported from England. But workmanship was poor and in contrast to the fine sixteenth- and seventeenth-century black-and-white half-timbered buildings which have survived in the clay lands of the English Midlands, for example, practically nothing has survived here in central Ulster. Thus the 'magpie' architecture which adds such character to the English scene is virtually missing from the Irish landscape and one is tempted to see a correlation perhaps between this and the missing Irish forests which were denuded so early in the country's history, although cultural and historical factors have also played an important part in the style of the domestic architecture.

4. County Londonderry and North Tyrone

The western tracts of the basaltic plateaux of Ulster rise gently from the Bann lowlands until they are abruptly terminated by the sheer cliffs which overlook the valley of the Roe and culminate in the summits of Binevenagh (1,260 feet) in the north and Benbradagh (1,535 feet) in the south. These are the west-facing equivalents of the Black Mountain–Cave Hill escarpment overlooking Belfast and of the deeply indented scarps of the Glens of Antrim. From the cliffs of Binevenagh the traveller will marvel at the view which unfolds beneath his feet, but with little realization, perhaps, that in a sense he is looking back through geological time. Across the glittering waters of Lough Foyle stand the hills of Donegal, famed in song and scenery alike, and composed of some of the oldest rocks in Ireland. The intervening Foyle depression, following a downfold or syncline in these older rocks, is filled with sandstones and shales of Carboniferous age, while immediately below the basalt cliffs lies a succession of Mesozoic rocks ranging upwards from the Trias through the Lower Jurassic clays to the Cretaceous Chalk (figure 7). The relationship between all these rock types, so contrasting in age and character, is not, however, a straightforward one. The fairly simple structure of the Antrim Plateau, where we saw the horizontal lava flows of Eocene age resting unconformably on the virtually flat-lying Chalk which in turn covers the Jurassic clays and Triassic sandstones, is repeated here only along the slopes of this western escarpment. Farther to the west, however, where erosion has destroyed these newer rocks a very ancient land-surface has been uncovered in much the same way as the older Palaeozoic and Pre-Cambrian rocks have been stripped and exposed near Torr Head in north-east Antrim.

The massive spreads of basalt in north-east Ireland can be likened to a blanket which has hidden from view the older rocks beneath. Only where there is a hole in the blanket, as in north-east Antrim, do we begin to suspect that these older rocks have very different structural trends to the relatively simple structures of the basalt and its underlying Mesozoic rocks. In the second chapter it was seen how the structural lines and

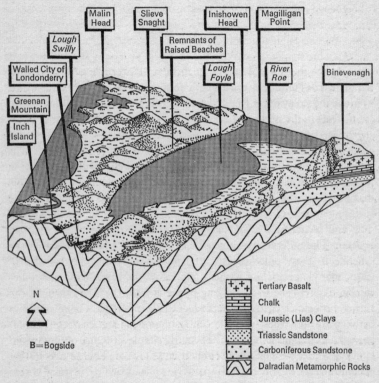

Fig. 7. *Lough Foyle and the City of Londonderry.*

faults of Scotland continued south-westwards into Ireland until they were lost to view beneath the basaltic cover of the Antrim Plateau. Below the western basalt scarp, however, these same structural lines, running from north-east to south-west as the so-called Caledonian trend, continue this 'grain' of the older 'basement rocks' as they emerge from beneath the blanket of newer 'cover' rocks (figure 1). The Highland Border Fault, which at Cushendun divided the older Pre-Cambrian rocks of the north from the relatively younger Palaeozoic rocks which lay to the south, was seen to disappear beneath the basalt and Mesozoic blanket. But it was visible long enough to establish that it marked a continuation into Ireland of the edge of the Highland Border Ridge which forms the northern shoulder of the Midland Valley of Scotland, itself a rifted structure. By the time that this feature reappears from beneath the basalt south of the Sperrins, the Highland Border Fault is composed of a series of parallel faults, which some geologists prefer to call the Highland Border (or Boundary) Fracture Zone, and this can be traced south-westwards through Omagh and Sligo to the town of Westport on Clew Bay in County Mayo. Thus the Sperrins (2,240 feet) can be regarded as the Ulster equivalent of the Perthshire Grampian Highlands, lower in elevation it is true, but with rocks of similar age (Dalradian) and with similar complex fold structures to those of the Caledonian mountains of Scotland. As in Perthshire such structures are suddenly terminated southwards at the northern edge of the central rifted trough by the Highland Border Fault (or Fracture Zone) which in Tyrone brings Old Red Sandstone and Carboniferous rocks of the faulted trough up against the older Dalradian rocks to the north. The latter are hard grits and mica schists which have resisted erosion more effectively than the Upper Palaeozoic conglomerates, sandstones and limestones, with the result that the older rocks have been left upstanding to form the Sperrin Mountains whilst the downfaulted Upper Palaeozoic rocks have been denuded to form the undulating plateau of central Tyrone. Although this is hardly equivalent in land form to the Midland Valley of Scotland, whose geological structure it reflects, its general surface is some 1,000 feet lower than the Sperrin summits. Furthermore, the geological connection with Scotland can be further established when it is realized that near to Dungannon in east Tyrone a heavily faulted but workable coalfield exists at Coalisland. This tiny patch of industrialization amidst the farmlands of the area is Ulster's equivalent to the major Scottish coalfields, for in both instances the Carboniferous Coal Measures have been preserved by virtue of the downfaulting in this central trough.

Because of the lack of local coal-mining expertise, Scottish and Cumberland miners were imported to Coalisland during the 1920s, although today the high quality fireclays of the Lower Coal Measures are of greater importance than the coal itself. Thus the chimneys and beehive kilns of the brickworks now dominate the landscape of Coalisland whilst the extensive brick pits and sand and gravel workings (from the glacial drifts) have devastated the scenery far more than the colliery waste on the outskirts of this small town (plate 5). Unlike the extensive dereliction associated with British coalfields the landscape of Ireland has suffered in this respect at only two localities, here at Coalisland and in the Leinster Coalfield (chapter sixteen), because of the dearth of workable coal seams.

The Sperrin Mountains and Slieve Gallion

The Sperrins form a broad ridge of high rounded hills, in direct contradiction of their name (Irish: *Cnoc Speirin*), which means 'pointed hills', but which nevertheless are an important physiographic divide between north-east and north-west Ulster (plate 6). East of here the drainage is to Lough Neagh and the Bann, west of the ridge it is to the Foyle. Their isolation has meant that this is a region of cultural survivals where innovations, particularly agricultural changes, have been slow to appear. Thus it is a region where traditional farming customs and land use have persisted, by-passed by the main roads and the bustle of the twentieth century. Rundale, that complex form of Irish land-tenure, has survived longer here than in most parts of Ulster and so have the clustered groups of dwellings known as 'clachans' (see p. 77).

The mountain summits are thickly peat-covered, giving miles of rather featureless, heathery bogland amongst which occurs one small treasured patch of cloud-berry, a small herbaceous blackberry, which is found nowhere else in Ireland. The plant is found on the Scottish hills and in Norway and no doubt it was common in Ireland during the cold of the Ice Age. But in the warmer climate of today we are told by the famous Irish naturalist, Dr R. Lloyd Praeger, that '... it has come to its final flicker, like half a dozen other Irish plants which belong to the Arctic, and in a little while it will join other former inhabitants of Ireland now known only from their remains entombed at the bottom of our bogs.'

The flanks of the mountains are deeply dissected by streams which drain northwards to the Roe and Faughan rivers and southwards to the picturesque Glenelly valley. Here, along the beautiful banks of the Glenelly river a road runs from the tiny settlement of Sperrin (Mount

Hamilton) through the charming village of Cranagh to the curiously-named hamlet of Plum Bridge. On the northern side of the road countless small burns rush down the steep flanks of the main Sperrin ridge and, although these slopes have not the precipitous nature of the cliffs which abruptly terminate the basalt country further east, they are another example of an escarpment. In this case, however, the southern flanks of the Sperrins have been carved from a fault-line scarp, where the river Glenelly has picked out a line of weakness created by one of the faults associated with the Highland Border Fracture Zone. The rocks to the south of the river have been 'down-thrown' by faulting many hundreds of feet below the crests of the high Sperrins, and the original sharp front of the fault scarp has now been smoothed and worn back by denuding agencies through millions of years of geological time, so that it has lost the freshness which one might otherwise have expected.

One of the major agents of denudation has undoubtedly been the ice-sheets of Pleistocene times and the Sperrins are high enough to have played an important role in the glacial history of Ireland. Yet, despite their favourable elevation, no glacial corries exist on the mountain ridge, which suggests that local glaciers never had time to form before the Sperrins were submerged by considerable thicknesses of central Irish ice-sheets moving northwards across the range. A recent study by Dr E. Colhoun of glacial erratics in the surrounding drifts has demonstrated that during the last glaciation (Midlandian) ice from three distinct centres crossed the Sperrins; that from Lough Neagh and eastern Tyrone moved north-west through the Glenshane Pass; that from the central Tyrone plateau moved across the central part of the high Sperrins; that from the Omagh basin and the Barnesmore granite area of south-east Donegal moved down the Mourne–Foyle valleys and crossed the western end of the Sperrin ridge before reaching the Faughan and Roe valleys.

There is no evidence to indicate that even the highest summits remained as nunataks above the ice-sheets at this time. Glacial erosion must therefore have been intense, as the Sperrin ridge would have presented an obstacle to the northward passage of the ice. Thus ice-breached cols are numerous, some of them having been lowered by as much as 200 feet with Glenshane Pass, the Altalacky Gap and the Cloghornagh Gap all now followed by picturesque mountain roads. Perhaps more instructive, however, is the deep through valley of the Letterbrat and Inver burns north of Plum Bridge, since it indicates the amount of glacial over-deepening which can occur across major pre-glacial watersheds on such occasions.

The upper slopes of the hills are covered by extensive sombre-coloured moorlands, given over to sheep, but lower down the mountain flanks a kaleidoscope of colour occurs where the thick, better drained spreads of glacial sand and gravel have allowed a variety of crops to be grown. Glacio-fluvial deposits have choked most of the valleys so that modern streams have cut deep gorges into the drift in their attempt to reach solid rock and these defiles are now thickly wooded. Otherwise the only woodland of any extent in the region is associated with the higher valleys to the south and east of Dungiven where large forestry plantations have imposed their unnatural geometric outlines on these gently rounded hills. Along the northern foothills of the Sperrins, between Strabane and Dungiven, the glacio-fluvial deposits are often associated with a different type of valley network for here we can distinguish a complex pattern of linked meltwater channels, carved deeply into solid rock by glacial streams which formerly ran beneath and around masses of southward retreating ice. Since the disappearance of the ice, however, many of these channels have been left streamless as the source of water supply has vanished.

Scattered amongst the glacial drifts of the Sperrins are a number of distinctive erratic rocks which must have been carried by ice from the area around Slieve Gallion (1,735 feet) which lies some ten miles to the south-east of the range. The erratics are distinctive because they are not sedimentary in origin nor are they from the Eocene basalts, although a small outlier of the basaltic plateau has managed to survive on the northern summit of Slieve Gallion; instead they are derived from what are termed the Tyrone Igneous Series. In chapter two we saw how a prolonged period of vulcanicity produced the Tertiary Igneous Province of Ulster with its great variety of volcanic phenomena. The tract of country between Omagh and Draperstown was also the site of important igneous activity, but in a much older period of geological time, as early as Ordovician times. These igneous rocks conceal a floor of Pre-Cambrian rocks and have been altered by subsequent granitic intrusions, of which the mountain of Slieve Gallion is the most striking example. In addition to the thick layers of lava, some of which are quite acid in composition (in contrast to the basaltic lavas), the Tyrone Igneous Series includes volcanic ashes and agglomerates, indicative of an explosive phase in the activity. But it is Slieve Gallion, with its twin summits, which is of most interest because of its position as a scenic viewpoint. Its northern top, where Eocene lava caps a thin outlier of Chalk, provides an opportunity to look across the dark green masses of Iniscarn Forest, eastwards to the waters of Lough Neagh and Lough Beg. The higher granite summit, some two miles to the south, however, has the added advantage of beautiful Lough Fea at its western foot. This little mountain lake, with pines, rhododendrons and willows round about it, is a jewel amongst the drab peat-covered moorlands which appear to stretch endlessly from here to the Sperrins.

The Foyle Lowlands

The complex Caledonian folding of the Dalradian and older rocks in counties Londonderry and Donegal has given a very marked north-east to south-west 'grain' to this part of Ulster. In Londonderry the majority of the rocks are composed of schists and gneisses, two rocks which geologists refer to as metamorphic rocks; in Donegal these metamorphics are accompanied by extensive granite intrusions and also by another extremely hard metamorphic rock known as quartzite. Such tough rocks as granite and quartzite have given to the Donegal landscape a ruggedness not found amongst the scenery of western county Londonderry, as we have already witnessed in the Sperrin Mountains. The line of the Foyle Valley can be taken as an approximate boundary, therefore, between the rugged scenery of Donegal and the more rounded whale-back hills which characterize that tract of county Londonderry which lies to the west of the basalt escarpment.

From Strabane seawards the river Foyle flows north-eastwards following the axis of a downfold or syncline which forms the Irish continuation of the Loch Awe Syncline of Scotland, itself part of the so-called Iltay Nappe formation, formed from a complex series of overfolded rocks. Such great overfolds, or nappes, like those of the Alps, frequently leave the bedded layers of rocks turned completely upside down by the enormous lateral pressures exerted during the mountain building period. Such structures are common in Donegal and may be present in the Sperrins, although the Upper Dalradian rocks of the Foyle region have not been inverted, so that the older rocks remain below the younger rocks following the order in which they were deposited prior to the folding.

The north-east to south-west striking syncline of the Foyle basin, described above, appears to have been a fairly persistent feature in the structural history of this region, for we find that the present waters of Lough Foyle submerge almost completely a basin of Carboniferous sandstone, similar in character and age to that at Ballycastle. The same type of sandstone also emerges from beneath the Mesozoic rocks which are capped by the Eocene basalts east of Lough Foyle and this sandstone outcrop at the foot of the basalt scarp has been in part picked out by the river Roe draining northwards from Dungiven (figure 7). Where the Roe passes temporarily on to the Dalradian schists it has cut a picturesque wooded gorge at the Dog's Leap south of Limavady, and it is here that the famous 'Londonderry Air' was first written down, an ancient folk tune inspired, perhaps, by this beautiful valley. The sandstone is generally a reddish coarse-grained rock, often associated with conglomerates below and shaley limestones above, suggesting that at the time of its deposition the Lower Carboniferous shoreline lay nearby. The large pebbles of the conglomerate cannot have been carried far from the shore and most of them appear to be quartzites probably derived from the Pre-Cambrian rocks of Donegal. Since pebbles of schist and vein quartz are also common in these Carboniferous sandstones it seems likely that the ancient rocks of Donegal emerged from the Carboniferous seas to form a high landmass to the north-west at that time. Finally, it has been suggested that during Tertiary times earth movements which assisted the break-up of the Tertiary Igneous Province, and which saw the downfaulting of the North Channel and the Lough Neagh lowlands, were also responsible for the faulting and sinking of the Lough Foyle basin along existing structural lines, thus preserving the Carboniferous sandstones.

The drainage pattern of the Foyle is significant, for it has been shown by Professor G. H. Dury that the majority of its western tributaries, including the Mourne Beg, Finn and Deele, exhibit a general disregard for the structures of the Dalradian rocks across which they flow. He suggests that these streams, together with several others which now drain eastwards from central Donegal into Lough Swilly, were all part of a series of east-flowing rivers which can be taken as an example of a superimposed drainage pattern (figure 8). We have already seen that the major axes of folding and faulting in this region lie in a direction from north-east to south-west, known as the Caledonian trend, and that the Foyle itself follows a line close to this orientation. Thus the main trunk stream of the Foyle is said to be adjusted to the structure. Its western tributaries, however, flow across fold-axes and faults at right angles and are dis-

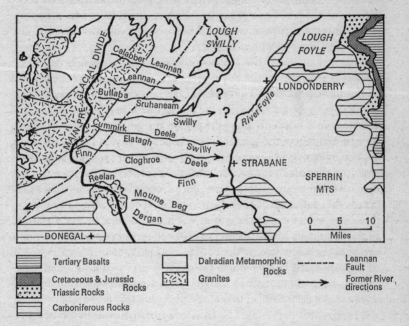

Fig. 8. *A hypothetical reconstruction of the Pre-Pleistocene drainage of the River Foyle, showing the Antrim basalts and Mesozoic rocks (after G. H. Dury).*

cordant to the structure. It seems probable, therefore, that these east-flowing streams originated on a 'cover' of newer rocks which formerly dipped or tilted to the east but which has now been totally eroded, leaving the streams, following their former easterly courses for the most part, superimposed on to the underlying older rocks that have now been exposed by erosion. It is impossible to do more than suggest the rocks that may have formed this 'cover' on which the east-flowing drainage was initiated. Only a few miles to the east we have the plateau basalts which almost certainly extended farther west at one time; we also have the Chalk, now surviving only where entombed beneath the basalt. Either of these rocks may have formed the surface in question but the evidence has been destroyed. Of one fact we are more certain, however, and it is that the north-east-flowing Foyle probably existed throughout the period of Tertiary time when the 'cover' rocks were present and, aided by the faulting and sinking of Lough Foyle described above, helped to integrate the east-flowing drainage network, which was probably initiated in response to Tertiary uplift in Donegal.

Towards the close of the Ice Age a large glacier is thought to have persisted in the valley of the Foyle after the northern slopes of the Sperrins had become ice-free. Thus some of the right-bank tributaries of the present Foyle were unable to join the line of the modern valley and were forced to turn northwards along the eastern margin of the valley glacier. The best example of this glacial diversion can be seen at Drumahoe village, two miles east of Londonderry city, where the river Faughan turns sharply northwards to run parallel with the Foyle before joining it some five miles downstream. Although the Burn Dennet today enters the Foyle directly, four miles north of Strabane, it is clear that during the melting of the Foyle-valley glacier the stream was forced to turn north-eastwards and flow through a narrow meltwater channel, now occupied by the tiny Burngibbagh, before joining the Faughan at Drumahoe.

The steep-sided hill, on which the old walled city of Londonderry is situated, owes its isolation to sub-glacial meltwaters which must have carved out the deep channel to the west of the hill (plate 7). Even in post-glacial times this depression has remained marshy, as demonstrated by its name Bogside, and it was in this unhealthy environment that the slums of Londonderry developed, until they were replaced by modern concrete tenement blocks in recent years. An expanding population has seen the city of Derry (as it is more colloquially known) extend on to the surrounding hillsides of Creggan, where a large modern housing estate overlooks the old city. The use of pebble-dashed walls and modern roof-tiling contrasts with the building material of the old city and its walls, generally constructed from the local schistose grit, mainly from Prehen quarry, although the houses are generally stuccoed in the tradition of urban Ireland. Only the larger civic buildings show the use of a contrasting building stone, but in these cases the stones are usually imported from afar; the Guild Hall, for example, is built of red calciferous sandstone from Scotland.

It appears that the last ice-sheet which occupied the Foyle Valley extended northwards as far as Moville, near the northern end of Lough Foyle, where the outwash from the moraine is seen to be interbedded with a red clay, thought by Dr N. Stephens and Mr F. M. Synge to be of marine origin. The clay is shown to be associated with an old shoreline which now stands abandoned at a height of some 70 to 80 feet along the indented northern coast of Donegal. The effect of the high shorelines on the landscape of Inishowen and the remainder of north Donegal will be looked at in more detail in chapter five, for at the moment we are concerned only with the landforms of the Foyle lowlands and especially with those flanking Lough Foyle. Some of the most striking landscape features of the southern shores of Lough Foyle are the wide expanses of virtually flat terraces which extend over a distance of some 20 miles from the basalt cliffs of Castlerock to the city of Londonderry. In north-west Ireland, a region of steep slopes and rocky terrain, such features have played a very significant part in the land-use of this northern coastline and it is important, therefore, to look more closely at their geological history.

The coastal terraces occur at various elevations and were formed at different dates during and after the retreat of the Foyle glacier (figure 7). The highest (70–80 feet) terrace is a late-glacial shoreline found only in a limited area to the north of the Moville moraine in Inishowen as mentioned above, but below it, at a height of approximately 50 feet, a clearly marked terrace extends almost the whole way round Lough Foyle. Although formerly providing good farming land this lower abandoned shoreline of late-glacial age became of the utmost significance during the Second World War. In a ten-mile stretch of coastline from Limavady to near Londonderry no less than four military airfields were built on this terrace, for here was one of the westernmost outposts of the United Kingdom in the battle to protect the Atlantic convoys. The tidal waters of the Foyle at Londonderry also played their part by providing a deep-water channel for an important naval base, now part of NATO. Since the end of the war the deserted military installations along the southern shores of Lough Foyle have witnessed an even greater change in the landscape, for at Maydown, one of the disused airfields four miles from Londonderry, a great industrial complex has sprung up, a scene unusual in rural Ireland. At the side of the large riverside Coolkeeragh power station (360 MW), which is fired by oil pumped directly from ocean-going tankers, two enormous chemical factories are located on the 50-foot terrace.

The sands and gravels which make up the 50-foot terrace were washed out of the downwasting Foyle glacier as it retreated southwards. They were carried by rivers into the sea, which appears to have been advancing slowly into the Foyle basin as the ice retreated, and were finally dumped as deltas and outwash terraces along the shoreline. How then, we may ask, are the terraces now situated some 50 feet above present sea level? It has to be remembered that when the ice-sheets were present in this region the crust was locally depressed by the excessive weight of the ice. Such depression is known as isostatic downwarping and appears to have reached its greatest extent in western Scotland and northern Ireland where the British ice-sheets were thickest. After the ice-sheets had disappeared, however, the land recoiled and started to return to its former level as the excess weight was removed. Although sea level rose in post-glacial times as water returned to the oceans, the isostatic recovery in north-west Britain is known to have outpaced it to such an extent that here late-glacial shorelines have been uplifted far above the present sea level.

Thus the high terraces and shorelines of Donegal and Lough Foyle can be explained, but what of the lower shorelines, below 25 feet, which also flank Lough Foyle? The marine shells of these lower raised beaches indicate that they are of post-glacial age and that they were formed at approximately the same period as those at Larne, when Mesolithic man first appeared in Ireland. It would seem most likely that about 8,000 years ago the rise of the post-glacial sea level overtook the rate at which the land was being raised in this part of Ireland so that for a short period of a few centuries the waves were able to cut cliffs in the fronts of the late-glacial terraces and leave shingle beaches at the foot of these cliffs. The marine transgression was short-lived, however, and before long the rate of recovery of the land proved greater than the rise of sea level, so that the sea receded from these cliffs leaving the marine clays and post-glacial beaches high and dry. They are best seen to the south of Lough Foyle between the railway and the 50-foot terrace, although the two sand-spits of Culmore Point and Magilligan Point are also of the same age. The latter is a remarkable feature, an enormous flat triangle of alluvium and blown sand which juts northwards from the basaltic cliffs of Binevenagh for a distance of five miles, thereby almost closing the entrance to Lough Foyle (plate 7). It is best viewed from the tops of these cliffs from where it will be seen how the small streams have been artificially culverted across this curious sandy foreland because of the impeded drainage on the flat terrain. It was because of its flatness that Magilligan was chosen as the site of the base line for the first topographical survey of Ireland. The sandy soils encourage tillage, and rye was once an important crop, particularly for its straw which was in great demand as a thatching material. The windblown sand forms high dunes along the northern coast and many of these were utilized as military installations during the Second World War. The foreland has been created on the glacial drifts of the Moville moraine which were later re-worked by the waves of the post-glacial high sea level.

The lowest and newest member in the staircase of Lough Foyle terraces dates from historical times, for during the nineteenth century hundreds of acres of 'polder' land were reclaimed from Lough Foyle by the construction of embankments along its southern shore. The rich alluvial soils of this so-called 'slobland' are amongst the most fertile in Ireland and excellent grain crops are common so long as the surplus water is pumped clear. In contrast to the tiny grouped settlements on Magilligan Point, however, we find that the sloblands are totally devoid of dwellings. Indeed their extensive hedgeless fields with the chimneys, oil tanks and pylons of the Maydown industrial complex as a background serve to remind us that here in the north-west of Ireland modern agricultural innovation and industrial investment came very late into the Irish scene.

In the centre of the lough, extensive shell-banks have long been a feature not only of the scenery but also of the local husbandry, for there is documentary evidence to show that the 'oyster, muscle [*sic*], cockle and cockspur' have been used since the seventeenth century for liming the acid soils of the surrounding land. These gleaming white accumulations, uncovering for more than two square miles at low tide, are a fossil feature since some of the mollusca (including *Turritella communis*) are very rare, if not extinct, in the lough today. It has been suggested that *Turritella* has decreased owing to a continued shallowing of Lough Foyle in post-glacial times in response to isostatic uplift of the land. But other types of mollusc appear to have accumulated when conditions in the lough approached those of the open sea much more than they do at present. Consequently the growth of the Magilligan sand-spit must have played an important part in the change from an open marine environment to that of a more confined estuarine type.

5. Donegal

From a geological point of view it is probably true to say that Donegal is the most complex of all the Irish counties. Antrim may possess a greater variety of rock types but is dominated by the great spreads of basalt; Mayo, too, can boast a lithological diversity but here the glacial drifts and blanket peats give a monotonous uniformity to the landscape throughout much of the county. Donegal, however, with its miscellany of rock types, its exceedingly complex structures and its fragmented coastline, has a landscape as irregular and as aesthetically stimulating as any in Ireland.

Lough Swilly and Inishowen

To appreciate the scenic contrasts between the counties of Londonderry and Donegal the tourist would be well advised to drive to the summit of Greenan Mountain, a few miles to the west of the city of Londonderry (figure 7). From the walls of the remarkably renovated ancient stone temple, which crowns the top of this small hill, it is possible to see both Lough Foyle and Lough Swilly, the one a structural downfold of Carboniferous rocks almost totally infilled with drift, the other a true fjord, ice-eroded and overdeepened between the steep walls of quartzite which flank its shores.

Lough Swilly is best viewed, perhaps, on a fine summer's evening when the setting sun silhouettes the stark, craggy ridge of the Knockalla Mountains, known locally as the Devil's Backbone, and the lumpy pyramids of the Urris Hills. Both of these heather-clad eminences would then be darkly mirrored in the gleaming waters of Lough Swilly which zig-zags to the open ocean. Clearly, these hills have been carved from the same band of hard quartzite, aligned in the characteristic north-east to south-west trend, but they have subsequently been separated by a deep glacial breach now occupied by the waters of the lough (figure 9). The twisting course of Lough Swilly results, in fact, from the disposition of such quartzite ridges amongst the intervening tracts of less resistant schistose rocks, for in some stretches the lough runs north-eastwards

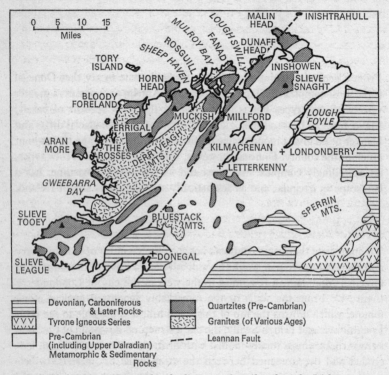

0   5   10   15
Miles

MALIN HEAD   INISHTRAHULL
MULROY BAY
ROSGUILL
SHEEP HAVEN
LOUGH SWILLY
FANAD
DUNAFF HEAD
TORY ISLAND
INISHOWEN
SLIEVE SNAGHT
HORN HEAD
BLOODY FORELAND
MUCKISH   MILLFORD
LOUGH FOYLE
ERRIGAL
ARAN MORE
THE ROSSES
DERRYVEAGH MTS.
KILMACRENAN   LONDONDERRY
LETTERKENNY
GWEEBARRA BAY
SLIEVE TOOEY
BLUESTACK MTS.
SPERRIN MTS.
SLIEVE LEAGUE
DONEGAL

Devonian, Carboniferous & Later Rocks
Quartzites (Pre-Cambrian)
Tyrone Igneous Series
Granites (of Various Ages)
Pre-Cambrian (including Upper Dalradian) Metamorphic & Sedimentary Rocks
– – – Leannan Fault

Fig. 9. *The geology of Donegal and adjacent regions (based on the Irish Geological Survey).*

with the strike only to turn abruptly at right angles where erosion has broken through the quartzite ridges. Some miles from the open ocean, between Soldanha Head on the Fanad shore and Dunree Head in Inishowen, the lough is at its narrowest and deepest, demonstrating that one of the characteristics of a fjord is a shallowing towards the entrance. The explanation is probably one of glacial overdeepening of the pre-glacial river valley wherever the ice had been laterally constricted by the valley walls. Farther seaward, however, where the valley widens, the glacier would have had room to expand laterally, downward erosion would have decreased and the valley entrance would not have been lowered to so great an extent. Thus, during the post-glacial rise of sea level when a valley such as the Swilly became drowned, a submerged rock sill would be left across the entrance of the lough, perhaps amplified by an accumulation of terminal moraine. To the west of the Fanad Peninsula the beautifully wooded Mulroy Bay exhibits another example of glacial overdeepening by ice tongues which followed these northern valleys in the Late Pleistocene. In this case, however, in contrast to the Swilly, the rock sill is at a higher elevation and the mouth of the valley is now blocked by glacial drift south of Ballyhiernan Bay. Thus the waters are forced to escape seawards by a devious ten-mile route past the Rosguill Peninsula. In chapters fourteen and fifteen it will be seen how the so-called ria coastline of south-west Ireland contrasts with that of north Donegal, for there the profile of the sea floor in the bays descends continuously seawards with no reversals of slope.

The curiously shaped peninsula of Inishowen is dominated by the high summit of Slieve Snaght (2,019 feet), composed, as one might expect, of the conspicuous Dalradian quartzite, in this particular instance the Crana Quartzite. But it is the much lower hill of Barnan More on its north-western flanks which catches the eye, for here the craggy King and Queen of the Mintiaghs rise like turreted castles from the peat-covered slopes. It has already been noted how the Dalradian sedimentary rocks became changed into so-called 'metasediments' by regional metamorphism and we now discover an example of a different type of rock, formed from the alteration of the igneous sills intruded into those former sediments, for the Mintiaghs crags are carved from 'metadolerites', once termed epidiorites or greenstones. Metadolerite exposures are common features of the Donegal landscape where, because of their hardness, they run as bare, rocky ridges for several hundred yards at a time. Although not very high they are formidable barriers to movement across the grain of the country. Such bare rock ribs projecting through the drifts are amongst the most prominent characteristics of Donegal and for a county so permeated by its coastline it is surprising how infrequently one gets a distant view of the sea. It is a landscape of closed vistas, tantalizing glimpses of peak and ocean being interspersed with a haphazard patchwork of ridge and valley, hill and hollow, rock knob and potato plot, with the cottages often tucked away from sight as if hiding from the stranger.

The eastern slopes of Slieve Snaght descend gently to a belt of lower land picked out by the drainage basins of the Crana and Glentogher rivers. This tract, which divides Slieve Snaght from the grits and slates of the high Scalp ridge, is in part due to the appearance of the Culdaff Limestone amongst the greatly faulted Dalradian metamorphic rocks. This relatively easily eroded rock occurs in a discontinuous, narrow band between Buncrana and Culdaff, with the latter village being sited on a lowland plain which forms the only breach in the cliff-bound northern coast of Inishowen.

West of Culdaff a road through Malin Town takes us past the shell beaches and yellow dunes of Trawbreaga Bay and the beautifully gleaming mica schists at the roadside near Cranny Hill, out to the northernmost tip of Ireland at Malin Head. Here too is a viewpoint that no visitor should miss, for in addition to the sheer majesty of the crashing waves on the fretted rocks and sea stacks the geological phenomena are of paramount importance. Malin Head itself is made of Dalradian quartzite, but ten miles to the north-east the tiny isle of Inishtrahull is composed of Lewisian gneiss, the oldest known rock in the British Isles. This is one of its few occurrences in Ireland and it is fitting, perhaps, that it appears at the point nearest to its type-site on the island of Lewis in the Outer Hebrides. Because of this tenuous link and the fact that the rocks of Inishowen match closely those of eastern Islay and Jura it has been suggested that the submarine valley which divides Inishtrahull from Malin Head was carved in part along the south-western extension of the Great Glen Fault of Scotland. Malin Head possesses what is probably the best collection of raised shorelines in Ireland. Below the high pre-glacial cliffline all three late-glacial shorelines described in chapter four can be seen, with the village of Ballyhillin perched right on the crest of the highest shingle ridge at 80 feet O.D. The colourful, striped, hedgeless fields of the village run seawards until they are truncated by the abandoned sea cliff of the post-glacial raised beach (plate 8).

The North West

The majority of visitors to north-west Donegal keep closely to the coast-line which, because of the complex intermingling of sea and mountain, is its chief glory. To understand the complicated geological history of the region, however, one must leave the superb beaches, sand dunes and sea cliffs and turn inland to the more austere uplands of the interior, for here is exposed a bewildering variety of Dalradian rocks.

These are best examined, perhaps, near the village of Kilmacrenan which is set amidst the drumlins of the Leannan valley, south of Mulroy Bay. From here several narrow twisting roads lead westwards into the bleak terrain of peat bog and bare rock. At first the eye is confused by the apparently haphazard arrangement of the rocks but generally four major rock types can be recognized: schists, marbles, quartzites and metadoler-ites. The first three were formerly sedimentary rocks but they have been so altered by regional pressures that they are now totally metamorphosed and are termed metasediments. The fine-grained argillaceous rocks were given a cleavage and were pressed into minute complex folds; the lime-stones assumed a crystalline structure and became puckered; the more competent siliceous ribs of the semi-argillaceous rocks were stretched out into lenticles or 'eyes'; the quartz-rich sandstones recrystallized into strongly lineated quartzites, whilst the pebbles of the coarser sandstones were elongated and squashed. As if this were not enough the whole area has been criss-crossed with faulting which has only added to the com-plexity. Thanks to Professor W. S. Pitcher and his colleagues, however, a picture has now emerged, a picture of strongly folded metasediments and their accompanying intrusions, generally following the normal Caledonian trend of the region and occurring in fairly well marked repetitive series of main quartzites overlying the schists which in turn succeed the limestones. To aid description these Dalradian rock series have been grouped into so-called 'successions', of which three have been recognized in north-west Donegal: first, the North-West Donegal (or Creeslough) Succession to the west of the Main Donegal Granite; sec-ondly, the Fintown Succession, south-east of the granite; and thirdly, the Kilmacrenan Succession, which stretches from Malin Head, through Fanad, south-westwards as a narrow strip to the Slieve League Peninsula.

The Kilmacrenan Succession differs from its neighbours because it includes amongst its basal rocks a remarkable conglomerate known as the Donegal Boulder Bed. This is a very distinctive rock, up to 200 feet in thickness, composed of rounded pebbles, cobbles and boulders of granite, quartzite, schist and limestone embedded in an indurated matrix of sandy clay. Its most striking characteristic, however, is the presence of glacial striations on some of the boulders, indicating that the deposit is either a fossil boulder clay (a 'tillite') or, more probably, that it was dropped from floating icebergs. Whichever idea proves to be true, the fact remains that since it is interbedded with Dalradian rocks we are dealing with evidence of a Pre-Cambrian glacial episode. It is best exposed at Tawny in the Fanad Peninsula but its outcrop can be traced intermittently past Lough Salt, Garton Lough and Lough Finn southwestwards to the Slieve League Peninsula. This unusual bed is generally regarded as equivalent in age to the 'Boulder Bed' of Achill Island, Co. Mayo (chapter twelve) and to the Portaskaig Boulder Bed of Islay and the Schiehallion Boulder Bed of Perthshire.

The folding of the Donegal metasediments was generally accompanied by large-scale sliding along low angle (15°–30°) thrust faults (figure 10a) and later complicated by severe tear-faulting or wrench-faulting (figure 10b). The intensity of the fractures suggests the scale of the tectonic forces which have subsequently affected the Dalradian rocks of the region, mangling the metasediments and metadolerites alike, cutting out or repeating rock series by faulting, and causing whole successions to be carried bodily forward by tangential pressure along enormous thrust faults. The Kilmacrenan Succession, for example, has been overthrust north-westwards on to the Creeslough Succession and has itself been sliced through by the Leannan tear fault.

A tear fault differs from a thrust fault because the pressures no longer force a moving block of rocks to travel tangentially forward along a low angle fault-plane across a stationary block (figure 10a), but instead cause a lateral movement which displaces rocks horizontally along a fault-plane which is almost vertical (figure 10b). The most important tear fault in Donegal from a geological viewpoint is the Leannan Fault, on which Kilmacrenan stands. South-westwards it has been picked out by the Leannan river, and it can be traced by way of Lough Ea and the north-western flanks of the Blue Stack Mountains before disappearing beneath the Carboniferous rocks of south Donegal (figure 9). North-eastwards

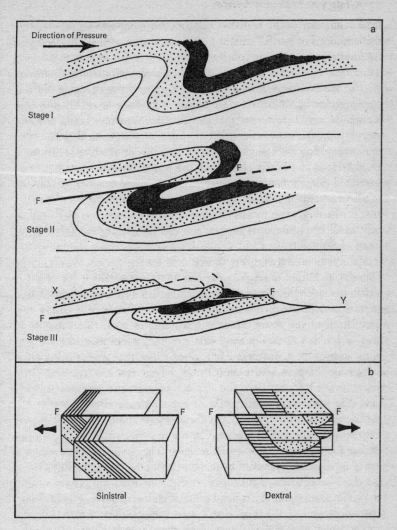

Direction of Pressure

Stage I

F

F

Stage II

X

F

F

Y

Stage III

a

b

F

F

F

F

Sinistral

Dextral

Fig. 10a. *Stages in the formation of a thrust fault. F–F marks the thrust plane. If denudation were to lower the land-surface to X–Y, older rocks would be seen to overlie younger rocks at the surface exposure (see Fig. 34).*

Fig. 10b. *A tear fault or wrench fault.*

from Kilmacrenan the fault has had an even more significant effect on the landforms of north Donegal for its lateral displacement has brought together rocks of strongly contrasting lithology and resistance to erosion. Thus near Millford the less resistant schistose rocks which lie to the west of the fault may have assisted in the glacial overdeepening of the upper reaches of Mulroy Bay. To the east of the fault, however, the tough Knockalla Quartzite forms the Devil's Backbone of Fanad, brought sharply up against the Old Red Sandstone of Ballymastocker Bay. On the eastern shores of Lough Swilly the fault cuts off the Urris Hills from Dunaff Head and Malin Head from the rest of Inishowen. It has been suggested that north-west Donegal may have moved as much as 25 miles south-westwards in relation to the country on the other side of the fault, and, furthermore, that its massive displacement and stratigraphic location may make the Leannan fault the Irish continuation of the Great Glen Fault of Scotland.

A correlation such as this is also claimed for another large tear fault in Donegal and from a scenic viewpoint the spectacular chasm of Glen Veagh has much to support the comparison with its more famous Scottish counterpart. Faults of this stature create a wide zone of crushing and brecciation of the rocks through which they pass so that subsequent erosion is able to pick out these shattered rock zones more easily. Such is the case of the Gweebarra Fault, along which the deep valley of Glen Veagh has been carved, essentially by glacial erosion. To view Glen Veagh castle standing dark and isolated amongst the pinewoods which flank the long narrow valley lake of Lough Beagh is an unforgettable experience. The towering valley walls of granite and the heather-covered Derryveagh Mountains across which the red deer roam, all add to the impression that here is a Scottish landscape. The geologists soon dash these romantic thoughts, however, by demonstrating that the Gweebarra Fault is a right-handed tear fault with less than one mile of displacement, whilst the Great Glen Fault of Scotland exhibits no less than 60 miles of lateral movement with a left-handed displacement similar to the Leannan Fault.

The valley of Glen Veagh neatly bisects the massive intrusion of the Main Donegal Granite which was the latest of four great granite units which invaded the metasediments of north-west Donegal. The Main Granite has a visible outcrop of 140 square miles and runs for 36 miles in a north-east to south-west direction, parallel to the regional strike of the Dalradian rocks into which it was emplaced. The high temperatures and pressures associated with the emplacement created a metamorphic aureole up to two miles in width, surrounding the granite like a halo; such a process is known as contact metamorphism. Granitic intrusions usually occur by an upwelling of deep-seated magma into crustal rocks which are frequently sedimentary in character. The contact metamorphism, therefore, changes these into metasediments which make up the metamorphic aureole. In Donegal, however, the granites were intruded into rocks which had already undergone an earlier metamorphic change by regional pressures so that the Donegal metasediments were merely given an intensified folding and cleavage, an increased schistosity and a development of new minerals. The granite itself is coarse-grained and porphyritic with prominent pinkish feldspars in its north-western outcrop but its character changes to a grey, medium-grained biotite-granite towards the south-east. Together with the other granites of this region it is thought to be of Caledonian age, i.e. contemporaneous with the granites of Barnesmore (south Donegal), Newry and Leinster, probably younger than the Galway granite, but considerably older than the granites of Mourne and Carlingford.

The most prominent of the landforms created by the Main Donegal Granite are the Glendowan and Derryveagh Mountains which flank the Glen Veagh trough. South-east of the glacial trench the Glendowan Mountains reach a modest height of 1,771 feet, although directly opposite, across the Barra river, the massive hump of Slieve Snaght (2,240 feet) achieves the status of Donegal's second highest mountain. Its title, like that of its Inishowen namesake, means 'peak of the snow', and in the Derryveagh case it is, perhaps, appropriate, for these granite mountains appear to have formed the centre of the local north Donegal ice-cap during Late Pleistocene times. The glacial smoothing and striations on their summits suggest that they were completely buried by ice which moved mainly north and north-westwards. The lack of granite erratics in the glacial drifts south-east of the Main Donegal Granite outcrop means that local ice movement in that direction was blocked by the larger ice-sheet which was centred over Tyrone and Fermanagh. Some local ice escaped northwards to Sheep Haven leaving trains of granite erratics, roches moutonnées and grooving obliquely across the strike of the Creeslough metasediments. The ice-cap surface gradient, however, must have been extremely steep for during this late advance ice failed to override the high Muckish Mountain (2,197 feet) or to reach the peninsulas of Rosguill and Horn Head (figure 9). Nevertheless its erosive powers were considerable judging by the magnificent glacial trough of the Poisoned Glen. This curiously named U-shaped valley, to the north of Slieve Snaght, is one of the most awesome and fascinating locations in northern Ireland. Its green marshy floor, where the poisonous Irish Spurge, said to have given its name to the glen, has long since disappeared, gives way to towering bare walls of pink granite whose polished cliffs and rain soaked slabs glisten in the fitful sunshine. The rock is seamed with numerous clefts which mark the lines of intrusive igneous dykes, many of Tertiary age, which have been picked out by erosion because they have proved to be less durable than the surrounding granite. The cliffs at the head of the glen have manifestly been overridden by ice from behind and we can visualize the magnificent ice-fall which must once have existed here when the glacier surged down the glen and on through the valley now occupied by the Dunlewy and Nacung lakes.

The Derryveagh Mountains are terminated steeply on their north-western side by the strike valley of the Calabber river. This is basically a pre-glacial valley carved by a drainage pattern well-adjusted to structure, for it has obviously taken advantage of the differential weathering properties of the granite and the altered rocks of its metamorphic aureole. Seawards of the Calabber valley, however, the land rises steeply once more where the Ards Quartzite of the Creeslough Succession appears. This thick (1,200 feet) silvery-white layer of coarse quartzite creates a series of outstanding landforms wherever it appears, ranging from the spectacular eastern cliffs of Tory Island and Horn Head in the north to the superb white cone of Errigal in the south.

Errigal (2,466 feet) deserves its title as Donegal's highest peak for it rises dramatically from the peat-covered lowlands of Gweedore through a shimmering splendour of frost-shattered screes, which skirt its flanks, to a jagged and bare summit (plate 9). From its airy, knife-edged top (which can be achieved most easily from the east) the traveller will be rewarded with a breathtaking view. Here is Atlantic Ireland at its best. The ocean waves have worked upon the intricate details of the geology to produce a wide variety of coastal landforms. Out to the far west the quartzite knob of Aranmore island rises above the older granodiorite which forms the scores of islands and the highly indented coastline south of the Bloody Foreland. The latter, whose prominent hill in northern Gweedore escaped glaciation in the last ice advance, is a bare granite feature whose glowing colours at sunset are said to be responsible for its singular name. The view to the north from Errigal is even more rewarding; the yellow sand dunes which almost enclose Ballyness Bay and climb high on to the slopes of Horn Head have been formed from material washed out of the end-moraine and the glacio-fluvial deposits of the last glaciation only to be re-fashioned by Atlantic waves and winds; the better drained sands and gravels of this moraine between Dunfanaghy and Falcarragh have allowed a tract of improved land to intervene in this poor ice-scrubbed landscape of bog, rock and lake. Seen on a clear sunny day the white cottages set in their bright green fields, the tawny colours of the unimproved land with the black slashes of peat-diggings, all backed by the yellow dunes and blue sea, create a picture which is difficult to surpass. North-eastwards, above the hump-backed quartzite ridge of Muckish, the Rosguill Peninsula can be seen, its quartzite and granite island now tied to the mainland by a narrow neck of sand to form what is called a tombolo. Here, on the beautiful Atlantic Drive, one can discover something of the ancient Irish settlement pattern known as the clachan. Instead of the haphazard scatter of isolated cottages, which is more common in the Irish landscape, it is possible to find here a cluster of simple cottages with up to a dozen dwellings grouped together with no apparent planning, to form what is still referred to as a 'town'. It is easy to see how the land unit, the 'town-land', is derived, a term more nearly equivalent to the English parish.

We must return, however, to the quartzite pyramid of Errigal, for along the ridge to the north it is possible to examine superb examples of glacial breaching by ice moving northwards from the Derryveagh Mountains. Altan Lough occupies one such breach, with some of the drainage of the Calabber structural trench now finding it possible to drain across the quartzite ridge by virtue of the glacial lowering. Lough Aluirg sits in a less spectacular col of similar derivation, north of Aghla Beg, but the most impressive breach of all, perhaps, is that followed by the road through Muckish Gap where the col has been lowered some 400 feet. The humpbacked mountain of Muckish itself has, at its northern end, a remarkable sand quarry, where weathering has leached out a calcareous cement which formerly bound together the quartzite grains. The resulting white sand is extremely pure (99·5% silica) and the grains so even that it is worked for high quality glassware and optical purposes.

Before leaving the fascinating geology and scenery of north-west Donegal it would be improper not to glance at the landscape of The Rosses, 'a land of innumerable lakelets, a windswept heathery region, with small peaty fields grudgingly yielding difficult crops of potatoes and oats and turnips, and roads meandering through granite hillocks' (R. Lloyd Praeger). Between Bunbeg and Dunglow this subsistence agriculture on tiny plots surprisingly supports one of the densest areas of rural population in modern Ireland and as such it has remained similar to one of the notorious Congested Districts of the nineteenth century. The country is a low undulating plateau at about 200 feet O.D., from which ice has scrubbed much of the soil and dumped thousands of large erratic boulders, but its main interest lies in the fact that it is also a granite terrain which has been greatly reduced by erosion, in contrast to the upstanding relief of the Main Donegal Granite. The Rosses granite is younger than the granodiorite into which it has been intruded but older than the Main Donegal Granite which cuts through it. It occurs as a circular outcrop, five miles across, known as a ring-complex. The intrusion was by means of a so-called 'cauldron subsidence', a process which will be examined in more detail in chapter eight.

South Donegal

In contrast to the wild and bare landscape of the north the tract of country around the town of Donegal, at the head of the bay which bears its name, produces a more gentle landscape with a softer type of scenery. The reasons for this are twofold: first, the Dalradian rocks are replaced by a basin of Carboniferous Limestone, the northernmost extension of the rocks which characterize the Central Plain of Ireland. Thus the ruggedness and the steep slopes so common in Dalradian country are replaced by rocks which on the whole have been less resistant to erosion than their northerly neighbours; secondly, the Pleistocene history of the area around Donegal town is one of glacial deposition rather than erosion, so that the landscape at the head of the bay is dominated by drumlins with their characteristic effects on land use and road patterns. The soils are generally deeper and less acid in this limestone tract so that farming is of a higher standard and trees return to the landscape. The river Eske, for example, flowing south-westwards with the regional strike which has, coincidentally, been followed by the lines of ice movement, traverses a region of great beauty. Its source, Lough Eske, is a particularly attractive lake, with a thick deciduous woodland mantling its western shores and with the bare summits of the Blue Stack Mountains rising behind the lower heathery hills which cradle the lake. The hollow in which the lake waters have accumulated seems almost certain to have been a product of glacial scouring for it occurs exactly at the junction of the hard Dalradian rocks with the less resistant Carboniferous rocks which lie to the south-west, in this instance Carboniferous sandstones which rim the limestone basin.

From the northern end of Lough Eske a track from Edergole bridge follows the Corabber river past the beautiful Eas Dunan waterfall deep into the heart of the rarely visited Blue Stack Mountains. Here is the lonely Lough Belshade surrounded by glistening slabs of bare granite which rise steeply to the highest summit of Croaghgorm (2,219 feet) or Blue Stack itself. The lake occupies one of a group of glacial cirques or corries, armchair-shaped hollows eroded by small glaciers which filled them during the later stages of the Ice Age when the thick ice-sheets had disappeared. In the northern hemisphere corrie glaciers lingered longest on east-facing or north-facing slopes where they were most protected from the rays of the sun and on the Blue Stack Mountains, as elsewhere in Ireland, this pattern is closely followed. Some of the corries are genuine rock basins, eroded by the rotational movement of the glacier as it moved out of the accumulation hollow, so that it is sometimes possible to see a rock bar across the lip of the corrie over which a stream usually tumbles, often from a corrie lake. In other cases small crescentic moraines stand on the lip, marking the final position of the glacier front prior to melting, and in these instances the corrie lake may be impounded by the moraines.

Other landforms created by glacial erosion may also be seen in the Blue Stacks, including glacial grooving, roches moutonnées and truncated spurs. The most spectacular features, however, are the deep glacial breaches which slash through this major pre-glacial drainage divide. These, like the majority of the other erosion features with the exception of the corries, were fashioned essentially during the period when the Blue Stacks acted as an ice-sheet centre and when even their highest summits were buried by ice. Five major troughs breach the divide, including three east of Lough Belshade: that followed by the Corabber and Cronamuck rivers; that followed by the Barnes river; and, most spectacular of all, Barnesmore itself. No traveller driving north-east from Donegal town will fail to be impressed by the stupendous gorge of Barnesmore through which he passes. There is little doubt that the river Lowerymore, which runs through the pass, was not responsible for the incision, as a glance at the glacially smoothed 1,000-foot walls will show. The pre-glacial spurs and ridges of the flanking peaks have been completely truncated by ice moving north-eastwards away from the thick ice accumulation zone around Lough Eske. Only a mile to the north of Barnesmore the Barnes river, closely following a fault line, as do many of the drainage lines of the Blue Stacks, flows north-eastwards through Barnes Lough as if to join the Mourne Beg river, a headwater of the Foyle. Quite abruptly it makes two right-angled turns and flows south-westwards through Barnesmore to the Lowerymore and thus to Donegal Bay. Its former course to the Mourne Beg is now blocked by mounds of glacio-fluvial outwash but its post-glacial course means that the major drainage divide of Donegal has been offset more than two miles to the north-east by this deep glacial breaching.

The granite of the Blue Stacks, known as the Barnesmore Granite, covers an area of about 20 square miles and everywhere forms an upland tract over 1,000 feet in elevation. Although there is evidence of four distinct phases of intrusion, each with a slightly different mineral composition, the age of the granite complex is known to be entirely Caledonian. Its generally pink colouring comes from the feldspars which together with quartz, biotite, plagioclase and muscovite are the major minerals of the Barnesmore Granite. The plutonic mass would have invaded the Dalradian rocks from below, updoming them to form a roof, and it is interesting to record that since eroded particles of this granite did not contribute to the later Carboniferous conglomerates of the region, erosion could not have succeeded in stripping off the roof by that time. But the granite is certainly unroofed now and we can see how it has subsequently been invaded by myriads of dykes, many of them of Tertiary age. The density of the dyke swarm has led some geologists to speculate on the presence of a buried Tertiary igneous mass nearby, not yet unroofed. The dykes are mainly doleritic and like the Tertiary dolerite dykes elsewhere in Donegal they tend to rot deeply and to be easily eroded. Thus they have been picked out by streams which exhibit a curiously angular pattern in their drainage network. Professor G. H. Dury, in his study of the landforms of Donegal, has commented on the importance of both dykes and faulting in guiding stream development in this area.

West of the Blue Stack Mountains and beyond the curiously shaped Carboniferous Limestone peninsula of St John's Point lies the broader peninsula of Slieve League which forms the westernmost tip of Ulster. If we were to travel on the coast road west from Donegal town we would soon become aware of a gradual transition in the scenery. At first the well-organized farmlands of the drumlins give an air of prosperity, even where these begin to be interspersed with the peat-covered ridges beyond Inver. But eventually '. . . every valley seems less fertile than the one before it; trees become fewer and the soils begin to possess the black colour of land wrested from the bogs' (T. W. Freeman). In fact, by Dunkineely we have left the Carboniferous Limestone and are crossing into the familiar terrain of the Dalradian metasediments; soon after passing the attractive fishing port of Killybegs we leave the drift limits of the last glaciation; by Kilcar the rugged metadolerite ridge of Crownarad is behind us and the high quartzite mountains of Slieve League ahead; we are back once more into Atlantic Ireland.

The special attractions of the outermost limits of the Slieve League peninsula are its sea cliffs which are at their most spectacular wherever the quartzites occur. Along the northern coast the cliffs of Slieve Tooey, Port Hill and Glen Head provide some of the wildest and most remote coastal walking in Ireland for there are no roads within miles of this stretch. But it is to the southern coast that we must turn for it is here on the flanks of Slieve League itself that we find some of the greatest sea cliffs in western Europe. Only Achill Island possesses higher cliffs but these are difficult to view, whilst the Slieve League precipices have a natural viewing gallery at Bunglass at their southern end. Only in a few places are the cliffs actually vertical, as at the Eagle's Nest (plate 10), but the summit cairn (1,972 feet) stands at the very edge of the main cliffs which stretch for more than two miles. Between the Eagle's Nest and the summit the coastal path traverses a narrow knife-edged ridge, appropriately termed the One Man's Path, which separates the sea cliff from the headwall of a corrie that bites deeply into the landward side of the mountain. It is a fine point to view the tiny corrie lake below the cliffs which are reputed to shelter the finest collection of Alpine plants in Donegal. Although the major ice-sheets failed to reach the western limits of the peninsula Slieve League was high enough to support its own small corrie glaciers during the last glaciation. It has been suggested, in fact, that the One Man's Path is a true arête, a frost-shattered ridge dividing the headwalls of two corries one of which is now drowned by the ocean.

6. The Fermanagh Lake Country

The eastern shores of Donegal Bay are very different from the cliff-girt coasts of the Slieve League peninsula described in the previous chapter. In part this is due to the low drumlin landforms which surround Donegal town, but more particularly to the presence of the more easily eroded lower layers of the Carboniferous Limestone series. The Lower Carboniferous rocks between Donegal town and Ballyshannon form the eastern flank of the so-called Donegal Syncline, a downfold of Carboniferous rocks now largely inundated by the waters of Donegal Bay. Although massive limestones occur in the coastal fringe (the Ballyshannon Limestone Group) they play no significant part in the landscape, for it is the overlying shales (the Lower Calp Shales of the Irish Geological Survey) which are more important in this respect. These rocks, composed of dark, micaceous, silty shales and mudstones, intercalate with thin limestone bands, suggesting that during 'Calp' times muds had invaded the Carboniferous seas. Despite the way in which the shales grade upwards into more durable, cross-bedded 'Calp' sandstones, including that of Mount Charles, whose building stones contributed to Armagh cathedral and the National Library in Dublin, it is the shales which are mainly responsible for the low relief near Bundoran and Ballyshannon.

An examination of topographical and geological maps will show that at Ballyshannon a low corridor of land, floored by Lower Carboniferous rocks, links the Central Lowlands of Ireland with the Atlantic seaboard. For the most part this lowland corridor has been carved by rivers and ice from the less resistant 'Calp' shales, more specifically the Bundoran Shales, which overlie the Lower Carboniferous Limestones. To the south-west of the corridor the massive limestones, with their overlying Namurian rocks, build the spectacular mountainland of Sligo and Leitrim (see chapter ten). To the north the terrain rises more gradually above Belleek and Pettigo to the lonely, heather-clothed south Donegal hills which surround Lough Derg. Here is one of the few outcrops of Moinian metamorphic rocks in Ireland and, owing to its lack of roads, it is one of the least frequented tracts of the country.

The lowland corridor is almost entirely contained within County Fermanagh and corresponds for the most part with the drainage basin of the river Erne, which has a catchment of some 1,500 square miles. The Erne rises well to the south, in the undulating Lower Palaeozoic hills of County Cavan which here make up the ill-defined northern limits of the Central Lowlands. Thus, such far-flung lakes as Lough Gowna (County Longford), White Lough (County Monaghan) and Lough Oughter (County Cavan) all contribute water to the Erne outflow in Donegal Bay. It is a most confusing area, so far as the drainage is concerned, since the stream divides are so inconspicuous and the gradients so low that it is anyone's guess whether the roadside ditch drains ultimately north to the Erne, south to the Shannon or east to the Irish Sea. Paradoxically, in this waterlogged, rushy, landscape of Cavan and Longford less than 10% of the households had piped water in 1945, and as late as the 1960s this featureless, amorphous tract was losing population more rapidly than anywhere else in Ireland. County Fermanagh is reputed to be more than one-third covered in water and a glance at any map tends to support such a suggestion (figure 11).

The river Erne meanders inconsequentially and dreamily from Cavan into Fermanagh where it gradually widens into the curiously shaped Upper Lough Erne. Downstream, as the river leaves the lake it flows deeper into the lowland corridor, past the town of Enniskillen and into the beautiful Lower Lough Erne. Here the valley is flanked to the east by the Old Red Sandstone plateaux which extend away into central Tyrone, and to the west by the harder Upper Carboniferous rocks which form the conspicuous highlands of the Fermanagh–Leitrim border country. Lower Lough Erne curves gradually from a north-west alignment to an east–west course, partly in response to the orientation of the so-called Omagh Syncline, a structure which has helped to preserve Carboniferous rocks, from Omagh to Kesh, in a downfold between the Old Red Sandstone of Tyrone and the Pre-Cambrian rocks of the north-west. The Castle Archdale fault, which in part defines the southern flank of the Omagh Syncline, runs north-eastwards towards the Sperrins and is generally

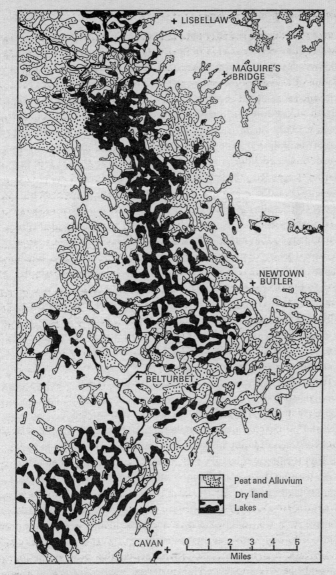

+ LISBELLAW

+ MAGUIRE'S
  BRIDGE

NEWTOWN
+ BUTLER

+ BELTURBET

Peat and Alluvium
Dry land
Lakes

CAVAN
+

0   1   2   3   4   5
        Miles

Fig. 11. *The distribution of dry land, of water and of peat and alluvium around Upper Lough Erne (based on the Irish Geological Survey). Dry land (white), water (black), peat and alluvium (stippled).*

regarded as an extension of the Highland Border Fracture Zone (see p. 55). Although the fault crosses Lower Lough Erne at right angles it appears to have played little part in the evolution of the scenery hereabouts and the Lower Carboniferous rocks extend right across it. Towards its western end the lake funnels to an outlet near Belleek as the flanking hills of harder rocks close in upon the narrowing corridor. To the north, the low Moinian schist hills approach the lake shores at Castle Caldwell and form the right bank of the Erne valley all the way to Ballyshannon. The southern wall of the corridor is much steeper where the river leaves the lake, for here the wooded northern cliffs of the Poulaphouca hills plunge steeply from over 1,000 feet in a series of prominent step-like cliffs. Each of these cliffs, with its accompanying fan of grey screes, represents the scarp of a gently tilted layer of Carboniferous Limestone which dips away at an imperceptible angle southwards. Each layer of limestone is succeeded upwards by a progressively younger layer until the whole system passes into yellow Namurian sandstones and shales of similar composition to that of nearby Cuilcagh Mountain (figure 23).

Below Belleek, the river Erne, having flowed for over 100 miles with scarcely any change in gradient, used to fall almost 150 feet in less than five miles to its Atlantic estuary. But the beauty and spectacle of the falls, and the gorge, like those on the upper Liffey near Blessington (see p. 270), are now no more, lost beneath the impounded waters of an artificial lake, Lough Assaroe, to feed the hydro-electric generating schemes of Cliff and Ballyshannon.

The heavy rainfall of this region, together with the relatively gentle gradients of the till-covered plain, have been responsible for the remarkable drainage pattern described above. The soils of these lowlands have developed from the ubiquitous till cover, which, having been formed very largely from the underlying 'Calp' limestones and shales of the corridor, produces a tenacious blue–grey clay–loam. Since the water table in the soil is permanently high its pore-spaces are closed and the soil is said to be gleyed, whilst in the hollows, which are permanently waterlogged, large patches of lowland peat can be found. It is no surprise, therefore, to learn that extensive flooding has characterized the Erne basin for centuries, having an adverse effect on farming, settlement and communications alike. Around Upper Lough Erne, for example, flood hazards and the waterlogged soils have restricted crop acreage to less than one-tenth of all improved land. With a shoreline of 100 miles and an area of 29 square miles this lake is reputed to double in size during every flood of more than ten feet rise. The typical Irish landscape of emerald green pastures with their darker rushy hollows is more prevalent along the Erne, perhaps, than almost anywhere else, and the lack of waterside settlement in the upper reaches, because of flood danger, is one of the most striking characteristics of this region. Since 1950, however, a major drainage scheme has alleviated many of the flooding problems and also given a more effective control of surface discharge rates which benefits the Ballyshannon power stations.

It has been seen from the geological description how the Fermanagh lake country is floored by limestones and shales of Carboniferous age and since the geological map depicts these as Carboniferous Limestone Series it is difficult at first to understand how the generally porous limestones can support such a waterlogged landscape. The answer, of course, has already been hinted at above, for the solid rocks hardly emerge at the surface because of their deep covering of glacial drift. The till has been moulded by ice-sheets into a typical drumlin landscape, so that the meandering channels of the Erne and the singular shape of Upper Lough Erne can now be explained. Drumlins also create the numerous islands which add so much charm to the lakeside prospect, although the traditional number of 365 islands is actually no more than 154 – 57 in the upper lake, 97 in the lower (See figure 23).

The reader will soon have realized that the small drumlin hillocks, rising above the water-threaded clay plains, must have offered the only sites for settlement in the Fermanagh lake country. Epitomizing this point is the town of Enniskillen (Inis = island) whose main street climbs over the drumlin island on which it is situated (plate 11). In an area where the lakeside reed swamps provide an endless supply of roofing material, it is no surprise to learn that two-thirds of Enniskillen's houses remained thatched into the latter half of the nineteenth century. Today, however, the town is slated and tiled, and one must travel off the main roads along the lake shores to see the thatched cottages standing white against the jet-black soil.

Most of the larger buildings in the region were constructed from Carboniferous Limestone, taken, perhaps, from the extensive roadside quarries which intrude into the thick ash and oak woods on the southern lake shore between Enniskillen and Belleek. One example of local stone-work is worthy of comment, that of the grey limestone round tower, one of the finest in Ireland, that stands majestically on the lake isle of Deven-ish, north of Enniskillen. But it is the mansion of nearby Castle Coole, arguably the greatest classical building in the country, which must take pride of place. Here the traveller will be astonished to see a house, de-signed by James Wyatt, built entirely of Portland stone. Quarried in Dorset, brought by ship to Ballyshannon, thence overland by bullock cart, the dazzling white stone helped to produce a late eighteenth-century building of supreme elegance, constructed regardless of cost by the first Earl of Belmore, amidst a landscape of silver waters and green meadows. It leaves one wondering whether the magnificence of the scene influenced the builder, causing him to ignore the dullness of the local stone, but, whatever the reason, Portland stone was never used again on such a scale in rural Ireland until the building of Stormont near Belfast, as a seat for the Northern Ireland government, in 1932.

There are many ecstatic descriptions of Lower Lough Erne where '. . . shelter, prospect, wood and water are here in perfection'. Its beauty appears to have been marred but little since the time of Arthur Young's visit in 1776 when he described the view from Castle Caldwell as the most pleasing that he had seen anywhere. It was from the Castle Caldwell estate that pottery clay was formerly mined to provide the basis of an important porcelain industry at nearby Belleek. The high feldspar content of the clay (probably derived from the nearby Moinian rocks) gave a fine finish to the Belleek lustre ware, although the clay is now imported from Norway. The civilized Georgian architecture of the Belleek pottery manufactory in its rural surroundings stands in sharp contrast with the smoke-blackened urban mills and factories of Belfast.

7. Belfast and the Down Lowlands

From the mouth of the Bann to the Mountains of Mourne the eastern seaboard of Ulster is broken by major indentations in only two places – at Belfast Lough and at Strangford Lough. Despite their geographical proximity the character of the landscape surrounding each of these marine inlets is very different. In part this is a result of their contrasting history, but the latter has to a large extent been governed by the detailed contrasts in geology, landforms and soils which characterize the two areas. In this part of Ulster, however, it is possible to recognize not two but three distinct areas: Belfast and the Lagan valley; Strangford Lough and the Ards Peninsula; and finally, to the south-west of these, the Mid-Down Lowlands.

Belfast and the Lagan Valley

The city of Belfast is cradled in the valley of the Lagan at the head of the sea lough which bears its name. Situated between the basaltic plateaux of Antrim and the rolling hills of Down there are few cities which can boast of so fine a setting. Whether one views it romantically from Cave Hill and ponders on '. . . its lean mill-chimneys stretched above the smoke haze . . . the Castlereagh Hills netted with lovely fields and skimming cloud shadows (with) the blue U-shaped lough covered with yachts . . .' (M. McLaverty), or bitterly, as a place to get out of quickly as did Sean O'Faolain in his notable *Irish Journey*, there is no doubt that Belfast has its own unique character. To some it is merely a drab, smoke-blackened, brick-built product of the Industrial Revolution, quite foreign to the dominantly rural personality of Ireland. Certainly its vast urban sprawl, based essentially on heavy industry, seems more closely linked with the industrial landscapes of the British coalfields, although there are no Coal

Measures here. So dominant has it become in the landscape of Ulster that it has been likened to a large house in a small garden, although it must be realized that the 'garden' was created long before the house was built.

To understand the landscape of the Belfast region one must turn once more to an appraisal of the regional geology of north-east Ireland. We have seen in earlier chapters how the structural lines of southern Scotland continue south-westwards into Ireland, this being especially true of the two great fault lines which delimit the downfaulted Midland Valley of Scotland. It is the more southerly of these, the Southern Uplands Fault, which concerns us here, for it is thought to run onshore in Ireland beneath Belfast Lough. It is certainly true that the Ordovician and Silurian rocks of County Down, to the south-east of the city, form a logical continuation into Ireland of the rocks which make up the Scottish Southern Uplands and it is clear that these Lower Palaeozoic strata are abruptly terminated along a linear boundary running beneath Belfast from north-east to south-west. These Ordovician and Silurian rocks, although forming hills of lesser magnitude than their counterparts in the Southern Uplands of Scotland, nevertheless create a distinct line of low bluffs running south-west from the Holywood Hills (644 feet) through Castlereagh (597 feet) to Hillsborough Forest (500 feet). The actual contact of these rocks with the downfaulted, buried Upper Palaeozoics (probably of Old Red Sandstone and Carboniferous age) is masked by a thick layer of Triassic rocks which in turn are overlain by Jurassic and Cretaceous sedimentaries preserved beneath the Antrim Plateau lavas (figure 12).

In chapter two it was seen how the Lagan valley at Belfast is overlooked from the north-west by a line of high hills, of which Cave Hill is the most prominent. These are the southern scarps of the basaltic terrain described in earlier chapters, but there seems little doubt that the basalts once extended much further south, possibly across the whole line of the buried Southern Uplands fault, judging by the tongue of basalt which still overlaps the Silurian rocks at Portadown. The lavas must therefore have buried much of the present outcrop of Triassic rocks, but denudation, largely by rivers, has subsequently caused the escarpment to be worn back to its present position over a period of some 40 million years.

The Lagan valley, then, has been carved essentially along a zone of structural weakness, where an outcrop of Triassic marls and sandstones some four miles in width has proved less resistant to downwearing than have the flanking masses of harder rocks to the north-west and south-east.

There seems little doubt that Triassic rocks also once existed over a much wider area of northern Ireland, although they were probably thickest in existing structural depressions such as the downfaulted Irish

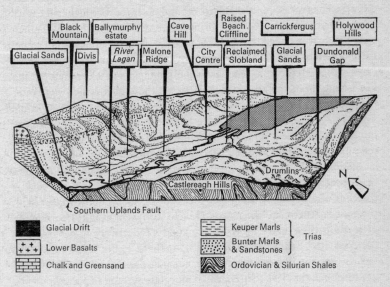

Black Mountain · Ballymurphy estate · Cave Hill · Raised Beach. Cliffline · Carrickfergus · Holywood Hills

Glacial Sands · Divis · *River Lagan* · Malone Ridge · City Centre · Reclaimed Slobland · Glacial Sands · Dundonald Gap

Drumlins

Castlereagh Hills

N

Southern Uplands Fault

- ■ Glacial Drift
- ⊞ Lower Basalts
- ▦ Chalk and Greensand
- ▤ Keuper Marls ⎱ Trias
- ▦ Bunter Marls & Sandstones ⎰
- ▨ Ordovician & Silurian Shales

Fig. 12. *The location of Belfast (after E. E. Evans).*

extension of the Midland Valley of Scotland or that now occupied by Strangford Lough. There are several reasons for this supposition, including the survival of the so-called Kingscourt outlier of Triassic rocks in south-east County Monaghan. There, some forty miles from the Triassic outcrop of the Lagan valley, a tiny strip of rocks of this age has survived by virtue of downfaulting. The likelihood is, therefore, that this tiny patch was once part of a continuous cover of Triassic rocks but that it has become increasingly isolated from the major surviving outcrop near Belfast by millions of years of denudation. Hence it is known as an outlier. Another reason for postulating a former cover of Trias is the red or purple staining of the Lower Palaeozoic rocks in many parts of northern and mid-Down. It is thought that this resulted largely from Triassic 'cover' rocks which have now been stripped off.

It is important to pause at this juncture and to attempt a reconstruction of the landscape which existed here in Triassic times in order to explain the ways in which the different Triassic rocks were created. The basalts of Tertiary times had not yet appeared, nor, of course, had the Jurassic or Cretaceous rocks, but the Palaeozoic and older rocks, which had earlier been folded and uplifted, now formed mountain ranges, heavily faulted and largely consumed by lengthy periods of denudation. The scene, therefore, must have been similar to one in modern Persia or Baluchistan; extensive deserts of low relief with the mountains of older rocks rising like islands from the sand plains. Between the dunes, which were later to form the typical dune-bedded sandstones, ephemeral lakes of saline water (playa lakes) existed in some of the hollows, helping to stabilize the wind-blown dust and convert it into thin layers of finely laminated clays or marls. The absence of organic matter because of the scanty vegetation, together with the great heat, meant that the grains of the dune-sands became coated with a thin film of red ferric oxide. Red or pink is therefore the dominant colour of the Triassic rocks, and together with those of the Permian sandstones (which are insignificantly represented in Ireland) these make up the rocks known collectively to geologists as the New Red Sandstone. The term is perhaps rather confusing to the layman, for the deposits are neither new nor are they always composed of sandstone, for clays (marls), conglomerates, gypsum deposits and even limestones occur within the so-called New Red Sandstone. Insofar as these red rocks were deposited immediately after the Coal Measures had been formed, however, they served as an important upper marker zone to the earliest mining geologists who were concerned primarily with the mineral wealth of the Carboniferous rocks. The New Red Sandstone, therefore, was a term adopted to distinguish it from the Devonian rocks which frequently lay beneath the basal sediments of the Carboniferous and which because of their red colouring have long been known as the Old Red Sandstone (figure 2).

The Triassic succession in the Belfast area consists of basal conglomerates which are rarely seen at the surface, more than 200 feet of silty Bunter Marls, with their remarkable evidence of sun-cracks and ripple marks, passing upwards without a break into the Bunter Sandstones, which are in turn succeeded by the Keuper Marls.

The Bunter Marls, which contain occasional thin bands of limestone, underlie the south-eastern part of the city of Belfast, thinning out as they are traced up the Lagan valley to Lisburn. There is a very great thickness of Bunter Sandstones (more than 1,000 feet) overlying these marls, and both dip gently north-westwards away from the Holywood–Castlereagh Hills, before disappearing beneath the Keuper Marls which make up much of the rising ground to the west of the city, below the frowning basalt escarpment (figure 12). The Bunter Sandstones underlie the greater part of Belfast and are well exposed along the shores of the lough. It has recently been suggested that the uppermost 100 feet of these sandstones ought now to be regarded as belonging to the Keuper series, and this particular horizon is important because of its water-bearing qualities; it is in fact known as a Waterstone. It is best seen, perhaps, as a yellowish-brown sandstone in the raised beach cliffline on the Shore Road. These sandstones have long been the main source of water for Belfast and they have been pierced by numerous wells not only for domestic purposes but also to supply the various mills and the distilling and mineral water industry. The massive, well-jointed sandstones have also been extensively quarried for use as a building stone, especially for the city churches and some of the larger secular buildings. Most of the modern quarrying, however, has occurred at Scrabo Hill near Strangford Lough and will be considered below. Nevertheless, it is important to note that despite the existence of this important building material, Belfast is one of the few Ulster towns in which stone was never in general use, largely because of the brick-making qualities of both the Triassic marls and the much younger glacial clays. There is documentary evidence to show that during the Plantation in 1611 the decayed Norman castle here was rebuilt in locally made bricks and that sufficient were left over to complete the domestic housing. At that period the marls and sandstones of the Lagan valley supported a flourishing oak forest which provided an excellent supply of timber for the buildings of the early settlement. The town, with its half-timbered and brick buildings, would have had much of the character of an English town of that time and as such must have contrasted sharply with the more Scottish character of stone-built Newtownards at the head of Strangford Lough.

The major brick-clay workings were in the Keuper Marls of the modern Springfield area on the slopes below Black Mountain. Some of the flooded brick-pits survive although these formerly wooded slopes are now mantled by a new 'forest' of modern housing estates, such as Ballymurphy, which have obliterated much of the green belt which formerly flanked the city on its western side.

The site and layout of Belfast, within the Triassic vale, is linked closely with the local physical factors, for here an ancient trackway crossed the Lagan just above its mouth. A wide area of estuarine clay, which had been uplifted by post-glacial upwarping to form a raised beach, of similar age to that at Larne (see chapter two), is more extensive on the left bank than on the right. Where this slightly raised shoreline stood above the estuary marshes a small stream, the Farset river, joined the river Lagan and it was at the resulting confluence sandbank that Belfast was born (Beal-Farset: 'The approach to the sandbank'). Like the river Fleet in London, the Farset river now flows underground and is carried in a conduit before entering the modern Lagan ignominiously through a pipe in the precipitous dockside wall. The curve of the present High Street below which the channelled river runs, is a reminder of this former river course, although the estuary of the Lagan has been considerably altered by the construction of artificial channels and islands. The extensive raised mudflats, known as sloblands, were reclaimed as early as 1800, putting into practice on a large scale the 1582 recommendations of Sir John Perrot who saw the estuary as 'the best and most convenient place in Ulster for shipbuilding'. Around the early town nucleus rectangular plots were laid out on the sloblands, later to be filled with the great mass of terrace housing which accommodated the industrial workers who crowded into Belfast. This gridiron plan was delimited by physical features, for it stops abruptly where the land rises sharply at the cliffline of the post-glacial raised beach. Above the change of slope, on the Triassic rocks and the glacial sands and clays, the street pattern, of the Shankill and Falls roads for example, rises irregularly up the western slopes. To the south, the Malone road, formerly the main route to Dublin, follows a low but distinct ridge of glacial sands, and on this well-drained eminence of lighter soils the more expensive Regency terrace houses and Victorian villas were built; this is the present University 'quarter' of modern Belfast. To supply the enormous demand for bricks during the latter half of the nineteenth century, when the city's population quadrupled, new brick-pits were opened on the Bunter Marls, on the floor of the Lagan valley near to the present Stranmillis College.

A much older town than Belfast, in a strategic position at the mouth of the Lough, is Carrickfergus, now almost a part of the Belfast conurbation. It is a neat little town, dominated by a splendid Norman castle which is perched on a Tertiary igneous intrusion on the shore itself (plate 12). The fabric of the castle is interesting for, whilst the majority of the building stones are of local black basalt, the blocks of cream Magnesian Limestone set in the walls remind us that at Cultra, near Holywood, on the far side of the Lough, there occurs one of the very few instances of this particular rock in Ireland. Of much greater importance, however, are the formerly worked rock salt deposits which occur here within the Keuper Marls. Just as in Cheshire in 1670, the discovery of the salt was made accidentally in 1850 during a fruitless boring for coal. Originally the salt was dug out from large underground caverns excavated in one of the three most economic beds, but in more recent years it was found simpler to pump it to the surface in the form of brine where it was purified and evaporated at Carrickfergus itself. Production has now ceased in this, the only salt mine in Ireland. The salt deposits serve to emphasize the great climatic oscillations which have occurred throughout the geological record, for in this area during Keuper times the climate was hot and dry, with salt lakes (salinas) forming in many of the basins, much as they do today in the state of Utah, U.S.A. The intense evaporation caused mineral salts to be drawn to the surface where they were concentrated as layers of rock-salt and gypsum, later to be buried by thick layers of marls. It is interesting to speculate on the reserves of rock-salt which probably exist in the Triassic rocks entombed beneath the Antrim basalts at depths too uneconomic to exploit.

Strangford Lough and the Ards Peninsula

To the east of Belfast the Holywood–Castlereagh hills are broken by one distinctive gap, the Dundonald Gap, now followed by the main road to Newtownards (figure 12). It has been suggested that during Late Pleistocene times this gap was used as an overflow by the pro-glacial lake waters impounded in the Lagan valley by a Scottish ice-sheet blocking the entrance to Belfast Lough. It must not be assumed, however, that the Dundonald Gap was formed by glacial meltwaters, for there is evidence to show that a valley feature has existed here for a considerable period of geological time. An examination of a geological map will show that the junction between the Ordovician and Silurian rocks is markedly displaced between Belfast and Newtownards by a fault line running almost east–west. Erosion must have picked out this weakness before Mesozoic times because the valley is floored by Triassic sandstones which link up the two major basins of Triassic rocks in Ulster, that of the Lagan valley described above and the drowned basin of Strangford Lough. Since the Triassic rocks have subsequently proved less resistant to denudation than the surrounding Palaeozoic strata, erosion has once more created an east–west corridor at this location.

The finest viewpoint in the area is undoubtedly the steep little hill of Scrabo (538 feet) near Newtownards where a knob of Bunter sandstone has been preserved by a thick dolerite sill which now caps the hill top. In the quarries which scar the slopes the well-jointed and cross-bedded sandstones exhibit excellent evidence of ripple-marks, sun-cracks and occasional rain-pitting, further proof of the arid environment which existed here in Triassic times and which was discussed in more detail above. The sandstone was formerly quarried extensively as a building stone, especially for Belfast, but working became increasingly difficult because of the overlying sill and has now ceased. To the south and east there is a fascinating view of Strangford Lough, its curiously sinuous coastline having been produced by the drowning of countless numbers of drumlins by the sea. It is a remarkable fact that this landlocked inlet of the sea has a coastline more than 80 miles in length and yet is linked to the Irish Sea by a channel only half a mile in width. Little wonder that the Norse raiders gave the name Strangford (the violent inlet) to this place, for the tide rips through the narrows at almost ten knots as 400 million tons of water pour twice daily through the gap at Portaferry.

Strangford Lough appears to be carved from a fault-controlled structural basin within the Silurian rocks, infilled at least in its northern part by a layer of Triassic rocks. Solid rock is rarely seen on its shores, however, for during the Ice Age the area was predominantly a zone of glacial deposition, mainly in the form of drumlins (plate 13). From Scrabo it can be seen how the drumlin landscape of mid-Down passes beneath sea level at the lough to create a multitude of whale-backed islands, the like of which is nowhere seen on such a scale in Ireland except in Clew Bay on the Mayo coast (chapter 12). The post-glacial rise in sea level has left its mark in the clearly defined raised beach which notches most of the seaward facing drumlins, the marine transgression being approximately the same age (7,400 years) as that at Larne. Many of the drumlin islands have now been linked to the mainland by artificial causeways, to incorporate their potentially valuable grasslands into the livestock-rearing economy of the surrounding farmlands. The raised-beach deposits also extend some distance into the Ards peninsula from its western coast, to provide broad fertile flats of shelly and pebbly soils amidst the heavier clays of the drumlins. There are fewer drumlin islands on the Ards coast of the lough for the prevailing westerly winds have facilitated more effective wave attack here than on the more sheltered western shore. Consequently some of the drumlins have been totally destroyed by marine erosion of the soft boulder clay, leaving behind boulder-dotted shoals and mudbanks, known as 'pladdies', which uncover at low tide.

Although of no great geological interest the Ards Peninsula is worthy of a visit to view its neat farmlands, if nothing more. The land is generally low-lying and is dominated by the drumlins except in the extreme south where a rocky ice-scoured plateau extends across the Portaferry–Strangford narrows into the Lecale Peninsula. A contrast in scenery becomes apparent, therefore, as we travel southwards down the length of the peninsula. The northern half of the Ards is one of Ulster's most important grain-producing areas, with the large wheat and barley fields and a couple of abandoned windmills adding a touch of the East Anglian scene to the Irish countryside. Almost one-third of the land is under the plough and the farms are larger than the county average. Favourable soil and climate, therefore, have contributed to a prosperous scene, and nowhere in Ireland does one find better farming than in this easternmost corner. As we move farther south, past the imposing monastic ruins of Grey Abbey, built of Scrabo sandstone, the true Ards landscape begins to unfold – 'all tilled fields and white cottages and little winding roads, and a low flowery coastline with alternating points of sharp upturned slates and bays of fine grey sand' (R. Lloyd Praeger). In the extreme south the trim hedged fields disappear as we pass on to the bare ice-scrubbed plateau near Portaferry, their place being taken by a more typical Irish landscape of small stone-walled fields. Here the soils are thin and stony, supporting a patchwork of rough heathland, marshy hollows and many clumps of gorse.

The Mid-Down Lowlands

Like most parts of eastern Down 'described above' the landscape of mid-Down is also dominated by drumlins with their characteristic effect on settlement and field patterns and it is this part of Ireland which inspired the analogy between drumlin topography and a basket of eggs. Nevertheless, although solid rock rarely appears at the surface, except in the south along the curving rim of the Slieve Croob upland (the metamorphic aureole of an ancient granite intrusion), wherever the Palaeozoic rocks do appear they are seen to be strongly folded. The majority of these rocks are grits, shales and slates of Silurian age, the Irish equivalent of the Scottish Southern Uplands. What strikes the visitor as so curious, however, is the fact that these self-same rocks are here planed across by an erosion surface at a height of 400–500 feet. The folds are part of a Caledonian synclinorium which crosses from Galloway into southern Down, following the characteristic north-east to south-west trend, but they play virtually no part in the present relief of mid-Down as the erosional plane cuts right across all their intricate detail with total disregard for anticlines and synclines alike. Some authorities have called this low plateau feature the County Down peneplain, reputedly the end-product of a lengthy period of base-levelling by rivers in Tertiary times. It might equally be the result of an extensive marine bevelling by waves of an early Quaternary sea. One fact remains indisputable, however; that the erosion surface was in existence before the deposition of the glacial drifts which have added local diversity to the plateau-like landforms.

Because of its low altitude and relatively deep soils the landscape of mid-Down contrasts sharply with the Scottish Southern Uplands. In place of the high peat-covered mountains, rough grazing lands and conifer plantations of Scotland, here is excellent agricultural land with a large number of prosperous farms and well-maintained roads and hedgerows. Peat bogs were never very extensive here and most of those which existed were soon cut away for fuel. Although this was once a thickly wooded area, natural woodland had disappeared by the late eighteenth century, to be replaced by planting only on the large estates, mainly south of Slieve Croob, two of which, at Castlewellan and Tollymore, now represent examples of Northern Ireland's Forest Parks. The northern part of the area, dominated by the proximity of the Belfast market, is essentially a landscape of dairy farms, with scarcely any tillage to be seen. Economic history has been the major cause of change in the landscape here, for the medium-textured soils once supported countless fields of flax when the demand was high. But the picturesque splashes of blue flowers have now gone, to be replaced by large herds of Friesian and Ayrshire cattle in the neatly tended fields. Most of the farms have small sheltering clumps of trees, often of beech or sycamore, and hedgerow trees are not uncommon here since the small areas of ploughland do not require the removal of hedges to facilitate mechanized farming. Thus the northern part of mid-Down has a well-wooded appearance, in contrast with the bare basalt plateaux which face it across the Lagan valley.

As one travels southwards in mid-Down, however, the prosperity of the scene diminishes. From Ballynahinch to Seaforde the villages look rather forlorn and the farmland less ordered. Perhaps this is because the Silurian rocks are never far below the surface in this tract and because the drumlin belt with its deeper soils virtually disappears. To the west Slieve Croob (1,735 feet) rises to a treeless moorland from the small mixed farms of the lowlands.

The southernmost part of mid-Down, between the Mournes and Strangford Lough, is an area of considerable individuality, different from any other part of the county. This peninsula of Lecale is bordered on three sides by the sea and on the north-western side by the marshes which stretch from the Quoile estuary to the inner bay of Dundrum. Its physical isolation, its fertile lime-rich soils and its natural harbours of Killough and Ardglass, combined to give Lecale an attraction not only to the earliest prehistoric population, but also to settlers from the Early Christian period right through to the sixteenth century. It exhibits a landscape chequered with historic remains for this is St Patrick's country, with seemingly every hill and valley having links with Ireland's patron saint. Suffice to mention two of the more important: first, Downpatrick, with its fine cathedral and splendid Georgian town-houses, one of the few pre-seventeenth-century towns in Ulster; secondly, the simple little church of Saul standing on the site of the earliest church in Ireland close to the spot at which

St Patrick landed in 432. In addition to the Early Christian associations Lecale was a stronghold of Anglo-Norman power. The ruins of their tower-houses in the area remind us that because of its Norman settlement Lecale was one of the few areas of Ulster to escape the seventeenth-century 'plantation' by Scottish and English settlers. The most significant feature in the agricultural scene is the unusually large size of the farms, with many being over 100 acres in area. A combination of the large farms and the exceptionally fertile soil, derived from the glacial deposits, enables large numbers of cattle and sheep to be grazed. But the ruined windmill and flour mill of Ballydugan near Downpatrick and the dilapidated grain stores at Killough quay serve as a reminder that the same exceptionally high-yielding soils once supported thriving cornfields all over Lecale. The fine texture of the soils in this part of County Down could well result from the fact that Lecale is crossed by a line of kame moraines, with associated glacio-fluvial outwash, marking the southern limit of the glaciation which produced the major Irish drumlins.

Across the bay from Lecale rise the magnificent sand-dunes of Dundrum which almost enclose the lagoon of Dundrum inner bay. Recent research has shown that the dunes, which attain more than 100 feet in height, stand on a complex shingle spit now almost inundated by sand. The pebbles of the spit decrease in size as they are traced from south-west to north-east, demonstrating that longshore drift of beach material by dominant waves from the south-east probably played a large part in the growth of the spit along the coast from Newcastle in post-glacial times. Archaeological excavations have indicated that Neolithic, Bronze Age and Iron Age settlers once dwelt at this coastal site which is now protected as a Nature Reserve. But the coastal scene cannot hold our attention for long, for the neat little resort of Newcastle is overshadowed by the soaring slopes of the Mourne Mountains to which we now turn.

8. The Mountains of Mourne and Carlingford

From any viewpoint in mid-Down one's eyes are constantly drawn to the southern horizon where the great massif of the Mourne mountains rises dramatically from the surrounding plains and plateaux. Famed in song and story, the Mournes are but one, albeit the largest, of three upland areas which dominate the scenery of south Down, south Armagh and north Louth. The unique character of the Mourne landscape has inspired a notable monograph, *Mourne Country*, in which Professor Estyn Evans has demonstrated the close relationships which exist between the physical and cultural landscapes of the area. Smaller in extent and markedly lower in elevation, the neighbouring mountains of Slieve Gullion (1,894 feet) and Carlingford (1,935 feet) complete an upland trio, remarkable not so much for their scenic charm as for their fascinating geological structures. As if to unify the three the basin of Carlingford Lough nestles between them, taking its tidal waters deep into the mountainland as a constant reminder that this is essentially a coastal environment.

Although the Mournes are best known from their northerly aspect, since most visitors approach them across the Down lowlands, one of the best prospects is that seen from the easterly tip of the neighbouring Cooley Peninsula, across the waters of Carlingford Lough. One advantage of this viewpoint is that the highest peak, Slieve Donard (2,796 feet), does not dominate the remainder of the peaks to quite the same extent as it does when seen from Castlewellan or Newcastle, whilst the impressive summit of Slieve Binnian (2,449 feet) can now be appreciated. Furthermore, one is now able to observe the so-called Kingdom of Mourne which lies between the mountain summits and the sea, a remarkably isolated corner of Ireland with its own way of life specially adapted to this maritime–upland environment.

The Kingdom of Mourne

The shape of the lowlands which border the south-eastern slopes of the Mournes is that of a crescent, its points narrowing to north and west until they are cut off near Newcastle and Rostrevor as the mountain flanks 'sweep down to the sea'. In a lowland area of only 40 square miles it seems unlikely that there would be major contrasts in the landscape, although in fact marked differences can be seen between the Greencastle Peninsula and the remainder of the lowlands. Greencastle is '. . . a land of fine, easily worked soils, free of the great boulders which litter the country nearer the hills. Farms and farm-houses are often larger than in other parts of the Kingdom, stone walls less common and the hedges more luxuriant, except along the coast' (E. E. Evans). Elsewhere, the deep incision of the rivers, the steep gradients of which carry the Mourne waters swiftly to the sea, has led to a scarcity of lateral roads along the slopes. For the surface drifts are thick hereabouts and the streams are forced to excavate some 50 feet to reach the Silurian shales and grey-wackes which underlie most of the lowlands. Thus, many of the routeways run parallel with the stream valleys from the mountains to the shoreline, reflecting not only the difficulty of bridging the chasms, but also the need of the inhabitants to look seaward for part of their livelihood. In such a landlocked situation their economy has been based partly on farming, with seaweed gathering to manure the acid, impoverished soils, and partly on fishing to supplement their diet. Despite the presence of the under-lying Silurian rocks the soils of the hillslopes achieve their character from the Mourne granites because the glacial drifts together with the later hillwash were derived very largely from the neighbouring mountains. Because of their lime-deficiency and stoniness the soils of these slopes require considerable labour to produce reasonable crops, although they are generally more rewarding to work than some of the heavy clay soils of the drumlin belt farther north. Along the coast, however, and farthest from the mountains (as at Greencastle) the soils get lighter and more friable, thus facilitating very high yields of potatoes. These deep sandy loams of the coast are in part a response to the gravelly moraines (of the former Carlingford glacier) that here sweep out from Rostrevor eastwards to Kilkeel before swinging southwards across the mouth of Carlingford Lough (figure 13). The curious lower course of the White Water river appears to have been influenced by the disposition of these moraines, while the three small headlands of Cranfield, Soldiers and Greencastle Points represent their wave-truncated ends.

Moraines are also found near Bloody Bridge, at the northern extremity

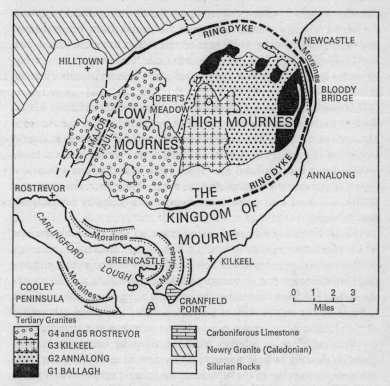

Fig. 13. *The geology of the Mountains of Mourne (after J. E. Richey et al.).*

of the lowlands, where former ice-sheets swung around the northern flanks of the Mournes. The steep, narrow, inhospitable, boulder-strewn slopes north of Annalong seem to have been avoided by settlers from prehistoric times onwards. Indeed such physical obstacles as these discouraged the Anglo-Normans from penetrating into the Kingdom of Mourne; instead they were content to build their castles at the two extremities of

Rostrevor and Newcastle and to turn their backs on this enclave of native Irish life.

The Mountains of Mourne

Covering an area of some 55 square miles the Mourne granites represent the largest Tertiary granite outcrop in the British Isles, being slightly more extensive than the Arran granite and almost twice the area of the Red Cuillins of Skye. The area of mountainland, however, is considerably larger for it will be seen how a great deal of the western Mournes granite is still 'roofed' by a gently sloping cover of Silurian rocks (figure 13).

It is possible to distinguish two broad topographical divisions within the highlands, referred to as the High Mournes in the east and the Low Mournes in the west. The different character of the two areas is largely a question of geological contrasts although their dividing line is a topographic break running from the Upper Bann past the Deer's Meadow reservoir and over the watershed to the White Water river. On a map the Hilltown–Kilkeel road provides an approximate boundary between the two divisions.

The Mournes are formed from no less than five granitic intrusions which themselves exhibit only slight petrological differences, although the three eastern granites of the High Mournes are generally more porphyritic than their two western counterparts in the Low Mournes. To understand their method of formation the reader is referred to figure 14 which is based largely on the work of Dr J. E. Richey. The actual mechanism of the plutonic intrusive phases is known as 'cauldron subsidence', when a cylindrical block of Silurian rocks, bounded by outwardly inclined faults, is thought to have subsided slowly into an underlying magmatic reservoir. In response to the subsidence the granitic magma is thought to have risen into the roof space and 'ring' cavity left behind by the subsiding block without destroying the undisturbed roof of sedimentary rocks (figure 14a).

When this first magma cooled and solidified it formed a coarse feldspathic granite (G1), known as the Ballagh granite, which has subsequently been exposed as denudation has destroyed the roof. This is the granite which has been most actively worked between the rivers of Bloody Bridge and Annalong, for it forms the easily accessible eastern slopes of the High

Mournes which here culminate in the prominent summits of Chimney Rock Mountain (2,152 feet) and Slieve Donard (2,796 feet) itself. The granite workers of these boulder-strewn slopes were also farmers and their neatly built whitewashed farm cottages, within the primly rectangular fields, testify to the skill of the Mourne stone-workers. Where the granite

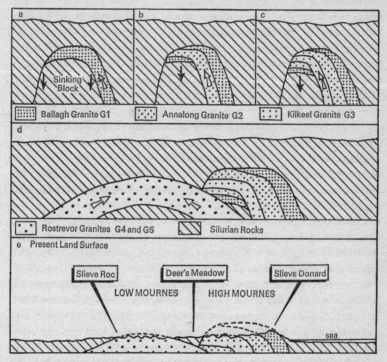

Fig. 14. *The theory of Cauldron Subsidence and the suggested formation of the Mountains of Mourne (after J. E. Richey).*

margin came into contact with the surrounding sedimentary rocks during its intrusion, not only did it convert the Silurian rocks into schists and hornfelses as part of the metamorphic aureole, but it also caused the granite margin to cool more quickly. Consequently the outermost zone of the Ballagh granite is generally finer grained, is easier to work and therefore produces the better 'setts'. Many of the latter were transported downslope to Annalong and exported to England where they are reputed to have 'paved Lancashire' during the Industrial Revolution. With more certainty, the setts are known to have been used extensively in the construction of Liverpool and Belfast docks, whilst the larger blocks were incorporated in London's Albert Memorial. During the later nineteenth century some of the returning stone boats brought cargoes of Welsh slates which gradually replaced thatch as a roofing material in this part of Ireland. The impact of the stone-working industry on the scenery of these slopes was only slight until after the Second World War, for the granite was originally procured from the screes, the moraines and the isolated erratic blocks which littered the area. Only as a result of post-war building were the demands great enough to cause the opening of large new quarries.

The second granitic intrusion (G2) is known as the Annalong granite, its most characteristic feature being the high proportion of dusky quartz which gives the rock a dark colouring (figure 14b). Where its margins cut through the older Ballagh granite the latter was baked and hardened by contact metamorphism to form tough bands of rock which were subsequently picked out not only by erosion to form impressive cliff faces, but also much later by the stone-workers who specifically sought these more durable rocks. Because it occupies the heart of the High Mournes, the well-jointed Annalong (G2) granite outcrop forms the high tor-capped summits of Slieve Binnian (2,449 feet) and Slieve Bearnagh (2,394 feet), although the lower summit of Ben Crom (1,721 feet) is no less spectacular when viewed from the Silent Valley. The Annalong granite (named from the Annalong river basin, not the town) is now being extensively quarried, especially on Slieve Bearnagh and Slieve Binnian, which are generally regarded as the two most picturesque peaks. Since the Second World War the demand for fine-grained granites has fallen and has been replaced by a preference for porphyritic rocks, the large crystals of which will take a high polish. This demand is largely a result of post-war rebuilding which has required a great deal of ornamental stone. But the whole character of the Mourne countryside has changed with this shift in demand, for the small stone-worker/farmer has been replaced by the large mechanized consortium, with its transport facilities at Belfast docks instead of at Annalong and Kilkeel, which are now more important as fishing ports. Thus the Mourne hillsides now echo to gigantic blasting operations and the rumble of heavy lorries as the quarry faces extend their scars across the slopes. The ringing of the solitary hammers using the 'plug-and-feathers' method of splitting, together with the rattle of the slipes (types of sledge) and the stone-carts, has virtually ceased in the Mournes, probably never to return.

The third granite of the High Mournes is exposed in the south-west and since it underlies much of the basin of the Kilkeel river it has been termed the Kilkeel granite (G3). It differs from the Annalong granite because of its lighter colouring and its finer grain. It was intruded in much the same way as the earlier granites (figure 14c) although, since its roof was originally lower, it has been less denuded than the others. Consequently, some of its sedimentary rock cover is still intact and can plainly be seen at Slieve Muck (1,931 feet). Here the cover is composed of Silurian shales which create a conspicious scarp facing east across the Miner's Hole river and the Silent Valley. Around Lough Shannagh, however, the roof of the Kilkeel granite (G3) is formed from the slightly older Annalong granite (G2) into which it was intruded, the surrounding horseshoe of hills being capped, therefore, by this older, darker granite.

Mention of the Miner's Hole river is a reminder that the Mournes have witnessed sporadic attempts to work the mineral wealth which one usually associates with granitic intrusions. Minerals such as lead, zinc and copper are often produced during the hydrothermal phase of granite emplace-ment, being deposited in fissures and cavities by gases given off by the cooling magma. But the mineralization of the Mournes is relatively poor and most prospecting for metals has met with little success. Nor does the hydrothermal alteration seem to have been sufficient to produce large-scale kaolin formation, in contrast to that of the much older Cornish granites. Nevertheless, it is known that kaolin, a white clay formed from the decomposition of feldspar, occurs at depth in the Annalong granite beneath Slieve Binnian, so that the currently extensive surface quarrying may one day expose an economic outcrop.

Before leaving the High Mournes it is necessary to say something of the cliffs, hollows and ridges which give such an intricate character to the mountain scene. Most of these features owe their final form to the effects of glacial and periglacial processes during the Pleistocene ice age.

The Mourne summits were almost certainly completely overridden by the earliest Irish ice-sheets which travelled south-eastwards to contribute their share to the enormous ice accumulation within the Irish Sea basin. During the later phases of the Ice Age, however, in the so-called Midland General (Midlandian) glacial episode in Ireland, it has been shown how the ice-sheets, emanating from centres further to the north-west, swept around the flanks of the Mournes to leave their summits isolated as nunataks above the ice. One such lobe created the Carlingford glacier in the west, whilst the eastern ice lobe left its marginal moraines on the slopes of Slieve Donard near to Bloody Bridge. But this is not to say that the high peaks remained entirely unglaciated at this time, for there is evidence to show that small glaciers existed in the highest hollows and valleys.

Many of the granite cliffs became freshly steepened, either by glacial overdeepening of the walls and heads of valleys or by the plucking action of corrie glaciers on the headwalls of their retaining hollows (plate 14). Ultimately these hollows were glacially scoured into armchair depressions or corries (cirques) such as that on the north face of Slieve Corragh. Small lakes were occasionally impounded in these high, lonely corries, sometimes due to their having been glacially overdeepened but partly by virtue of the moraines which often mantle the corrie lip. These moraines represent the final phase of the Ice Age in Ireland, for by this time the major ice-sheets had virtually disappeared elsewhere in the island. Thus the last cold period saw only tiny corrie glaciers forming on the highest Irish mountains although a large ice-sheet still persisted in the Highlands of Scotland. In addition to the Mournes, there were corrie glaciers at this stage in the Wicklows, the highest Mayo hills, the Reeks and the Dingle mountains of Kerry.

Above the corries and on the intervening ridges the granite slopes must have been subjected to intense frost-shattering and solifluxion during the several cold phases of the Midland General glaciation. Consequently some of the summits now support extensive spreads of shattered rock waste, whilst enormous screes have formed beneath the crags. But it is the tors, crowning the summits and the ridges, which catch the eye of the climber and walker. Although tors can form in any well-jointed rock, granite lends itself better than most to tor-formation. There is much disagreement concerning the way in which tors are created, some authors claiming that they are entirely a product of rock rotting at great depth during a period of pre-glacial time when tropical conditions prevailed, whilst others would see their pinnacles and towers as being the result of a periglacial frost climate only. Despite this divergence of views on their genesis it remains possible that both hypotheses may be correct in part. The same type of deep tropical weathering which rotted the surface of the Eocene basalts in Antrim may have had a similar effect on the freshly unroofed Mourne granites, while the glacial and periglacial processes of the Quaternary may have helped to strip off much of this regolith (see glossary), leaving only the unconsumed relics to remain as tors, later to be freshened-up by frost shattering. Be that as it may, there is no doubt that the summits of Slieve Bearnagh, Slieve Binnian and the less lofty Doan are enhanced by their granite tors whilst the pillars known as the Castles of Commedagh offer a variety of scrambles to the rock climber.

As already noted, the road from Hilltown to Kilkeel, across the centre of the mountains, marks the division between the High Mournes and the Low Mournes. The geology map (figure 13) shows that the granite out-crop narrows to a 'waist' at the point where the road passes the reservoir of the Deer's Meadow. The visitor may not realize that the shining lake waters impounded behind the Spelga dam, like their counterparts in the Silent Valley, introduce an element into the Mourne landscape which is totally foreign, despite its enhancement of the scene. Unlike the English Lake District, Snowdonia or even Donegal, the long, narrow valleys of the Mournes have remained devoid of major lakes until the advent of the urban water board authorities, perhaps because the valley glaciers failed to overdeepen the valley floors. The reservoirs, however, are now as much a feature of the Mourne landscape as the incredible 'Mourne Wall' which delimits the catchment; the Silent Valley lake was a creation of the 1930s; the Crom Dam, in the upper reaches of the same valley, was completed in 1957; the Deer's Meadow was inundated in 1959.

The curiously flat upland basin of the recently submerged Deer's Meadow is believed to have been fashioned by rivers when it lay near to sea level, prior to uplift of the whole region in early Quaternary times. Such a process of levelling by rivers is termed 'peneplanation' and the resulting surface a 'peneplain', although many modern authors are questioning the whole of this concept, which was defined by W. M. Davis many decades ago. Because of its gentle gradients this extensive basin appears to have become an area of impeded drainage in post-glacial times, for there is evidence of several phases of peat-bog growth after the final disappearance of the Mourne glaciers. Much of the peat had already been cut away for fuel long before the Spelga dam was built and this serves to remind us that the Deer's Meadow has not always been deserted. Although sheep now graze the surrounding hills this was once an important area of rich cattle pasture, used by the inhabitants of the mid-Down lowlands who drove their herds up to the Deer's Meadow during the summer months. Such a movement of people and animals to the high summer pastures is known as transhumance (or 'booleying' in Ireland) and remains common today in mountain regions of central Europe. Booleying appears to have died out in Ireland during the nineteenth century (except in Achill Island, see chapter twelve), but it is interesting to record that the relative fertility of the lush grassland surrounding the Deer's Meadow results from the preservation of a tongue of Silurian shales which here still caps the roof of the granite and replaces its acid, impoverished soils.

The Western, or Low Mournes, extend south-westwards from the Deer's Meadow and are composed very largely of two non-porphyritic granites; the older (G4) being pink in colour, whilst the newer (G5) is a blue-green microgranite. These granites were intruded at a later stage than those of the High Mournes but they have not been uplifted by earth movements to quite the same extent. As a consequence they have retained large patches of their Silurian shale roof, which means that their landforms are more subdued and their relief not as high as that of the Eastern Mournes. Nevertheless, the outcrop of what may be termed the Rostrevor granites (G4 and G5) is considerable, almost equal in area to the combined outcrop of the High Mourne granites (figure 13). At the scarp of the contact-hardened Silurian rocks of Gruggandoo (1,263 feet) the Rostrevor granites pass westwards beneath the Silurian sedimentary rocks which here form only a low plateau, some 1,000 feet in elevation. The flatness of the plateau and the accordance of its summits have suggested to some writers that here on the western flanks of the Mournes is another example of an uplifted peneplain of approximately the same age as that of the Deer's Meadow. In complete contrast to the deserted heather-clad granite country farther east this plateau of Silurian rocks, to the north of Rostrevor, is a region of improved land where a network of lanes helps to link the small scattered farms which have managed to survive at heights of 1,000 feet because of the more fertile soils. In the High Mournes, on the other hand, settlement rarely rises above the 600-foot contour because of the poorer soils and steeper slopes of the eastern granites.

The central area of the Low Mournes has been considerably affected by faulting, most of which follows a direction somewhat to the east of north, parallel to one of the principal joint orientations of the granite. Not only have these fault and joint directions had an important effect on the local drainage pattern but they have often been picked out by erosion to form important lineaments in the topography. The most striking of these is the Rostrevor fault scarp which overlooks the picturesque valley of the Killbroney river. Whilst the valley has been carved from the down-faulted Silurian rocks the Rostrevor Mountains are made up essentially of the youngest (G5) granite. At their southern end these mountains plunge steeply to the sea at Carlingford Lough, so steeply in fact that the slopes have been given over entirely to forestry.

Carlingford Lough

With the exceptions of Killary Harbour and Lough Swilly, both on the rugged Atlantic coast, Carlingford Lough is more fjord-like than any of the other coastal inlets of Ireland. Lying between the Mountains of Mourne and Carlingford the 'Cairlinn fjord' is named more aptly than its neighbour of Strangford (Strang fjord) amidst its low drumlin-covered plains (see chapter seven). There seems little doubt that its character was achieved by lengthy periods of glacial overdeepening from ice-sheets compressed between the mountains of Mourne and Carlingford (plate 15). The Silurian and Carboniferous rocks which occupy this narrow tract had previously been affected considerably by faults trending north-west to south-east, so it is little wonder that a combination of less resistant rocks and parallel faulting was destined to produce a deeply incised corri-dor at this point. The Pleistocene ice-sheets, in the form of the Carlingford glacier, scoured out the floor of the trough at its narrowest part but as in all true fjords the entrance to the lough is marked by a shallowing of the sea bed. This is the submarine rock bar or 'threshold' resulting from the decreased downward cutting power of the ice as its lateral restriction was diminished at the coast. Unlike Lough Swilly and Killary Harbour, parts of the rock bar can actually be seen as a series of limestone reefs across the entrance to the lough, between Greencastle and Greenore (figure 13).

In earlier days this rock-strewn entrance, which leads through the coastal mountains to the fertile lowlands of mid-Down, would have had considerable strategic significance, as shown by its numerous ruined military installations. Greencastle on the northern shore and the island blockhouse off Soldiers Point both testify to the troubled history of the area, but it is the gaunt ruin of King John's Castle which, standing grim and massive on the rocks above the quay at Carlingford, epitomizes the character of this remarkable sea lough.

The faults which gave some structural control to the formation of Carlingford Lough must also have played a part in the development of the curiously linear course of the Newry river which enters the head of the Lough. Although taking its name from its waterside position (Iubhar-cinntragh = the yew tree at the head of the strand) Newry is so far from the sea that its function as a port is rapidly being replaced by Warrenpoint on the lough itself. Thus the decaying quays and warehouses create a melancholy aspect in this sombre granite-built town. Not far to the west lies the planned industrial village of Bessbrook, built as a flax-spinning centre in 1845 by a Quaker family, the success of which inspired the model village of Bourneville near Birmingham in England. Both Newry and Bessbrook are examples of the early use of granite as a domestic building stone, although both exploited the underlying Newry granite, not the better-known Mourne granites described above. The Newry granite, of Caledonian age, extends for some distance to the north-east of Newry where it culminates in the rounded eminence of Slieve Croob which rises darkly above the pastel green fields of mid-Down. The Newry granite also runs, to a lesser extent, south-westwards from Newry where it forms Camlough Mountain (1,389 feet), although its outcrop is less important in its scenic effects than that of the so-called Slieve Gullion Ring Complex.

Slieve Gullion and the Carlingford Mountains

The country to the west of Newry is dominated by a group of isolated hills which rise dramatically from the undulating lowlands of the Newry granite and Silurian shale country. Only from the highest parts of Slieve Gullion (not to be confused with Slieve Gallion, chapter four) would it be possible to distinguish the semblance of a regular pattern in the layout of these hills. From the summit cairn (1,894 feet) a visitor would be able to distinguish a curving pattern of ridges and hills which encircle Slieve Gullion at a distance of some three to four miles. Rising above the farmlands of the plain to heights of between 700 and 1,000 feet these heathery hills make up the famous ring-dyke of Slieve Gullion. The ring-complex is a structure similar to that of the Mournes, described above, for it resulted from the subsidence of a cylindrical block of rocks within a circular fracture. The major difference lies in the fact that the Mournes were formed from an underground cauldron subsidence which failed to reach the surface, the granites being unroofed only by later denudation. Slieve Gullion, on the other hand, is a much denuded example of a ringdyke which had a surface manifestation in a caldera (see glossary) and several small volcanoes.

The sequence of events which led to the formation of the remarkable ring phenomenon is extremely complex although the simplified structure is shown in figure 15. In early Tertiary times, slightly before the formation of the Mourne granites, a circular fracture, some seven miles in diameter, appeared in the Slieve Gullion area, slicing through the floor of Newry granite and Silurian slates. This was followed by the initial rise of acid magma into the lower part of the ring fracture to form the porphyritic granophyre of the ring-dyke. Its mineral composition is similar to that of the Ballagh (G1) granite of the Mournes and is best seen exposed at Sturgan Mountain at the north end of Cam Lough. Further igneous activity manifested itself at the surface in the form of small volcanoes associated with the ring fracture (figure 15), chiefly in the south-western area (where the village of Forkhill stands today). The volcanoes extruded basaltic (and some trachytic) lavas, similar to those of Antrim but on a much smaller scale, until their vents became blocked by a combination of collapsed lavas and agglomerates, the latter composed of a shattered mixture of Newry granite and Silurian metasediments. This agglomerate had been created suddenly by an explosion sparked off by a second phase of acid magma intrusion in response to further subsidence of the central floor enclosed by the ring-dyke. In contrast to the intact roof of the Mournes cauldron subsidence, the vapour pressure built up at Slieve Gullion was sufficient to shatter the overlying older rocks and create a large surface caldera. This enormous amphitheatre acted as a receptacle for further lava extrusion until hundreds of feet of basic lavas had accumulated in the central area. The well-known Ngorongoro 'Crater' (more accurately 'caldera') of the Serengeti Plains of East Africa illustrates the type of scenery which must have existed at Slieve Gullion during early Tertiary times. After the felsites had been added to the ring-dyke a final phase of subsidence of the central block allowed acid granophyre

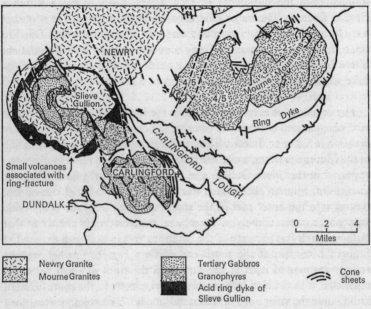

Newry Granite
Mourne Granites

Tertiary Gabbros
Granophyres
Acid ring dyke of
Slieve Gullion

Cone
sheets

Fig. 15. *The igneous complexes of the Mourne and Carlingford Mountains and of Slieve Gullion (after F. H. Hatch and A. K. Wells).*

to rise once more and sills of dolerite and gabbro to be intruded into the lava pile of the central arena. The mountain of Slieve Gullion owes its dominance very largely to the successive layers of dolerite and gabbro, which, together with the summit granophyre, have withstood denudation more successfully than the older rocks which surround them within the ring-dyke (figure 15). Thus whilst the Newry granite has subsequently been worn down by rivers and ice to form the broad, curving corridor which separates Slieve Gullion from its circle of ring-dyke satellite hills, the latter rise steeply above the valleys and lowlands by virtue of their harder rocks.

Since the ice movement closely paralleled the Tertiary faulting pattern of the region it is interesting to note how the river courses and the superficial drifts exhibit a marked north-west to south-east alignment, which has had a marked effect on the road pattern of the region. Nowhere is this drift orientation better seen than on the southern flanks of Slieve Gullion itself, for here can be found an excellent example of a 'crag and tail' feature. The 'tail', composed entirely of drift, is best seen from the village of Forkhill, its two-mile length having been deposited in the lee of Slieve Gullion by ice-sheets which moved south-eastwards around the flanks of the mountain.

The lowland which separates Slieve Gullion from the eastern half of its ring-dyke, which here abuts on to the northern slopes of the mountains of Carlingford, is of great historical importance. It forms the only break in the line of hills which from time immemorial has represented the southern frontier of the ancient province of Ulster. Known as the Moyry Pass or the Gap of the North, it has witnessed many a battle between warring Irish chieftains and later between English and Irish armies, for this was the northern limit of the notorious 'English Pale' of the early sixteenth century. It is now followed by the main road and railway between Dublin and Belfast.

Beyond the beautiful parklands and forests of the Ravensdale demesne the Carlingford Mountains rise to form the backbone of the Cooley Peninsula. These uplands have a similar geological history to those of Slieve Gullion, since they represent the last of the three major Tertiary igneous complexes which we set out to explore.

The geological sequence is again difficult to describe concisely but can be outlined as follows: the first phase was one which saw thick spreads of basaltic lava extruded on to the Silurian slates and Carboniferous Limestone which make up the 'country-rock' of the peninsula; thick sheets of basic gabbro were then intruded as a saucer-shaped structure, known as a 'lopolith' (see figure 16) between the underlying sedimentaries and the overlying basalts; a late cauldron subsidence allowed the acid granophyre to rise in the form of a ring-dyke although it never succeeded in reaching the surface. As in the case of Slieve Gullion, the presence of such contrasting lithologies as gabbro and granitic rocks in the same

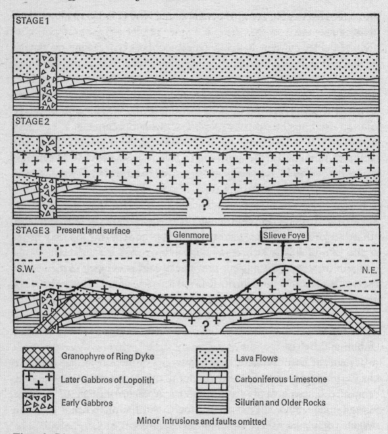

STAGE 1

STAGE 2

?

STAGE 3   Present land surface

Glenmore

Slieve Foye

S.W.

N.E.

?

☒ Granophyre of Ring Dyke	⋮ Lava Flows	
⊞ Later Gabbros of Lopolith	▦ Carboniferous Limestone	
◬ Early Gabbros	▤ Silurian and Older Rocks	

Minor intrusions and faults omitted

Fig. 16. *Diagrammatic cross-section of the Carlingford Igneous Complex showing stages in its structural history (after J. K. Charlesworth).*

igneous complex is uncommon and needs an explanation. It has been suggested that a lower, heavier, basic magma reservoir was initially predominant in the sequence but that ultimately it was replaced by an upper, lighter, acidic magma reservoir which fed the ring-dyke. The scenery which we see today is the result of the differing rock hardnesses and their varying resistance to denudation. Much of the basalt cover has been destroyed by erosion and although denudation has penetrated through the gabbroid lopolith to expose the roof of the granophyre ring-dyke in the centre of the complex (figure 16) these granitic rocks today form the relatively low basin of Glenmore, although farther north they succeed in building the hill of Clermont Carn (1,674 feet). The main feature in the scenery is the circle of gabbroid hills which overlook Glenmore on all sides, their craggy summits and precipitous cliffs contrasting markedly with the subdued and rounded slopes of the granophyre. Slieve Foye, the highest peak of the Carlingford Mountains (1,935 feet), is itself formed from gabbro and in the metamorphic aureole of its eastern slopes it is possible to examine the great number of cone sheets (see figure 15) which sliced through all the existing rocks, rather in the manner of concentric dykes, at a late stage in the sequence.

Surrounding the bleak igneous uplands of the Cooley Peninsula the Palaeozoic shales and limestones have been denuded to form a lowland fringe which is of great importance to the settlement and economy of the region. The limestones and their calcareous drifts, which occupy the easternmost tract of the peninsula, have been especially significant in their effect on the agriculture. Like the neighbouring lowlands of the Kingdom of Mourne, with which it can be compared in many ways (not least in its isolation), the agricultural viability of Cooley rests very largely on the fertility of this clay plain. The easily worked soils along the northern shores of Dundalk Bay, for example, are really an extension of the fertile drift-covered plains of the Central Lowlands, described in the following chapter. Thus we discover that by the nineteenth century a prosperous farm in northern Louth would possess '. . . a complement of extensive outbuildings, orchards and carefully maintained gardens, and the whole was frequently contained within a miniature park, hidden by tall trees' (T. Jones-Hughes). But as the number of small-scale holdings has increased in the present century, at the expense of landlordism and the great estates, so the landscape itself has changed. Many of the demesne walls have tumbled, the parks and orchards become overgrown, while the roofless mansions now serve only as shelters for the livestock. Paradoxically, some of the smaller cottage holdings on the poorer soils of the more marginal land of the Carlingford Mountains have flourished, for these were worked by families or kin-groups and have remained largely self-sufficient.

9. The Central Lowlands

The Central Lowlands are roughly rectangular in shape, with the long axis running eastwards from the Irish Sea to the Connacht Uplands, and, together with their various appendages, cover an area of no less than 8,000 square miles, (3,000 to the east of the Shannon and 5,000 to the west). Only in the east is there a complete absence of the upland perimeter of Ireland and here the coastal plains of Louth, Meath and Dublin face eastwards across the Irish Sea to Wales and England. Elsewhere the peripheral mountains are broken only by a few important corridors: the Erne basin in the north; Clew Bay and Galway Bay in the west; the lower Shannon and the upper Barrow in the south. The Central Lowlands are generally thought of as a monotonous landscape with low gradients and little scenic attraction, although there is some diversity of relief, especially east of the Shannon. This diversity is partly in response to the geology but is largely due to the heterogeneity of the glacial drifts. Before looking at the general geological structure of Central Ireland, therefore, it would be important to note the significant differences which result from this latter phenomenon. The drifts vary in their thickness from place to place, occasionally reaching depths of over 100 feet, but they effectively clothe the solid rock except in the plains of Galway. The character of the glacial drifts also differs throughout the Central Lowlands, so that the undulating till sheets of the Dublin region give way north-westwards, westwards and south-westwards to wide expanses of glacio-fluvial landforms (including the well-known esker topography). Beyond the latter, in Ulster, Connacht and north-west Munster, drumlin landscapes dominate the fringes of the Central Lowlands, but it should be clearly understood that drumlins are generally absent from the central areas of Ireland and do not seem to occur south of the so-called Kells moraine (figure 17). From figure 17 it can be seen how the last glaciation of Central Ireland, the Midland Gen-

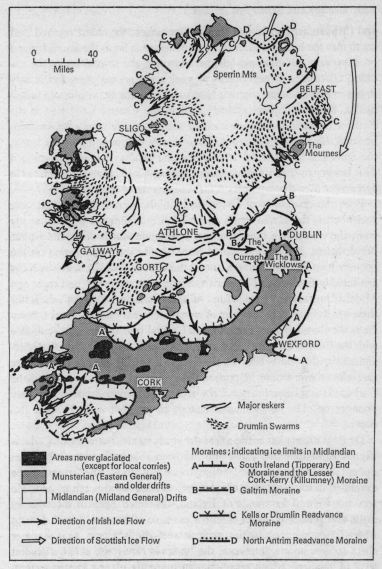

Fig. 17. *The Pleistocene geology of Ireland (based on the Geological and Soil Surveys of Ireland, and the works of J. K. Charlesworth, E. Colhoun, A. Farrington, G. F. Mitchell, A. R. Orme, N. Stephens, F. M. Synge and W. A. Watts).*

eral (Midlandian), exhibited three major stages: the oldest reached well south into the hills and vales of north Munster as far as the South Ireland or Tipperary end-moraine (chapter sixteen); the second stage, the so-called Galtrim moraine, appears to mark a recessional phase but is only found in east Leinster, where it runs south-westwards for some 40 miles; finally, the most important line of all in the Central Lowlands, is the Kells or Drumlin Readvance moraine for it not only marks the southern limits of the Irish drumlins but also the limit of the largest eskers. Clearly, the ice-sheet which stood at this moraine produced more pronounced drift landforms than its predecessors, although authors are by no means in agreement over the explanation for such a state of affairs.

With the exceptions of Cavan and Louth, where Lower Palaeozoic rocks occur, the glacial drifts of the Irish midlands are derived largely from the ubiquitous Carboniferous Limestone which floors the plains. Nevertheless, it should be noted that, despite their designation on the geology map (see back cover), not all the Carboniferous Limestone rocks are actually limestone. This is particularly true wherever the Lower and Middle 'limestones' (the 'Calp' of the Geological Survey) occur, for these are frequently in the form of arenaceous or argillaceous rocks. Insofar as the Carboniferous Limestone of Central Ireland appears to coincide with the Central Lowlands, however, it is manifestly clear that an important relationship exists between the two. It is equally clear to the traveller that almost every time he crosses the geological boundary between the Carboniferous Limestone and the rocks of different lithology, be they younger or older, a significant change in gradient and elevation also occurs.

Dr P. Williams has made a lengthy study of the character of Carboniferous Limestone in Ireland and has been able to distinguish between upland and lowland karstic landforms (see glossary). The former will be examined in more detail in chapter ten, so need not concern us here. He sees the Central Lowlands of Ireland, blanketed beneath their glacial drifts and peat bogs, as an excellent example of 'covered karst'. Except where limestone irregularities, such as 'reef-knolls' (see p. 148) or major chert accumulations, intervene, the lowlands rarely rise above a general level of 300 feet, which represents an unevenly planed karstic surface, albeit drift-covered. Dr Williams is led to conclude that the Central Lowlands represent the end-product of a lengthy period of karstic denudation, probably by river action and chemical solution, which may have commenced as early as Oligocene or even Eocene times. A word is necessary on the effectiveness of chemical solution in Ireland, for it must be remembered that not only does dissolved carbon dioxide increase the solvent action of water by forming carbonic acid (H_2CO_3), but that the extensive Irish peat bogs create their own organic acid, humic acid, so that surface lowering by solution is still continuing today. Various authorities have suggested that the rock surface of the Irish midlands may have been lowered by solution between one and three feet since the end of the Ice Age.

Following the writings of the geologist Edward Hull, in the nineteenth century, it has generally been accepted that many of the larger lakes in Central Ireland could owe their form to limestone solution. At various times, loughs Ree, Derg, Corrib, Mask and Conn, to name only the largest, have been thought of as solution lakes. It is now believed, however, that solution may be only one of the factors, and not necessarily the most important, involved in their formation. Denudation by ice and running water may also have played an important role in many of the cases in question.

Although we have seen how the Central Lowlands of Ireland exhibit uniformity in their general characteristics of low relief, minimal gradients and sluggish drainage, it is possible to distinguish two contrasting areas within the Irish midlands, divided by the valley of the upper Shannon. Such a dichotomy in the central Irish landscape has long been recognized, for the Shannon is the provincial boundary between Leinster and Connacht. Leinster includes some of the richest soils and many of the most prosperous farmlands in Ireland, especially in the belt of grazing and fattening pastures of Meath and Kildare. Here, to the east of the Shannon, on the deeper drifts, only 40% of the farms are less than 30 acres in extent. In contrast, on the Connacht lowlands west of the Shannon, where more than 60% of the farms are smaller than 30 acres, the drifts are thinner and frequently leave bare limestone pavements of little agricultural value. In a sense the contrasting rural landscapes, with their differing soils, husbandry, history and culture, are epitomized in the 'townscapes' of their respective cities – Dublin and Galway.

Dublin and the Eastern Lowlands

Standing astride its east-flowing river, Dublin has been regarded by some as the city most like London, in its situation, its street plan and its architecture. But there the resemblance ends, for the character of the city is decidedly Irish and even its 'ruby-bricked nucleus' of fine Georgian terraces is Irish Georgian, not English Georgian. Apart from Belfast, Dublin is the only major city in Ireland but the contrast between the two is most striking, for whilst the former was essentially a product of the Industrial Revolution, Dublin was not an industrial creation, indeed, its historic nucleus was completed before the end of the eighteenth century as an administrative and commercial centre.

In much the same way that most English roads radiate from London, so Dublin is the natural focus for the routeways of the Central Lowlands of Ireland. Sited at the mouth of the river Liffey, one of the few natural harbours between Carlingford and Cork, 'Dubh-linn' (= the black pool) reminds us that the Norse invaders utilized the haven of the estuary to create one of the first urban settlements in Ireland in the year A.D. 837. Nevertheless the site was already known to the native Irish as Atha Cliath * (= the ford bridged by hurdles), a crossing point of some significance between the ancient kingdoms of Meath (to the north) and Leinster (to the south). At that time the river Liffey could only be forded about one mile above its mouth, and here, where a narrow strip of marshy alluvium flanked the channel between the bluffs of glacial till, the first bridge was constructed (figure 18). Although gravel river terraces stand above the floodplain upstream from the earliest crossing point, these appear to have played little part in the earliest settlement, and it was on the southern bank of the boulder clay bluffs (formed by a 50-foot incision of the Liffey, as it nears the sea) that the Normans chose to build their castle in the thirteenth century, on the site of the Norse stronghold. To the east, the medieval Liffey floodplain graded into a coastal delta which had been uplifted in post-glacial times to form a marshy raised beach, whilst the coastline of the time stood where the Custom House is now located. Some two miles down the coast the smaller river Dodder also

* Dublin is officially known in Gaelic as Baile átha Cliath, and this name appears on modern Irish maps.

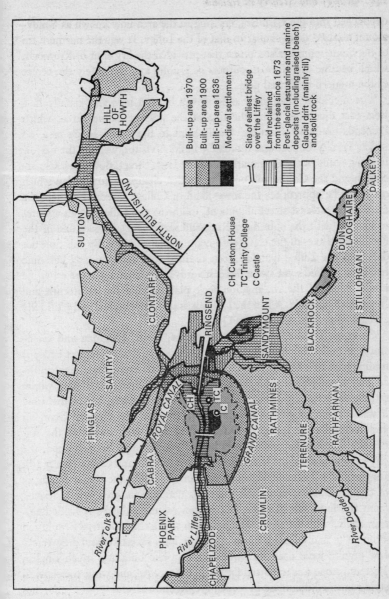

Fig. 18. *The Site of Dublin.*

Built-up area 1970
Built-up area 1900
Built-up area 1836
Medieval settlement

Site of earliest bridge
over the Liffey

Land reclaimed
from the sea since 1673

Post-glacial estuarine and marine
deposits (including raised beach)

Glacial drift (mainly till)
and solid rock

CH Custom House
TC Trinity College
C Castle

HILL
OF
HOWTH

SUTTON

NORTH BULL ISLAND

CLONTARF

DALKEY

FINGLAS

SANTRY

RINGSEND

DÚN
LAOGHAIRE

CABRA

ROYAL CANAL

SANDYMOUNT

BLACKROCK

STILLORGAN

PHOENIX PARK

GRAND CANAL

RATHMINES

TERENURE

RATHFARNAM

CHAPELIZOD

River Liffey

CRUMLIN

River Dodder

River Tolka

debouched into the Irish Sea, creating in the area now known as Sandy-mount a raised delta similar to that of the Liffey. It was the northern tip of the Sandymount raised beach that provided the dry spur of Ringsend, which became the Norman outport of Dublin and ultimately the centre of the modern industrial port.

The medieval town grew only slowly beyond its walls, mainly in a west–east direction, along the line of the present Dame Street which descends gradually from the Castle bluff to the raised beach area, on which Trinity College was ultimately built. A visitor, walking the narrow twisting roads of the Cornmarket and the High Street, down past Christ-church and the Castle, will note the sudden change in street plan which occurs as he approaches the lower land of College Green. For here the medieval west–east street alignment, following the Liffey (in an attempt to link up with the subsidiary Ringsend settlement), crosses one of the north–south axes of the eighteenth-century planned city. By this time not only had the Liffey marshes been drained, but the pre-1673 coastline had been pushed some two miles eastwards by reclamation of the estuarine muds. Most of the reclamation took place during the eighteenth and nineteenth centuries, when the Liffey was also straightened and artificially embanked to form the famous Quays.

Georgian Dublin, the Dublin of Burke, Swift, Sheridan and Gold-smith, is built from beautiful red bricks imported from Somerset by ships trading with Bristol, and provides one of the finest examples of eighteenth-century town-planning in the British Isles; less dramatic in its physical setting on the plain, perhaps, than Edinburgh or Bath, but at that time it was the second city of the Empire (plate 16). The classical Georgian architectural style lasted in Dublin until 1860 and, owing to the few physical constraints, once the estuarine marshes had been drained, the city expanded slowly to the encircling Royal and Grand Canals (figure 18). Its planned suburbs of Victorian refinement, unlike the earlier buildings of central Dublin, were built more frequently from grey bricks derived from the local glacial clays, but in general the suburbs remained un-trammelled with the clutter and pollution which the Industrial Revolution brought to many British cities. Although local limestone and grey Wick-low granite were used for some of the public buildings much English Portland stone was imported for use in the façades, and while the classical style remained dominant in secular architecture several 'gothic' churches also appeared, including the curious 'Black Church' (St Mary's Chapel of Ease) built of local black 'Calp' limestone.

The nearby peninsula of Howth is clearly an example of a former island of Cambrian slates and quartzites now tied to the mainland by a tombolo of gravel and sand, moulded by wave action. The low neck of land, on which Sutton is built, has been shown to be a post-glacial raised beach of similar age to that described in Dublin, whilst northwards the low, till-covered limestone coastline, with its post-glacial spits and sand-dunes, continues as far as the river Boyne.

The limestones of county Dublin are gently folded in a north-east to south-west direction, but, except where they emerge from beneath the drift along the coastline, they play little part in the scenery. Occasionally, where 'reef' limestones occur, there is a tendency for the rocks to protrude through the drift as small hills in an otherwise undulating plain. Some of the hills owe their form to the local lithology, for patches of pure calcite mudstone, known as 'reef-knolls', appear to resist denudation more successfully than the adjacent less pure limestones. The origin of 'reef-knolls' will be examined below (p. 148), where the landforms created by such phenomena are more comparable with the distinctive Pennine hill features of England; suffice to say that near Dublin such hillocks as Feltrim Hill (190 feet), near Dublin airport, and Bray Hill (324 feet), near Trim, are 'reef-knoll' structures.

Some of the anticlines of these eastern lowlands have been denuded sufficiently to expose the pre-Carboniferous rocks at a few localities; the smaller anticlines, both here and to the west of the Shannon, reveal only Old Red Sandstone, but the larger ones bring up the Lower Palaeozoic rocks as well. Such structures, where the older rocks are revealed through 'holes' in the overlying blanket of younger rocks, are known as inliers. On the coast at Ballbriggan, for example, not only Silurian rocks but Ordovician greywackes and slates are also exposed in the low coastal cliffs. Both here and further south at Portrane (between the martello towers), the sedimentary rocks are seen to be interbedded with Ordovician volcanic rocks. The Ordovician volcano, from which they were derived, appears to have been situated near the island of Lambay which itself is made up of a complex mixture of sandstones, limestones, slates, andesitic lavas, tuffs and a particularly attractive green porphyry. It must be remembered, however, that these older, scattered volcanics have failed to produce landforms in east central Ireland comparable in stature with the Cumberland fells, many of which owe their craggy splendour to the qualities of the much more widespread Ordovician vulcanicity of that area. Nor can they hope to compete, of course, with the spectacular scenery created by the Tertiary igneous rocks of eastern Ulster, described in previous chapters.

The valley of the Boyne can be taken as an approximate northern boundary of the Central Lowlands, since north of An Uaimh (Navan) and Drogheda the Carboniferous Limestone is replaced by the undulating hill country formed by the Lower Palaeozoic rocks of Louth. Furthermore, just to the north lies the Drumlin Readvance moraine with its marked change in topography as we cross the Ulster borders. The drainage basin of the river Boyne coincides with the fertile pastureland of county Meath where grazing cattle, coppiced woodland and prosperous farms help to create a scene not unlike the Cheshire Plain on the opposite side of the Irish Sea. At Drogheda, a picturesque and romantic town, the river has cut a gorge into the limestone some 100 feet in depth, a result, no doubt, as in the case of the Liffey, of a late phase of tectonic uplift along this eastern coast. Not many miles up-river is Newgrange, the royal burial-ground of Neolithic and Bronze Age Ireland, which Dr Praeger believed to be the finest thing of its kind in western Europe. Blocks of vein quartz and granite boulders used in the construction of the enormous tumulus may have been brought from the Kingdom of Mourne (chapter eight). Radio-carbon dating of samples of burnt soil, used in packing the roofing slabs, indicate that the tomb was erected about 2500 B.C. A more famous historic centre, the Hill of Tara, lies to the south, built on one of the undulating hills of the Galtrim moraine which sweeps south-westwards into county Kildare, but nothing remains except cattle-trampled earthworks.

The Galtrim moraine, which marks a recessional phase of the last major ice-sheet to affect the Central Lowlands, is in reality a belt of ice marginal deltas formed by glacial meltwaters pouring into pro-glacial lakes. The ice-sheets and their marginal lakes have now disappeared and the deltas left high and dry as sandy hillocks in the landscape. The better drained sandy soils which were derived from this glacio-fluvial outwash go a long way towards explaining the fertility of the Meath–Kildare pasturelands, although one must not forget that here, in the so-called English Pale, the wealth and expertise necessary for improved husbandry were readily available. Nevertheless it would be instructive to note the impact that the drift landforms have had on the landscape and land use in the country of west Kildare. In this area a slightly older branch of the Galtrim moraine runs southwards towards the prominent Ordovician volcanic hills known as the Chair of Kildare (768 feet). To the east of the moraine, the enormous quantities of sand and gravel washed out from the former ice-front have created the sweeping, well-drained expanse of the Curragh with its close-grazed springy turf and clumps of yellow gorse. Here is the Epsom and Aldershot of Ireland rolled into one, for on the lighter soils of this heathland, which creates the divide between the Liffey and the Barrow rivers, the most famous racecourse and military centre in Ireland are found side by side. A marked contrast is seen when one crosses to the west of the moraine, however, for in the wide zone once occupied by the ice-sheet its impervious tills have given rise to a waterlogged environment in which post-glacial peat has built up to considerable depths.

This area has long been known as the Bog of Allen and it demonstrates quite clearly the landscape contrasts which occur as one travels westwards from Dublin towards the Shannon. Whereas in the eastern margins of the Central Lowlands it can be seen how the emphasis on cattle grazing has virtually excluded arable farming from the landscape, west of the Curragh one notices how cultivated lands, pastures and bogs intermingle and how farms get smaller as the soil fertility decreases. Nevertheless pastureland is still predominant, as store cattle are kept in counties Longford, West Meath and Offaly before they are sent east for fattening on the better pastures of Meath and Kildare. Because of the increasingly varied land-use of these boglands nearer to the Shannon one soon becomes aware of a patchiness of colour in the landscape, a patchiness which results from the contrasts in both soils and terrain; in short the contrasts are between dry ground and wet ground (plate 17). The black slashes of the peat cuttings in the hedgeless and treeless boglands alternate with the less sombre tones of the better-drained lands where the fields exhibit the contrasting greens of various arable crops amidst the yellow hayfields.

Although some of the dry ground is formed from Carboniferous Limestone hills, especially west of Mullingar, it is really the presence of the glacial drift hills, and especially the eskers, which has been of the greatest significance so far as settlement and routeways are concerned. Whilst the more recent railways and canals, by virtue of modern engineering techniques, can cross directly across the boglands, the ancient trackways were frequently confined to the sinuous esker ridges which, in this part of the Central Lowlands, run conveniently from west to east (figure 17).

It is noteworthy that as late as the 1890s many geologists still believed that the glacial drifts were remnants of the Biblical Flood, this being particularly true of the eskers. Today, however, eskers are thought to have been formed beneath an ice-sheet by glacial meltwaters, and a cross-section will generally reveal rudimentary bedding formed as the stream deposited its load within the sub-glacial ice-tunnel. Thus, as the ice-sheet thinned and retreated, these tunnel infills were exposed and if, as appeared quite common, the ice-front became temporarily stabilized the melt-stream built either a delta or an outwash fan, depending on whether or not it flowed out into a lake. In these cases the width of the ridge would increase owing to the greater mass of accumulated material at this point. The esker chains of the Central Plain of Ireland reach their finest development in eastern Galway, West Meath and Offaly where, east of the Shannon, the majority terminate at the line of the Drumlin Readvance moraine (plate 18). Although the latter was formed during the general recession of the last major ice-sheet to occupy the Central Lowlands, in fact it represents a temporary ice readvance phase which over-rode the slightly older Galtrim moraine in the vicinity of the Shannon (figure 17). Such a fluctuation would not be uncommon in Pleistocene times when a transient climatic variation could result in a major ice-front oscillation. It has been pointed out by Professor T. W. Freeman that the Shannon crossings at Athlone, Shannonbridge and Banagher are all associated with eskers which provide firm ground on either bank (figure 19). The ancient cathedral 'town' of Clonmacnoise, on the other hand, although reached by a pilgrim's road along its adjoining esker, is not a bridging point because of the lack of firm ground on the western bank of the Shannon at this point. Not far from here the great 'Esker Riada' which runs from west to east, once acted as a natural boundary in ancient Ireland, dividing the Kingdom of Tara in the north from that of Cashel in the south.

Between the eskers stretch the bogs, although it is fair to comment that they are not as extensive in the Central Lowlands as one might imagine.

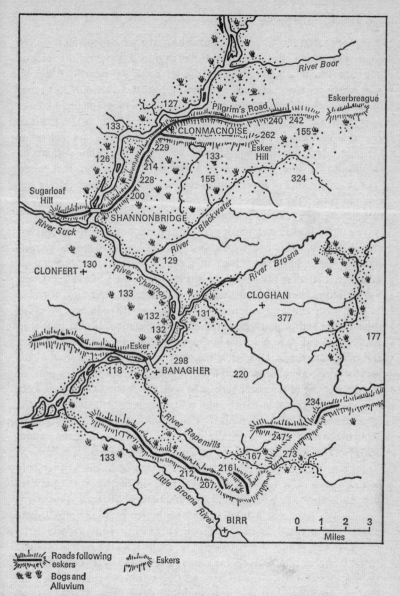

River Boor

Eskerbreagué

127

Pilgrim's Road

133

240 242

CLONMACNOISE

262

155

229

Esker
Hill

126

133

214

155

324

228

200

Sugarloaf
Hill

SHANNONBRIDGE

River Suck

Blackwater

River

129

CLONFERT

130

River Brosna

River Shannon

133

CLOGHAN

132

131

377

132

177

Esker

298

118

BANAGHER

220

234

River Repemills

247

133

167

273

216

212

207

Little Brosna River

BIRR

0   1   2   3
Miles

Roads following
eskers   Eskers

Bogs and
Alluvium

Fig. 19. *The influence of the eskers on the road pattern and the Shannon crossings
in the Central Lowlands (after T. W. Freeman).*

The type of peat bog which develops in any area will depend on the plant association which has created it and this in turn depends on the mineral nutrients available both in the ground-water and the rainfall. Although many attempts have been made to classify bogs there are only two types of bog in Ireland: first, those of the Central Lowlands which are known as 'raised' or 'high bogs', corresponding more nearly to the German *Hochmoore*; secondly, those of western Ireland, which are known as 'blanket bogs', but the high altitude bogs of the Wicklow Mountains would also fall into this category. Although it will be seen that raised bogs occur in areas of lower rainfall they are generally much thicker (up to 20 feet) than the blanket bogs (*c*. 8 feet) which occupy the wetter and cloudier western margins (figure 20).

The differences in terminology reflect differences not only in form but also in genesis and in age, for the two types of bog were created in contrasting ways. The raised bogs of Central Ireland commenced their existence soon after the ice-sheets had melted in the Central Lowlands, for the large, badly drained basins of calcareous boulder clay provided an ideal environment. Numerous water bodies would soon have occupied these basins and in post-glacial times a fen vegetation, similar to that in East Anglia today, would have begun to flourish in the base-rich waters and calcareous muds. Ultimately the open water of the lakes would have become obliterated, either by the infilling of the basin with fen-peat, or by the covering of the water surface by a mat of floating vegetation. Late in post-glacial times, in the climatic zone known as 'Atlantic' times, the large tussocks of certain fen plants seem to have built up the surface of the fen above the level of the alkaline ground water, so that the natural acidity of the decaying vegetation was no longer neutralized. This allowed *Sphagnum* moss, and other plants such as *Eriopherum*, which thrive only in more acid water habitats, to gain a hold on the fen surface and to flourish in the cooler, wetter climatic conditions of 'Atlantic' times. It is easy to see, therefore, how the surface of the fen peat grew upwards to change into a typical raised bog, the surface of which became characteristically convex, sloping gently from the centre towards the periphery where it was bounded by a watercourse which received the water draining from the bog. Radio-carbon dating suggests that in Ireland the change, from fen-peat growth to 'Atlantic' sphagnum-peat growth, took place around 5500–5000 B.C.

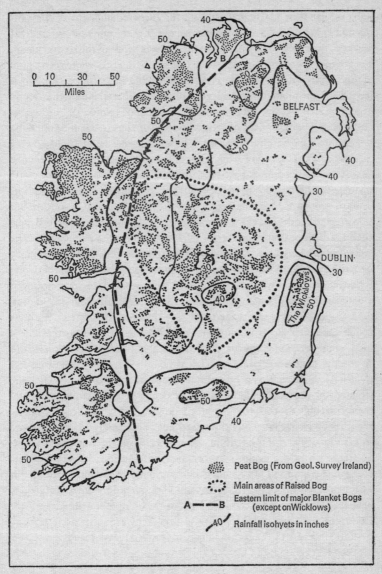

Fig. 20. *The distribution of the Peat Bogs in Ireland (after H. M. S. Miller).*

In the far west of Ireland (and on the higher mountains of the east) the rainfall is so high and the air so moist that acid peat growth has become the typical vegetation or 'climatic formation' of the coastal plains. Its growth began on a large scale during the cooler, wetter 'Atlantic' period referred to above, but as it did not need to arise from existing local fen basins the ubiquitous acid peat blanketed the whole of the terrain except on steep slopes, hence its name, blanket bog (plate 24). For blanket bog is largely independent of ground-water supplies, depending more on high rainfall and humidity; raised bog, on the other hand, seems always to have built itself upon a pre-existing fen-peat which had depended almost entirely upon a base-rich aquatic habitat. Nevertheless, once established the raised bog requires sufficient atmospheric humidity if its upward growth is to be maintained.

Owing to its deficiency of coal supplies, Ireland is fortunate in having such a wealth of peat deposits, for peat bogs cover about 15% of its total area. Peat has long been the only fuel available for rural Ireland, especially in areas away from the coal-importing ports of Belfast and Dublin, and until recent years it was cut almost exclusively by hand. In 1934, however, a state-directed board launched a limited programme of machine-cut peat, then, in 1946, this was superseded by the state-sponsored 'Bord na Mona', a much larger commercial enterprise with massive machinery producing peat not only for domestic and industrial use but also for electricity generating stations. Today more than 25% of Ireland's electricity is derived from peat-fired power stations, most of which are situated on the edges of the raised boglands of the Central Plain, for mechanization on this scale is suited only to flat-lying, deep bogs free from rocky obstacles. Thus the raised bogs are rapidly being consumed in Central Ireland, especially in the area between the Shannon and the Curragh, whilst the shallower, more undulating blanket bogs of the West are being 'harvested' to a much lesser extent; in Atlantic Ireland the turf spade and the donkey cart are still very much in evidence. The city of Galway, standing on the boundary of the Central Lowlands and the Connacht Uplands, marks the transition between the raised bogs of Central Ireland and the blanket bogs of the Western Uplands.

Galway City and the Western Lowlands

Whilst Dublin is essentially a brick-built city Galway is a city of quarried limestone blocks, in a region where the drifts are thin and rock is ever-present. Little wonder that Galway city has been regarded as the key to the whole of Connacht, even before the Normans settled there more than eight centuries ago, for it stands at the meeting place of two contrasting regions, right astride a major geological boundary. To the east lie the Carboniferous Limestone lowlands, here almost driftless and exposing large areas of stony surface, '. . . at its worst an arid karst covered with little vegetation except for hazel scrub and ashwood, but at its best a good natural pasture with patches of soil on which excellent crops can be grown' (T. W. Freeman). To the west, the uncompromising Galway granite, the boulders, the peat bogs, the pocket-handkerchief fields, the treeless wastes of Atlantic Ireland. A traveller journeying from this historic city will carry with him many memories of the landscape contrasts, not least of which would be the differing colours: the tawny browns, the sombre blacks and purples of the west – the sparkling greens and glinting greys of the east.

To the north of Galway city the broad waters of Lough Corrib create a continuous barrier of water for almost 30 miles, so that the city has always commanded the most direct routeway from the Central Lowlands into Connemara. Here, where the Corrib river meets the sea in a deep tidal lagoon which offered safe anchorage, a small midstream island served as an early bridging point. Thus the earliest settlement grew up on the rocky spur of the eastern bank, just below the rapids which now form the famous salmon weir, and ultimately became linked to the west bank fishing village of the Claddagh (Cladach = the stony sea-shore) by a bridge.

The domestic architecture of ancient Galway reminds one of the contemporary mercantile houses of medieval Bristol, whose Spanish wine trade it almost emulated. The great stone-gabled houses of Tudor-Gothic style still survive in the town centre, with the well-known Lynch's Castle demonstrating quite clearly that the emphasis was on defensive strength rather than on elegance of style. Nevertheless, the Carboniferous Limestone building-stone lent itself well to carving, so that enough heraldic decoration, dripstones and corbels of intricate design remain to confirm the former commercial prosperity of this intriguing town. The advent of the railway was the final blow to its earlier importance, for it virtually killed the sea-borne trade and substituted Dublin as the distributing centre for the lowlands west of the Shannon. The warehouses down by the quays now stand gaunt and derelict, the walls and gateways have all but gone, save for the so-called Spanish Arch. But Galway remains a bustling, vital city, and a word must be said of its fine new cathedral in which extensive use has been made of the local black Galway 'marble'. Quarried at Angliham, on the southern shores of Lough Corrib, the 'marble' is in reality a facies of the Lower Carboniferous Limestone which can take a high polish. It has not been altered by metamorphism and is not a marble in the true geological sense.

The tract of country that extends south-eastwards from the city of Galway, skirting the limits of Galway Bay and thence into the so-called Gort Lowlands, is rather different from any which we have so far encountered. The low-lying plain of Upper Carboniferous Limestone is generally driftless, except near Athenry where eskers appear, until one passes into a familiar drumlin landscape near to Gort. Away to the south-east the mountains of Slieve Aughty (1,207 feet) terminate the limestone plains and because of the impervious nature of their Lower Palaeozoic and Old Red Sandstone rocks a simple radial drainage pattern has developed on this upland area. No sooner do the west-flowing rivers debouch on to the Gort limestone lowlands, however, than they disappear beneath the surface into numerous swallets. One of the best-known examples lies about a mile to the south of Gort itself where, at the Punch-bowl, a series of striking, grassy depressions can be seen enclosed in a woodland of beech and chestnut. These mark collapsed areas along the subterranean course of the stream which flows for a short distance in a deep gorge from Lough Cutra before disappearing underground. The water table (see glossary) appears to be close to the surface on the Gort lowlands for the elevation of the area is little above sea level. For this reason there are numerous, intermittently occupied, lake-hollows in this tract, their surface waters depending in part on the seasonal rainfall and even on tidal ebb and flow for their ephemeral existence. The level of Caherglassaun Lough, for example, some four miles from the sea, fluctuates synchronously with the tides of Galway Bay. The periodically flooded depressions are known as turloughs (Tuar Loch = dry lake) and are reported from nowhere else in the world except Ireland. Much of the research on turloughs was carried out by Dr Praeger, who not only explained the mechanism of their intermittent flooding by virtue of a fluctuating water table, but also made a detailed investigation of their vegetational characteristics. He described how '. . . the most conspicuous indication of a turlough is the abrupt cessation of all shrubby growth below a well-marked contour. The herb vegetation, which extends from this level to the bottom of even the deepest turlough, which may measure as much as twenty feet, is very closely nibbled by rabbits or sheep, and forms a dense fine green sward'.

It has been suggested that turloughs are similar to the karstic poljes, which are found particularly in the Yugoslavian karstic areas, and which owe their existence to surface stream erosion on a large scale. Dr P. Williams has argued, however, that turloughs are considerably smaller in size and often result from irregularities in the glacial drift rather than actual hollows in the limestone. Dr Williams emphasizes that unlike poljes the turloughs do not possess planed rock floors and, insofar as the only karstic attribute common to all turloughs is subterranean drainage, they would be better regarded as landforms of glacio-karstic origin.

A few miles to the east of Gort, in the valley of the Boleyneendorrish River which drains the Slieve Aughty Mountains, lies a site of some importance to the geologist. For in this isolated valley the river has cut down deeply into the glacial drift to reveal a bed of peat buried beneath two distinct layers of grey and red boulder clay. Quite clearly, from its stratigraphical position, the peat is much older than the post-glacial peats of the raised bogs of the Central Lowlands, described above. It is generally thought that the overlying tills represent local equivalents of the Eastern General and the Midland General glacial phases in Ireland and thus that the peat must belong to the so-called Great Interglacial period of the Ice Age, having been formed when the ice-sheets temporarily disappeared from the island. Botanical investigation of the organic remains has supported such an interpretation, for the peat contains remnants of a wide variety of vegetation types which are no longer found in close association in modern Ireland. The abundance of pollen from yew, alder, silver fir and rhododendron, together with the sparseness of pollen from spruce, hazel and elm in the peat deposit, is regarded as being especially diagnostic of its Great Interglacial age, and as such the Gort example has been taken as the Irish type-site for this important Pleistocene strati-graphical horizon.*

Woodland is uncommon on the plains of Galway today and many of the bare limestone areas have never borne trees. Instead, thickets of hazel and ash are common on the poorer soils and in some places these are so impenetrable as to recall a 'maquis' type of landscape. But some of the limestones carry sufficient soil cover to provide excellent sheep pastures, so that on the plains of Galway lowland sheep farming is more extensively developed than anywhere else in Ireland. During the last century the lowlands of eastern Connacht have witnessed a considerable extension of improved land, mainly by the reclamation of boglands after they had been cleared for fuel.

Some of the more extensive raised boglands which have survived on the plains of Galway flank the shores of Lough Corrib. Here the glacial drifts appear to thicken, especially at the northern end where a drumlin swarm has been partly inundated by the lake waters to form an archipelago of tiny islands. Second only to Lough Neagh in area, Lough Corrib's length actually exceeds that of its Ulster counterpart, for a sinuous western arm reaches far into the metamorphic terrain of Connemara. The presence of these harder, older rocks of western Connacht along the Atlantic peri-meter of the Central Lowlands goes a long way towards explaining the form and the location of both Lough Corrib and its smaller northern neighbour, Lough Mask. Although limestone solution appears to have played some part in the formation of these lake basins, their great depths and their position astride a major geological boundary suggest that so far as their genesis is concerned other factors were of greater importance than chemical solution. The most obvious explanation appears to lie in selec-tive glacial erosion of the more easily removable limestones, at a time when Connemara ice-sheets crossed the boundary between the older, harder rocks of west Connacht and the Carboniferous Limestone terrain to the east. To seek a parallel for this type of differential glacial erosion we must turn to the 'glint-line' lakes, which occupy the marginal areas of the Scandinavian Shield, or to the extensive Canadian Prairie lakes at the edge of the Laurentian Shield.

Apart from its importance as a viewpoint to appreciate the singular

* The so-called Gortian period in Ireland is now regarded as equivalent to the Hoxnian of Britain or the Holsteinian of Northern Europe.

beauty of these lake shores, where the blue hills of Connemara are mirrored in the silver waters, the isthmus which separates Lough Corrib from Lough Mask is worth a visit if only to witness a monument to the folly of man. Near to the town of Cong the superbly finished masonry of a canal wharf with associated locks marks the terminus of a canal which was excavated during the mid-nineteenth century to link the waters of Corrib and Mask. A short excursion will demonstrate to the traveller, however, the incredible lack of foresight in the planning of such an enterprise, for the canal which can be seen stretching away to the north is entirely waterless! After five years of enormous toil, in which millions of tons of limestone were removed by hand labour, the opening of the canal saw the water flow into it for only a few yards before disappearing underground. A geologist, Mr J. C. Coleman, has subsequently mapped some 44 swallets on the Cong isthmus and no less than 30 of these lie within half a mile of the ill-fated canal, a fact which should have warned the navvies of the cavernous nature of the limestone. In hindsight it is easy to point to the impervious Silurian rocks, which form the isthmus a few miles to the west, and ask why the canal was not routed across these?

The Upper Shannon

We have already seen how the Shannon has long been regarded as both an administrative and a cultural boundary, and the landscape contrasts between the eastern and western tracts of the Central Lowlands have been described in some detail. There are also scenic contrasts between the country drained by the headwaters of the Shannon and the lands which surround its estuary. From Lough Derg seawards, however, the Shannon has effectively escaped from the Central Lowlands, so the latter section of its course will be treated separately in chapter thirteen. Its upper reaches, on the other hand, flow through a countryside which for the most part resembles that of the Central Lowlands. Only near its source does the scenery change as rocks of Upper Carboniferous age appear in the landscape.

The town of Athlone, located on an esker ridge where the river leaves Lough Ree and situated midway between Dublin and Galway, is a natural starting-point for any account of the Upper Shannon landscapes. To the north '. . . the Spacious Shenan spreading like a sea' (Spenser) has created the wide expanse of water known as Lough Ree, cradled in its basin of limestone and long thought to be the epitome of a solution lake. Although some doubt has been cast on the efficiency of chemical solution to produce, unaided, lakes of such magnitude, particularly since the discovery of carbonate deposition in some south Clare lakes, the fact remains that in Lough Ree undercut mushroom-shaped rocks testify to the importance of post-glacial limestone solution in the moulding of the lake shores. Near to the northern end of Lough Ree a planned village has sprung up at Lanesborough, to accommodate the employees of the milled peat bog workings. This is only one of eight such housing schemes created by Bord na Mona in the Central Lowlands, in association with its programme of mechanized peat cutting.

To the north of Lough Ree a line of low hills crosses the Shannon from south-west to north-east. This is Slieve Bawn, created from a denuded anticline of Old Red Sandstone and Silurian rocks which protrudes through the limestone cover, to remind us that the Caledonian tract of folded Lower Palaeozoics now lies to our east in southern Ulster. The northern horizon is also closed by a range of hills around Lough Allen, and as we follow the Shannon towards its source across the drumlin landscape of south Leitrim, we slowly become aware that these mark the northernmost limits of the Central Lowlands. The great river meanders slowly through the countryside with little fall in gradient, its water meadows, known as callows, rendered practically useless by the growth of rushes. Leitrim is '. . . a boggy, soggy, rushy land, full of burrowing streams, tiniest crevices of water everywhere' (O'Faolain), and it is little wonder that south Leitrim and Roscommon form one of the lowest income areas in Ireland. To the west lie the bare limestone plains of Boyle, but for the most part the Shannon meanders through a waterlogged drumlin landscape where some 75% of the farms are less than 30 acres in extent and there is a shortage of great demesne lands suitable for redistribution.

One demesne which is being redeveloped is that of Rockingham House, on the shores of Lough Key east of Boyle. Although the great Nash mansion is a melancholy shell, its position on the thickly wooded lake shores, with the romantically named Curlew Mountains of Old Red Sandstone as a backdrop, is so picturesque that it is now to be incorporated as part of the Lough Key Forest Park. Roads have been driven through the demesne to enable the public to view the magnificent vistas of islands, promontories, castles and noble trees. It is encouraging to see an attempt being made by the Irish government to recreate the thickly wooded landscape which once existed in the Upper Shannon valley. It is, perhaps, difficult to conceive that some 300 years ago there was a good deal of woodland between Athlone and the Shannon's source. West of Lough Ree, for example, lay the Feadha or Faes oakwoods which stretched westwards to the Connacht Uplands. Farther north, near Boyle, the thick woods of Coill Conchobhair have left some important survivals around Lough Key, as noted above. The nearby Fasach-Coille near Lough Allen, however, has been virtually destroyed, very largely to supply the ironworks of Arigna, Boyle, Drumod, Drumshanbo and Drumsna. Historically, since the best charcoal for iron smelting comes from immature coppiced oakwoods, the ironmasters of England had practised coppicing to ensure a continuous supply, but in Ireland, except in Wicklow, no such provision was made. Thus, in the Upper Shannon area, the works were moved from one forest to another until the fuel became exhausted.

The small abandoned furnaces and slag heaps near to Lough Allen, through which the Shannon flows, bear witness to the former iron mining of that area. The iron occurs in the form of nodules or nodular bands of ironstone bedded within the Namurian shales of this area. For here Carboniferous rocks younger than the limestone have managed to survive the periods of denudation which elsewhere in central Ireland have lowered the land surface by stripping off the younger rocks to expose the Carboniferous Limestone beneath. Thus, on the hillsides which surround Lough Allen, the limestone can be seen to give way upwards to dark shales, flagstones and sandstones of Namurian age which now build the high Leitrim plateaux. The ironstones accumulated as iron solutions in former swamps and lagoons, in a Carboniferous environment equally conducive to the formation of their lenticular coal seams. These Namurian coal bands are not, however, of Coal Measures' age, but are merely forerunners of the more extensive swamps which were to develop later in Upper Carboniferous times. The two chief seams were originally worked to supply the local iron furnaces, following the invention of the coke-smelting process and the reduction of the Lough Allen forests. But today the small coal production from the so-called Leitrim field is used almost exclusively in the nearby power station. The coal seams crop out in parallel bands high up on the slopes of the surrounding flat-topped mountains, for the bedding of these Namurian rocks is virtually horizontal and the seams have only been exposed by virtue of the deep incision of the Shannon drainage system. In detail, however, the strata dip inwards in a saucer-like arrangement, so that seepage of subterranean water has made working very precarious. Today most of the coal mining is found on the flanks of the Arigna valley, a tributary of the Shannon, and, owing to the disposition of the strata, the shafts are driven horizontally into the mountainside in the form of adit-mining.

It is a sobering thought that despite the local supply of raw materials, limestone, coal and iron ore, the Lough Allen ironworks have all closed down. The high plateau of Slieve Anierin (= mountain of iron) east of the lake is known to have considerable ore reserves, but the high phosphorous content of the ores has made their working uneconomic. Consequently, these flat-topped Leitrim uplands have survived as dark heather-covered moorlands, free from the colliery and furnace slag heaps which dominate the scenery of the British coalfields. The valleys too, with one exception, remain free from the inimical scars which the Industrial Revolution brought to the mining areas of Britain, and here the waters of Lough Allen and the Upper Shannon are unsullied by the industrial waste so common in many British rivers. Only in the tributary streams are the waters iron-stained, for the iron nodules have gradually been weathered out of the friable shales and redeposited in the valleys.

A few miles more and our journey up the Shannon comes to an end, for north of Lough Allen, in a basin fringed with the precipitous gritstone scarps of the Leitrim plateau, lies the source of Ireland's longest river. Here, an insignificant pool, known as Shannon Pot, is situated on the boulder-strewn slope of Cuilcagh Mountain, which is itself an airy ridge of Millstone Grit. It can hardly be regarded as part of the Central Lowlands but it is significant that Shannon Pot is the exit of an underground river, a fact which suggests that limestone is not far away and limestone has been the recurrent theme throughout this lengthy excursion in central Ireland. Furthermore, it serves to demonstrate that Carboniferous Limestone is not always associated with lowland terrain: on occasion it creates upland landscapes of remarkable grandeur.

10. Carboniferous Limestone Landscapes

In the previous chapter it was seen how the widespread distribution of Carboniferous Limestone in central Ireland was in part responsible for the form and location of the Central Lowlands. Nevertheless, Carboniferous Limestone cannot everywhere be regarded in terms of lowland relief and subdued landscape. Indeed, in Britain limestone of Carboniferous age is often referred to as Mountain Limestone, for there it frequently projects itself as a series of positive landforms in the highland zone, landforms which are famous for their spectacular scenery. This is equally true in those parts of Ireland where exceptional thicknesses of Lower Carboniferous rocks occur. Regional uplift has helped to raise these rocks in some areas, as in Sligo and Leitrim where a limestone succession well in excess of 5,000 feet occurs, whilst the thickness in the Burren is more than 3,000 feet. When one adds to this the fact that in both these regional examples massive, pure and remarkably resistant limestones occur high up in the succession, one begins to understand why the Carboniferous Limestone can sometimes create such positive relief. Facies differences within the Carboniferous Limestone (figure 21) can also lead to contrasting resistance to erosion, despite the apparently uniform distribution shown on the geological map on the back cover. The Fermanagh Lakes, for example, occupy basins carved for the most part from the less resistant shales and the so-called 'Calp' limestones of the Lower Carboniferous succession. In contrast, the high relief and spectacular plateau scenery which overlooks the Erne valley from the west is built up largely from the thick, hard, and relatively pure limestones of Sligo and Leitrim, a region to which we must now turn.

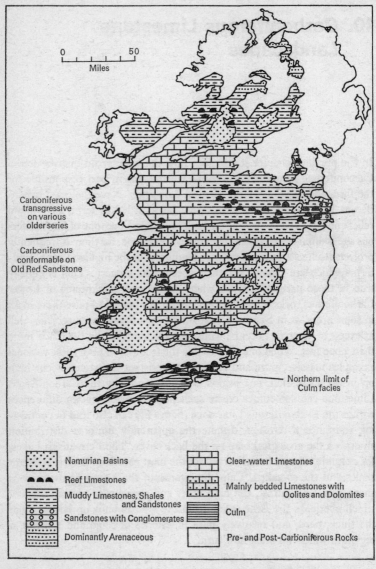

Fig. 21. *Facies distribution in the Lower Carboniferous rocks (after J. K. Charlesworth).*

Sligo and Leitrim

After having experienced the magnificent limestone scenery of northern Sligo and Leitrim it is difficult to conceive how, in 1843, Mrs S. C. Hall could state quite baldly that '. . . Leitrim presents no particular feature for comment', and that one may ignore Sligo since '. . . its scenery and character so nearly resemble that . . . of Mayo'. A view of Ben Bulbin from the Sligo coast road is sufficient in itself to belie such a statement, and this fine mountain is only the outer portal of a veritable storehouse of geological treasures which stretches eastwards through Leitrim into Fermanagh, for more than 30 miles.

Ben Bulbin (1,730 feet) is not a high mountain, nor in many eyes even a true mountain, for in reality it is nothing more than the scarped edge of a limestone plateau. But approach it from north or south and one cannot fail to be impressed by its implacable presence in the landscape, like the prow of a battleship thrusting westwards towards the Atlantic waves (plate 19). It is the upper capping of very pure unbedded limestone (the Dartry Limestone) which gives rise to the sheer precipices that characterize the upper slopes although the subjacent Glen Car Limestone, with its thin shaly partings, is also significant in this respect. Equally important, however, in the sculpting of the present landforms are the underlying Ben Bulbin Shales for these are so much less resistant to denudation that they have been greatly eroded, wherever they appear on the lower slopes, by ice-sheets moving outwards from the mountainland. We can understand, therefore, how the partial removal of this underlying material caused undercutting and ultimate collapse of the upper limestones. Landslipping appears to have been particularly common at the close of the Ice Age, for bereft of their supporting ice walls the unstable, oversteepened cliffs broke away in enormous slices and slid bodily down the lower slopes as gigantic rotational landslips (see figure 22), similar to those of the Antrim Plateau (chapter two). One of the largest and most picturesque is that which forms the so-called Swiss Valley in Glen Car, where the vertical cliffs, waterfalls and fir trees recall the splendours of the much larger Swiss valley of Lauterbrunnen. Today the upper cliffs are freshened mainly by rock falls, which add to the enormous apron of limestone screes which surrounds the plateau.

Where the bedding planes can be distinguished in the Carboniferous

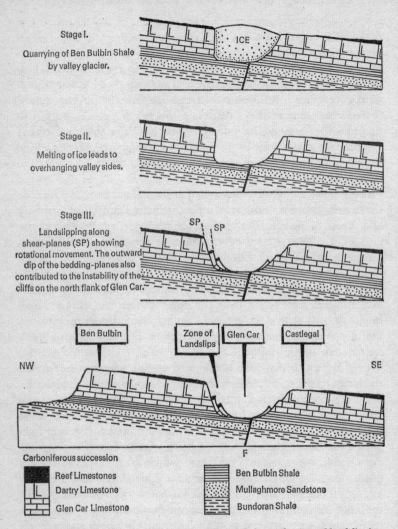

Stage I.

Quarrying of Ben Bulbin Shale by valley glacier.

Stage II.

Melting of ice leads to overhanging valley sides.

Stage III.

Landslipping along shear-planes (SP) showing rotational movement. The outward dip of the bedding-planes also contributed to the instability of the cliffs on the north flank of Glen Car.

Ben Bulbin

Zone of Landslips

Glen Car

Castlegal

NW

SE

Carboniferous succession

Reef Limestones

Dartry Limestone

Glen Car Limestone

Ben Bulbin Shale

Mullaghmore Sandstone

Bundoran Shale

Fig. 22. *The structure of the Sligo Mountains and the mechanism of landslipping in Glen Car.*

succession of these uplands around Ben Bulbin it is possible to see that the strata are almost flat-lying and relatively undisturbed except where landslips have occurred. The erosion of the valleys and cliffs has not been entirely the work of ice-sheets, for streams have also played their part by cutting down deeply into the horizontal limestone beds to form steep-sided gorges. Thus the verticality of the Sligo cliffs is very largely due to the presence of the well-developed joint patterns of the limestones, so that rock walls and pinnacles, such as the remarkable Eagle's Rock and other great monoliths of Glenade, are not uncommon features in the scenery of this region. On the precipitous slopes of naked grey limestone a wide variety of rare Alpine plants has survived; for example, this is the only site within the British Isles where the Fringed Sandwort grows. Dr Lloyd Praeger wrote affectionately about the Ben Bulbin cliffs with their Alpine Saxifrage, Mountain Avens, Cushion Pink, Green Spleenwort, Holly Fern and Maidenhair Fern, all of which flourish in this calcareous environment. The steepness of the cliffs has meant that the few streams which rise on the plateau fall dramatically over its edges as spectacular waterfalls, the most famous being that in Glen Car known as 'the stream against the height'. Here, an Atlantic gale will often blow the water back against the cliffs, so that '. . . the cataract smokes upon the mountain side . . . that cold and vapour-turbaned steep' (W. B. Yeats).

Sligo is Yeats country. Its scenery and legends have been woven into the richly coloured tapestries of his early poems in much the same way as the romantic landscapes of the Lake District have been translated into the poetry of Wordsworth. It is almost impossible to travel anywhere in this beautiful limestone country around Sligo without finding some links with W. B. Yeats. The best viewpoint in the region is the isolated limestone dome of Knocknarea (1,078 feet) to the west of Sligo town. From this '. . . cairn-heaped grassy hill', with its massive stone tumulus, estimated to weigh some 40,000 tons, we can see not only the whole of Sligo but much of Leitrim too, whilst the hills of north Mayo and south Donegal provide a fitting backdrop to a panorama of such grandeur and elegance. At our feet are the yellow sand-choked estuaries of Sligo Bay washed by 'the crawling tide of the Rosses'; beyond lies the bustling town of Sligo on an ancient ford where the Garvogue river broadens to the sea, and 'where every side street seems to lead to a bridge'. Above the wooded river course the beautiful expanse of Lough Gill intrudes an arm of lowland into the Sligo uplands, although only its northern shores are flanked by limestone. To the south the eastern arm of the Ox Mountains thrusts a ridge of bare quartzites and gneisses into the limestone country as if to remind us that the metamorphic terrain of Mayo lies not too far distant. These older rocks, through which road and rail break at the well-known Collooney gap south of Sligo town, are exposed at the core of a faulted anticline from which the Carboniferous rocks have been denuded. The high, wooded bluffs which flank the southern shores of Lough Gill mark the narrow faulted outcrop of this metamorphic ridge and include the famous Slish Wood ('Sleuth Wood') with its profusion of ferns and mosses. At the foot of the ridge at the eastern end of the lough a tiny wooded island is perhaps the best known of any in Ireland for this is the 'lake isle of Inisfree', epitomizing in the mind of the poet not only the islands and tree-garlanded peninsulas of Lough Gill but the whole of the beautiful Sligo landscape with its aesthetically pleasing combination of rock, wood and water.

The highest point of the Ben Bulbin plateau, Truskmore (2,113 feet), is built from Carboniferous rocks somewhat younger than the limestones and shales so far described. As the limestone beds give way eastwards to these overlying Glenade shales and sandstones, so the landscape changes from one of bright green fields enclosed by walls of rough, grey limestone blocks to one of featureless moorland, its heather-clad peat bog interspersed only by patches of dark rush-choked pasture. We are now in County Leitrim and east of Manorhamilton the landscape loses something of the freshness and sparkle of Sligo. This is largely because the Carboniferous Limestone is capped by thick layers of rocks similar in character to the English 'Yoredales' and 'Millstone Grit' with their accompanying acid soils and concomitant peat bogs. There is an affinity between these high Leitrim moorlands, with their gritstone edges rising to tabular summits, and the high Pennine moorlands of northern England.

Around Lough Allen and at Cuilcagh Mountain the shales and sandstones pass upwards into shales and gritstones of Namurian age (including the Millstone Grit), but this area has already been described in the previous chapter, and now only serves to lead us just across the Fermanagh border to the remarkable limestone country around Marble Arch.

Halfway along the Belcoo–Florence Court road, above the attractive waters of Lower Lough Macnean, the tiny river Cladagh tumbles through a deep, forested, limestone gorge on its way to join the Erne drainage. This is the entrance to one of the most intriguing landforms in Ireland, the famous caverns of Marble Arch. A remarkable arch of limestone, some 30 feet high, marks the emergence of the Cladagh river after its subterranean journey of one mile from the northern slopes of Cuilcagh Mountain (2,188 feet). At various points along this underground course the waters of the Monastir river and the Sruh Croppa river (which combine at depth

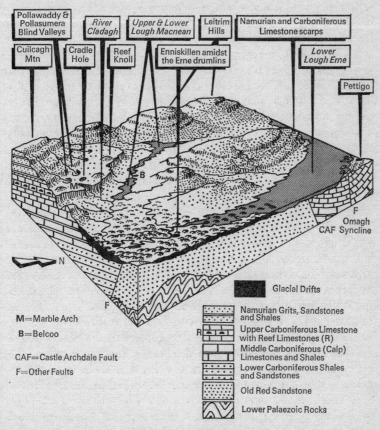

Fig. 23. *The Marble Arch upland and the Enniskillen region.*

to form the Cladagh river) can be seen through gigantic vertical shafts in the limestone. These are shown as depressions in figure 23 which depicts the general structure and karstic features of the Marble Arch region. A closer examination of a depression such as the Cradle Hole, which is more than 100 feet in depth, would show that it was formed by the collapse of a cavity in the limestone created in part by solution and partly by stream erosion at depth. Quite clearly the coalescence of a number of these depressions, the alignment of which marks the courses of the underground streams, could lead to the appearance of a deep surface gorge in place of a subterranean cave system. Their genesis may be similar to that of such well-known features as Cheddar Gorge and Gordale Scar in England.

The Marble Arch region is composed of a narrow limestone shelf, varying in width between one and three miles, which stands between the Cuilcagh ridge and the Erne lowlands of Fermanagh. To the south the limestone shelf dips gently away beneath the Upper Carboniferous shales and flagstones of the Leitrim plateau country and to the north and east it is terminated abruptly by a scarp overlooking the lake-studded lowlands around Enniskillen (figure 23).

Of the streams which rise on the impervious rocks of the Cuilcagh ridge, only those which flow northwards exhibit the characteristic features of karstic drainage, for the remainder run as surface streams south-westwards to the Shannon or south-eastwards to the Swanlinbar river. The northward-flowing streams disappear into swallow holes (or swallets) soon after crossing the junction of the shales and the porous limestones, in a manner similar to the streams of Ingleborough in the Pennines. But in place of the vertical shafts of Gaping Ghyll and Alum Pot the Marbel Arch rivers disappear more gradually down the great clefts of Pollawaddy and Pollasumera which are impressive examples of 'blind valleys' (figure 23). Dr P. Williams has demonstrated how the acidity of the stream waters from the Cuilcagh ridge has played a large part in the creation of the deep solution features seen in the Marble Arch region. Along the northern flank of the limestone shelf, however, there are landforms which appear to show little sign of karstification and therefore need an explanation. These take the form of prominent hills which rise above the limestone shelf, including Gortmaconnell Rock near the Pollasumera blind valley, and which are composed of a different type of limestone known as a reef-knoll. A reef-knoll appears to shed water rather than absorb it for it is made up of a very pure calcite mudstone with steeply dipping structures and widely spaced joints. In some knolls the limestone is particularly rich in fossil shells and this has led some geologists to regard them as shell banks formed in the Carboniferous Limestone seas. The more resistant character of the rock has left it projecting as a hill as the surrounding well-jointed limestone has been slowly dissolved and denuded.

Below the line of reef-knoll hills the bounding scarp of the Marble Arch upland drops steeply away to the Erne lowlands. In places the cliffs are 400 feet high, as at Hanging Rock, and because of their steepness the slopes are generally given over to forestry. Whilst the limestone upland is a region of swallets so the scarp foot is a zone of springs or 'risings' where subterranean drainage reappears at the surface. Spring-sapping by these streams must have played an important part in the general retreat of the scarp, leaving the outlier of Benaughlin isolated from the main upland shelf. Some of the streams flow through the demesne of Florence Court, a magnificent Georgian mansion, cradled in its woods of silver fir which flourish on the deeper soils of the glacial drift beneath the bare limestone escarpment.

The Burren

The limestone plateaux of north-west Clare appear to have been notoriously barren throughout most of recorded time, and it is here that the Cromwellian troops claimed there was neither wood to hang a man, water to drown him, nor earth to bury him. The reasons for this are based on its geological and denudational character, for the porous qualities of the Carboniferous Limestone and the scouring of the Pleistocene ice-sheets have combined to inhibit the presence of surface water and soil; it is generally regarded as a splendid example of glacio-karstic landforms.

The scenic attractions of the Burren are well known, its bare and lonely hills of pale grey limestone contrasting vividly with the narrow slashes of bright green valleys where pockets of drift support thickets of oak, ash and hazel. The ordinary tourist will be astonished at the miles of bare limestone pavements in the rock-strewn fields, and the geologist rewarded by its remarkable landforms, but it is the botanist who will be compelled to return time and again to examine the profusion of calcium-loving plants which thrive in the Burren. The Bloody Cranesbills, creamy Mountain Avens, blue Spring Gentians, white Anemones and yellow Primroses help create natural rock gardens in the spring, to say nothing of the more widespread carpets of less exotic flowers such as the yellow Bird's Foot Trefoil, blue Milkwort and purple Thyme. To view these kaleidoscopes of colour in the ever-changing pearly light of Atlantic Ireland is an experience never to be forgotten. For this is a botanical 'metropolis', a meeting-place of plants from the Arctic, the Alps and the Mediterranean, all flourishing in the mild climate and lime-rich environment provided by the Burren. The fact that this remarkable ground flora has survived is probably explained partly by the treelessness of these bare coastal plateaux and partly by the lack of agricultural improvement. We might be surprised to see Alpine plants thriving at elevations near to sea level but it is thought that this is due to lack of competition and overshading by Ling, Gorse and Bracken which are so common in the generally acid soils elsewhere in Ireland.

The geological structure of the Burren is quite simple for it is composed largely of great thicknesses of relatively pure and massively bedded Upper Carboniferous Limestone (Burren Limestone Series) in which chert bands are common but shale partings thin and infrequent. The limestone dips gently southwards until it disappears beneath the black shales and flagstones of Namurian age which dominate much of south-western Clare. It is the impermeable nature of the latter rocks in contrast with the porosity of the limestone which leads to the remarkable drainage characteristics of the country to the north and east of Lisdoonvarna (figure 24). The Burren appears as a dissected tableland rising to over 1,000 feet in the north, with the highest point occurring on the dark Namurian rocks of Slieve Elva (1,134 feet) in the north-west. It appears that the Namurian rocks once covered the limestone everywhere but have been stripped off by denudation, mostly in pre-glacial times, to create a remarkably accordant summit plane which descends southwards as an exhumed fossil surface before passing beneath the Namurian rocks. Only at Slieve Elva and its easterly outlier of Poulacapple have the overlying shales and flagstones resisted the general stripping. It is thought that the Galway granite may extend southwards to pass beneath the limestone and although the granite is much older than the limestone some later thermal activity may have helped to create the fluorspar of the Burren. This beautiful purple mineral, found in cavities in the limestone, was produced from the chemically active gas, fluorine, which combined with the calcium of the limestone to form calcium fluoride.

The geographical limits of the Burren are clearly defined: in the north the coast of Galway Bay terminates the limestone terrain, whilst in the west the Atlantic Ocean serves the same function; in the south the boundary is a geological one, following the sinuous boundary of the limestone and the Namurian rocks; only in the east is the boundary some-what obscure but is generally regarded as the edge of the Slievecarran highlands where they overlook the limestone plain of Gort (figure 24). Owing to the porosity of the limestone most of the drainage is under-ground, although, where it can be traced, the streams follow the southerly dip of the rocks, south-west to the sea or south-east to the Shannon via the Fergus river. The curious Caher river, in the north-west, is an excep-tion since it flows on the surface, north-westwards, as an obsequent (anti-dip) stream, but it is known that its valley is infilled with glacial drift and is therefore a special case. The only other surface streams of any magnitude in the Burren are those which rise on the impermeable, peat-covered Namurian rocks, but which disappear down swallow holes im-mediately after crossing on to the limestone. This is best seen around Slieve Elva (figure 24) which exhibits a drainage pattern not dissimilar to that of Ingleborough in the Pennines, although the vertical 'pots' are not as deep as their Pennine counterparts.

Much of the work on karstic landforms in the Burren has been carried out by Dr Marjorie Sweeting and Dr P. Williams who have described the detailed character of the region. Although the limestone caves are very far-reaching in their lateral extent, it appears that they possess few vertical pitches, possibly owing to the lack of faulting, to the many chert bands which channel the water-flow horizontally, and to the generally close proximity of the permanent water table. Indeed, the south-eastern tract of the Burren descends to the current water table so that near to Corrofin the closed depressions in the limestone are occupied by perma-nent lakes, such as the Ballyeighter Loughs. Frequently the streams dis-appear into horizontal bedding-plane swallets (locally known as 'sluggas') in this south-eastern zone, a good example being where the upper Fergus river disappears near Killinaboy. But generally, in the higher tracts of the Burren, the water table does not break the land surface so that visible drainage is rare, except on the Namurian rocks. Some of the most interesting landforms of the limestone areas are the closed depressions, of which there are two varieties. The smaller depressions, up to 600 feet in

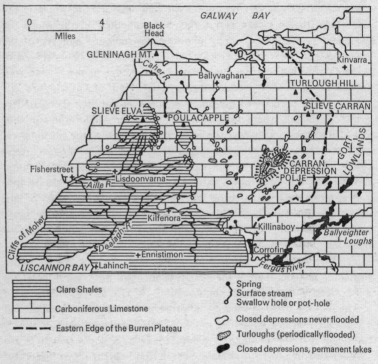

Fig. 24. *Geology and landforms of the Burren, Co. Clare (after M. M. Sweeting).*

diameter and with depths of some 60 feet, are probably due to subsidence associated with underground cavern collapse and in this case are known as collapsed dolines. Any of the depressions larger than 600 feet across, however, fall into a second category, known as poljes, which may have initiated as collapse structures but which have subsequently been enlarged by solution and erosion at a time when their floors coincided with a higher regional water table. All the large closed depressions of the Burren contain glacial drift which suggests that ice-sheet erosion may have played a part in their overdeepening. The most spectacular is the Carran depression, situated almost in the centre of the limestone Burren. Here is the finest polje in the British Isles, and from whichever direction one approaches it, this 200-foot-deep depression never fails to impress. Its steep bare limestone slopes, its circle of neatly walled fields and cottages and its central dried-up marshy lake-floors with their grey muds and alkaline peats, all contribute to a landscape unique in the British Isles. Periodically, after periods of heavy rain, the Carran depression carries an ephemeral lake, but this rapidly drains away into a swallow hole at the southern end from whence the water is known to drain underground to the Fergus river. Dr Williams believes that the Carran depression was initiated in Pliocene times by the coalescence of collapsed dolines at a period when a thin Namurian shale cover still survived on the surrounding hills. Thus, the surface streams of that period, flowing off the Namurian rocks, would have been relatively acid and therefore attacked the limestone more vigorously than today; once the shale cover had been totally removed (perhaps by ice during the Pleistocene) then the streams would have ceased to flow at the surface and the Carran depression would have become 'semi-fossilized', reaching the stage at which we see it today.

Whilst there is still doubt concerning the extent to which ice assisted in the lowering of the Carran depression, there seems little doubt that the widespread limestone pavements of the Burren owe much to the scouring of a former ice-sheet. Pavements seem to be found only in areas of dense, pure and massively bedded limestone which has been heavily glaciated (in this case by Connemara ice, judging by the granite erratics present on the Burren hills), so that despite its widespread occurrence elsewhere in Ireland the Carboniferous Limestone does not exhibit bare limestone pavements of this stature very commonly. In the grikes, which were subsequently created by solution of these bare pavements, the Maidenhair and Hart's Tongue Ferns now find refuge from the Atlantic gales. The deepest glacial grooving is found along the northern edge of the Burren, nearest to the former Connemara ice centre, and Dr Lloyd Praeger has drawn attention to the way in which these limestone hills and scarps are gently rounded and subdued. He contrasts such features with the angular scarps and fresh cliffs of both Ben Bulbin and the basalt plateaux of Antrim and concludes that it is not simply a matter of the efficiency of glacial erosion. Instead he points to the fact that in both the Sligo and Antrim cases the hard, cliff-forming rocks of the escarpments overlie softer and more easily eroded rocks, which, by their gradual removal, have caused the undermining and repeated collapse of the upper-most rocks. Thus, Ben Bulbin and the Antrim basalt scarps are kept constantly freshened up, but since the rocks which underlie the base of the Burren Limestone Series are nowhere exposed, the slopes are more stable and more subdued in form owing to the uniformity of the lime-stone.

The Aran Isles

If Sligo is Yeats country then the Aran Isles belong to John Millington Synge. It was on these fascinating limestone rocks, which straddle the entrance to Galway Bay, that this great Irish writer found his inspiration and came to intellectual maturity. The aesthetic quality of the Aran land-scape, from the '. . . great cliffs of Aran Mor [Inishmore] to the exquisite white-housed, white-sanded curve of the bay at Kilronan and Killeany' so entranced him that his writings were influenced ever afterwards.

The structure of the islands is extremely simple, that of a cuesta with the dipslope facing south-westwards to the Atlantic and the scarp north-eastwards to Galway Bay. The affinities of their geology and landforms with those of the neighbouring Burren are manifest, and although it is very gentle the general dip of the rocks is in the same southerly direction. So low is the dip, however, that the bedding of the rocks appears to be virtually flat, so that with the lack of faulting and folding the land has been sculptured into gigantic limestone terraces along the bedding planes. Each of the terraces is separated from its neighbours by a step, or riser, sometimes up to 20 feet in height, and this invariably acts as a field boundary. The general lack of major folding both here and in the Burren is often attributed to the presence of the Galway granite at depth, which appears to have given some stability to the area. Although the highest points of the islands are located near the centre, the most dramatic scenery occurs along their south-western shores. Here, in places, the sea cliffs rise to almost 300 feet in height and owing to the enormous power of the Atlantic waves they are being constantly eroded and undercut. Consequently the virtually horizontal limestone beds often overhang the ocean and have been used as fishing stances by the islanders from time immemorial. On one of the highest of these south-western cliffs in Inishmore the remarkable stone fortress of Dun Aengus is situated, its enormously thick drystone walls running in a half-circle right to the 250-foot cliff edge. This is not only the greatest antiquarian structure in Ireland, but also one of the most magnificent prehistoric structures in Europe. The limestone blocks, some of which are up to seven feet in length, have been removed from the bare pavements on which Dun Aengus stands. Each of the islands has its stone forts and one can only wonder at the enormous labour involved in their building. Even a cursory glance at the Aran landscape serves to demonstrate that the arduous way of life has continued up to the present day, for virtually every single field has been 'made' by the islanders, owing to the dearth of soil on the bare limestone (plate 20).

The Pleistocene ice-sheets, spreading outwards from Connemara, have scoured away most of the soil of these islands, and when one adds to this the porosity of the limestone terrain and the inhibiting effect of the salt-laden winds, it is little wonder that the vegetation is represented only by a ground-hugging flora. By prodigious effort the islanders have, over the centuries, carried thousands of tons of sand and seaweed from the low-lying north-eastern shores and piled it on the limestone pavements near the villages. To preserve their 'soil' the solution joints in the limestone were first filled with rubble and the small artificial plots surrounded with drystone walls, as a protection against the wind. A visitor to the islands will therefore gain an impression of a grey limestone desert, honeycombed with miles of stone walls within which cattle are grazed or potatoes grown on the artificial soil. Trees are entirely absent on the Aran Isles, although hazel and hawthorn scrub survives in sheltered corners. The ground vegetation, however, is almost as rich as that of the Burren, with many exotic plants flourishing in this curious environment, for reasons similar to those suggested above. Unlike the mainland of Clare, however, there is no peat left on the islands, although there is reason to believe that it once existed. Fortunately, the acid peat-covered lands of Galway are not too far distant and supplies of peat for fuel are sent regularly by boat across Galway Bay. The large granite boulders which are strewn across the Aran limestone terraces are obviously glacial erratics which have also come from Galway, and most of them, being too large to clear from the fields, are enclosed by the drystone walls, many of which follow the joint patterns of the limestone. The houses, which are sited along the sheltered north-eastern coasts, are all built of limestone blocks, although thatch is now disappearing as a roofing material, its place having been taken first by slate and latterly by artificial roofing imported from Galway city.

11. The Connacht Uplands – Galway

Next to Killarney and its lakes, there can be no more famous region in Ireland than that of western Galway. Connemara is a name which conjures up a vision of Atlantic Ireland, a land of whitewashed cottages set against a background of mountain, bog and ocean; a land of muted colours, in which the ochres, violets, pearly greys and misty blues mix together in countless combinations as if to resemble the fabric of the local tweeds. The name of Connemara is so well known that some mistake it for the name of a county, although in fact it is only a district of county Galway. The physical contrasts which obtain in the Galway section of the Connacht Uplands enable us to distinguish three regional subdivisions, for in addition to Connemara we must also examine the granite lands of Iar Connacht and the Lower Palaeozoic rocks of the Joyce Country.

Iar Connacht

The Galway granite, long thought to be of Pre-Cambrian age, is now known to be Palaeozoic, thanks to radiometric dating. Its main outcrop is extensive, covering some 500 square miles between Galway city in the east and Bertraghboy Bay in the west. In addition there are several smaller granitic bodies of similar age near to the northern and western perimeters of the main granite (figure 25). In the south the granitic terrain ceases abruptly along the remarkably linear northern coast of Galway Bay, a fact which has led some geologists to suggest that the coastline has been carved from a fault scarp. Nevertheless, it is thought by certain geologists that the Galway granite extends southwards beneath the Bay to pass unconformably below the Carboniferous Limestones of the Aran Isles and the Burren. In the east the relationship with the limestone is more clearly seen, for the granite descends beneath the limestone of the Corrib country, north-west of Galway city. To the north the granite is bordered by a tract of gneisses and schists which form a narrow corridor between the Pre-Cambrian quartzites of the Maumturk Mountains and the granite itself.

When we come to examine the lands of Iar Connacht in some detail, one characteristic of the granite terrain stands out more than any other.

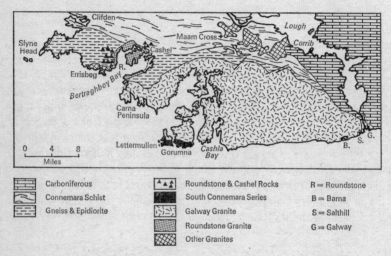

Fig. 25. *The distribution of the Galway granite and adjacent granites (after J. K. Charlesworth).*

This is the way in which the Galway granite has been denuded and dissected to become an area of relatively low relief. It is difficult to understand such an apparent anomaly, for in almost every other granite outcrop in Ireland the rocks form a landscape of steep, positive relief. Indeed granite is often spoken of synonymously with the term 'toughness', and is generally regarded by most laymen as being the least yielding of rocks. How come, then, that this wide exposure of granite creates so few positive landforms and only once overtops the 1,000-foot contour in Iar Connacht? It is not simply a matter of age, for the Palaeozoic granites of Donegal create higher mountains than those of Iar Connacht. But herein lies part of the answer, for it was seen in Donegal how the granite hills of the

Derryveagh Mountains were overshadowed in absolute height by the neighbouring quartzite peaks of Errigal and its satellites. The same is true here in the Connacht Uplands, for against the high Pre-Cambrian quartzite pyramids of the Maumturks and the Twelve Pins of Connemara, the granite country appears to be both low and subdued. This cannot be the entire explanation, however, for along its western perimeter the Galway granite has been deeply dissected by the Atlantic to form the remarkable archipelagos around Gorumna Island and Bertraghboy Bay. Quite clearly the granites of western Galway must exhibit mineralogical compositions and structures which lend themselves to erosion at a rate more rapid than that of most of their neighbouring rocks.

After the angularity of the bedded limestone of the Burren and the Aran Isles, the gently rolling granite hills of Iar Connacht come as a sharp contrast as we follow the coast road along the northern shores of Galway Bay. After passing through the bustle of Galway city and the prosperous hotels of Salthill, we are soon into the uncompromising granite country. Settlement and the improved land hug the coast, leaving the interior of Iar Connacht virtually deserted. Sean O'Faolain noted this dichotomy in the landscape and pointed out that the lack of any signs of prehistoric culture inland suggested that this had always been the case. Nevertheless, local tradition has it that in earlier centuries one could walk on the tops of the trees all the way from Letterfrack in west Connemara to Galway city. There are certainly records to show that woodlands existed in the interior of Iar Connacht in the seventeenth century, but these woods had all disappeared prior to the introduction of government plantations which have recently changed the face of the landscape around Lough Lettercraffroe. On these exposed western coasts the natural trees and shrubs, where they have survived the depradations of man and his animals, are stunted and deformed owing to the salt spray being carried far inland. Only on some of the inaccessible lake-islands in western Galway can we see survivals of the natural climax vegetation of low dense scrub. Here, in a habitat protected from grazing, Professor Tansley has listed an interesting combination of rowan, birch, willow, yew and occasionally oak, together with the more typical heather and gorse found at frequent intervals in this environment of acid bogland.

It is not so much the character of the vegetation but that of the granite itself which strikes one on a journey along the Iar Connacht coast road.

The large crystals of pink potash feldspar give the rocks their distinctive colouring, although they have often been dulled by a lichen growth on the drystone granite walls. The profusion of granite boulders scattered over the landscape is the most remarkable feature of the country near to Spiddal, and it was here that J. M. Synge commented how 'the fields looked so small and rocky that the very thought of tillage in them seemed like the freak of an eccentric'. It is true that the drystone walls enclose little more than crops of boulders, with grass appearing only as veins amongst the rocks, but a relatively large population is supported on this stony coastal margin. The coastal fringe of Iar Connacht was part of the notorious Congested Districts, where 'cottages swarmed by the roadside and in the boreens'.

The remarkable stoniness of Iar Connacht is largely a result of glacial erosion during the Ice Age, for whilst scouring away most of the pre-glacial regolith the ice left behind a mass of enormous glacial erratic blocks. A local ice-cap was centred over the Joyce Country so that in west Galway ice movement was generally in a radial pattern, carrying the massive blocks south-westwards across Iar Connacht as far as the Aran Isles (see p. 105). The ice was such a powerful abrasive agent that only at one place, near Roundstone, has the rotted granite (known as 'growan') survived. This rotting took place in earlier, warmer, climatic episodes, possibly in pre-glacial times, when tors may also have been created by deep weathering (if we are to accept one particular concept outlined on p. 108). But the fact that the Galway granite today lacks any tors or thick layers of 'growan' reflects the intensity of the glacial erosion. The Galway granite scenery, therefore, can be contrasted with that of Dartmoor in south-west Britain, where ice-sheets failed to reach the granite outcrop and left the tors upstanding above extensive aprons of clitters which themselves mantle the deeply rotted granite.

The way in which the Galway granite is decomposing in the present-day mild oceanic environment may be demonstrated by the ease with which the sea has broken into the granite terrain on the borders of Iar Connacht and Connemara. West of Costelloe stretch more than one hundred square miles of island-studded water, a labyrinth of land and sea unparalleled elsewhere in Ireland. Little wonder that the tortuous coastline is reflected in the local place-name of Camus Bay (Camas = crooked sea-shore). The islands of Gorumna and Lettermullen, at the southern end of the archipelago, are built partly from non-granitic rocks, known collectively as the South Connemara Series (figure 25). Their calcareous shales, volcanics, greywackes and amphibolites are so similar to the rocks of Murrisk, to the north of Killary (chapter twelve), that they have been tentatively dated as Ordovician. More important, however, is the suggestion that they may represent a remnant of the older 'roof' of rocks into which the Galway granite was intruded. Not that this has any significant effect on the scenery, for like all the other islands the landscape is one of bareness, since the stripping of the bogland for fuel has revealed the glacially polished, mamillated topography beneath. But the tiny fields, where the two-acre plots are divided equally between potatoes and oats, support a surprisingly large population, with a density as high as anywhere in the Gaeltacht. Home industries of knitting and tweed-making supplement the meagre income from fishing, but fishing on a commercial scale has never succeeded, for the Atlantic swell is continuous and submerged rocks and sandbanks in the serpentine channels are severe hazards.

Many of the islands have been linked by bridges to each other and thence to the mainland, largely in the widespread scheme of 'Relief Road' building during the famine years of the nineteenth century. Thus, there is easy access to the unspoiled coastal landscape of Atlantic Ireland, which, with its blue waters, white 'coral beaches', picturesque thatched cottages and hand-dug peat stacks, reaches one of its finest climaxes in this peninsular stretch of south-west Galway. Only the peat-fired power-station at nearby Screeb reminds us that modern innovations are waiting, just off-stage, to change the age-old scene at some undecided future date. Nevertheless, the landscape may be more resilient than one thinks, for in 1750 Screeb was the site of a local iron industry, based possibly on 'bog-iron ore' (from iron nodule deposits developed beneath the peat) or, more likely, on imported ore. No sign of this remains, except for the name of Lough na Furnace.

Connemara

West of the Carna Peninsula the main Galway granite disappears with a final defiant ridge of low hills overlooking Bertraghboy Bay to the west. Here, the so-called Roundstone granite, mineralogically and chemically similar to the main Galway granite, forms a circular outcrop some five miles in diameter (figure 25). It has been intruded into the main granite but has suffered the same fate, so far as marine erosion is concerned, for the Atlantic waves, possibly exploiting the granite jointing, have carved out the sinuous creeks and inlets of Bertraghboy Bay as far inland as the perimeter of the pluton.

The bays and creeks of Connemara (plate 21), which contribute so much to its scenic beauty, may have given their name to the region, for one interpretation of its name is Cuain na Mara (= harbours of the sea). But whatever its true derivation, there seems little doubt that the post-glacial marine transgression has caused the flooding of this low-lying landscape, for in places the Holocene peat is now submerged. But the drowning has not been sufficient to create the deep ria coastline which characterizes Kerry and Cork. The reasons for this contrast are difficult to explain, but may lie in the lithological differences and the degree of glacial downwarping experienced in the two areas. Nevertheless, the scale of the two coastlines is vastly different.

Overlooking Bertraghboy Bay on its northern and western sides are the two isolated hills of Cashel Mountain (1,024 feet) and Errisbeg (987 feet), their dark gabbroid rocks frowning over the paler granites of the lowland. The fact that these rocks are mineralogically very different from the granites and are also considerably older, signifies that we have left the Galway granite country and are now in a different geological tract. It would be instructive, therefore, to summarize the major geological structures which build the remainder of Connemara, before exploring its spectacular scenery.

The oldest rocks of the region appear to be the Pre-Cambrian schists and quartzites which are folded into a complex east–west striking anticlinorium. To the north lies a parallel syncline which brings in the unconformable Ordovician and Silurian rocks near to Killary Harbour, while to the south is the Cashel—Errisbeg group of basic and ultrabasic intrusions together with a narrow band of gneisses and migmatites (figure 26). The quartzite core, which is thought to be of similar age to the Dalradian quartzites of Donegal, has been given the name of the Twelve Pins (or Bens) Quartzite, which helps to build not only the most distinctive peaks in Connemara but also the equally steep-sided Maumturk Mountains. On the flanks of these high peaks the Connemara Schist series is complicated by folding and faulting, but its east–west alignment is retained. Included within these metasediments, between Clifden and Recess, is the well-known green Connemara Marble, which has been quarried for many

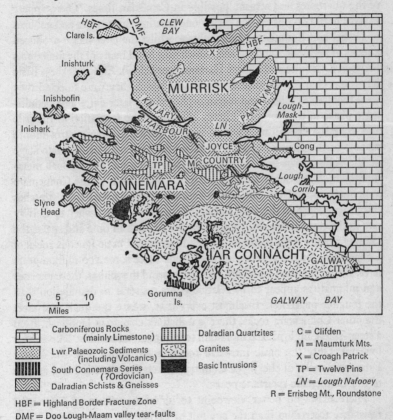

Fig. 26. *The geology of south-west Connacht (based on the Irish Geological Survey).*

years at Lissoughter, Derryclare and Streamstown. Its calcite and serpentine composition has resulted from the multi-phase metamorphism of an ancient dolomitic limestone, partly in association with the much later intrusion of the Galway granite, so that it represents a true marble. The marble is currently used mainly in the construction of souvenirs for the tourist trade, but on a larger scale its use as a decorative stone is well seen in the National Library and National Museum in Dublin.

The period of ultrabasic and basic intrusions came after the formation of the quartzites and schists, possibly in Cambrian times. There appear to have been two phases, the earlier one creating the diorites and gabbros of Cashel and Roundstone noted above, whilst the later phase produced a series of peridotites and eucrites which now build many of the mountains between Kylemore and Killary Harbour (see below). Although these basic intrusions changed the country rocks into which they were injected they were themselves folded and metamorphosed at a later date. The penultimate phase in this complex history came with the formation of the pale and coarsely crystalline gneisses and migmatites. The quartz–diorite magma of the gneisses appears to have been injected during a late stage of the schist formation, at the close of the period of regional metamorphism. Their main outcrop occurs on both flanks of the Connemara anticlinorium, but the one to the south is more marked as it stretches from Slyne Head in the west, through Roundstone and Cashel, to Galway city in the east (figure 26). It serves to divide, both in time and space, the Galway granite from the older metasediments and basic igneous rocks of Connemara, for the granitic intrusion took place some 100 million years later. But in common with both the granites and the schists, these gneisses and migmatites appear to be relatively less resistant to denudation than the tougher quartzites. In almost every case, where the quartzites meet the other Connemara rocks, there is a distinct change in landform, from a steep-sided, high-peaked mountain terrain to an undulating, lake-strewn lowland. Only the basic intrusive rocks, noted above, and the Lower Palaeozoic rocks of the Joyce Country, match the elevation and stature of the Connemara quartzite peaks.

There exists no better viewpoint to judge the effects of differential resistance to erosion than the summit of Errisbeg at Roundstone. From this isolated, breezy top not only can one view the entire length of the Iar Connacht granite country and its fascinating coastline, but also it is one of the finest points from which to see the Twelve Pins. There, to the north-east, across 40 square miles of the most desolate lake-riddled bogland to be found anywhere in Ireland, rise the splendid quartzite pyramids, their cloud-dappled hillsides in the luminescent Atlantic light creating a kaleidoscope of colours never to be forgotten. The bogland, developed on the outcrop of the schists, gneisses and migmatites to the north of Roundstone, has been studied in some detail by Professor Tansley, who described it as a classic example of a blanket bog, formed in a different way from the raised bogs of the Central Lowlands. Although blanket bog is the present climax vegetation of these parts, there is evidence to show that this has not always been the case. Beneath the peat a layer of pine stumps can often be seen (the bog 'oak' of local tradition), and this has been ascribed to a drier period of post-glacial time, known as the Sub-Boreal, when pine forests covered Connemara. They finally succumbed, however, to the wetter conditions of the present Sub-Atlantic climatic period, which commenced some 2,500 years ago.

The summit of Errisbeg also gives us a chance to view the dazzling white tombolo of Dog's Bay which lies to the south. Here a white strand of shelly sand has tied a low granite island to the shore. The 'sand' is not formed from the usual quartz grains but from countless numbers of foraminifera, tiny shells of microscopic creatures (no less than 124 species have been recognized here), which formerly lived in deeper water off-shore. It has been suggested, by Professor C. A. M. King, that the absence of quartz sand at this locality is in response to the difficulty of longshore movement of beach material on this intricate coastline.

At Mannin Bay between Ballyconneely and Clifden, and at a few other localities in Connemara, there are more white beaches, known locally as 'coral strands', which we must distinguish from the Dog's Bay beach described above. In the case of Mannin Bay the foreshore is composed of countless tiny fragments of broken branch-like material. It is certainly very like coral in appearance, but experts tell us that in reality it is not an animal product (like true coral) but is of vegetable origin. It is in fact derived from a species of calcareous seaweed, known as *Lithothamnion*, which thrives on the sea-floor beneath the clear waters of western Connemara.

The trim, twin-spired town of Clifden is the best centre to explore western Connemara or visit the offshore islands of Inishbofin and the deserted Inishshark. Clifden stands at the head of a long coastal inlet, at a point where the Recess–Ballynahinch lowland corridor reaches the sea (plate 22). To the east of the Twelve Pins the imposing lakes of Glen Inagh occupy a curving valley, carved out of a belt of schists which divides the quartzites of the Twelve Pins from those of the Maumturks.

Although such valleys were probably in existence prior to the Ice Age they must have been greatly overdeepened by glacial scour. It has been suggested that during the last glaciation the Twelve Pins' summits stood as nunataks above the ice-cap which wrapped around their slopes, although the larger corries of the eastern slopes almost certainly contributed to the glacier which moved both north and south down the Glen Inagh corridor. All the major corries of the Maumturks show a similar preferred orientation to those of the Twelve Pins, between north and east, for these were the slopes most sheltered from the sun in the northern hemisphere. In addition, if the prevailing winds in the Late Pleistocene were similar to those of today, then they would have served to blow the thick accumulations of snow off the quartzite summits into the lee of the north-eastern facing slopes, thus nourishing the corrie glaciers.

Eight of the Twelve Pins rise to over 2,000 feet, with Ben Baun (2,395 feet) the highest, being also the most central. The hard quartzite weathers slowly, despite the heavy rainfall (more than 100 inches), so with the lack of soil and with slopes too steep for peat growth, the bare light-grey rock sparkles in sunlight and rain alike. Only at one place (Muckanaght, 2,153 feet) do the schists rise up to the summits, and it is here, in the deeper regolith and more hospitable habitat, that the few Alpine plants occur.

To the north of these quartzite uplands lie the rugged hills formed from the basic intrusions of Currywongaun and Doughruagh (1,736 feet). But it is the narrow valley of Kylemore, drained by the Dawros river, which captures our attention in this part of northern Connemara. Here, the beautiful lake, with its castle of granite faced with limestone (now Kylemore Abbey), is cradled in the lush verdure of Kylemore woodlands (Coill Mor = the great wood). Apart from its sheltered position the dense woodland may owe its splendour to the thickness of the glacial drifts hereabouts.

The Joyce Country

To the east of the Maumturk Mountains a series of narrow valleys has been carved into the less resistant schists by the headwaters of the Lough Corrib drainage system. An arm of the great lake twists far into the Connacht Uplands at this point, around the picturesque island of Hen's Castle, until it is joined by the Joyces' River. The name of this remote mountainous district of western Galway is derived from a Welsh family settled here by the Anglo-Norman conquerors. The peaks of Bunbeg and Bunnacunneen, to the east of the Joyces' River, fail to reach the heights achieved by the quartzite Maumturks, nor is their shape so remarkable, for they are built of Silurian greywackes, shales and conglomerates lying unconformably on the Connemara Schists. To the south of Lough Nafooey, however, at the junction of the Silurian and Ordovician rocks, the greywackes and conglomerates have been reinforced with layers of agglomerate containing volcanic bombs. The presence of these tougher volcanic rocks has helped to build the sharp ridge of the Kilbride penin-sula, which divides the two parallel arms of Lough Mask as they bite deeply into the Connacht Uplands. Here, on the borders of Galway and Mayo, is some of the least known but most picturesque mountain scenery of Connacht. The glacially deepened valleys, the waterfalls, the corrie lakes, together with the wooded peninsulas and islands of Lough Mask,

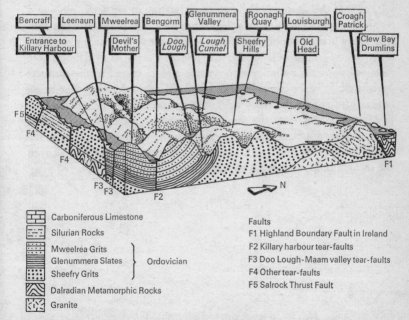

Fig. 27. *Killary harbour and Murrisk, south Mayo.*

in the blue waters of which the high mountains are reflected, all contribute to a scene reminiscent of Derwentwater in the English Lake District. Is it mere coincidence that the age and character of the rocks are similar in both cases?

To the north-west of the attractive waters of Lough Mask the frowning cliffs of the Partry Mountains form the eastern bastion of the Connacht Uplands, overlooking the Central Lowlands. Corries have fretted the edge of this extensive tableland of Lower Palaeozoic grits (mainly the Mweelrea Grit) and although the summits rise quite high by Connacht standards (Maumtrasna, 2,207 feet), they are little more than a dreary wasteland of eroded peat hags. The western satellite of the Devil's mother (2,131 feet), however, overlooks a scene as spectacular as any in western Ireland. For here, at last, is one of the highlights of the Connacht Uplands, the great fjord of Killary Harbour.

In the mountain-girt hollow of Leenaun it is difficult to appreciate that the waters which wash the walls of the pretty colour-washed village are salt, or that the Aasleagh Falls, in their 'setting of clustered pines and reef-sown rapids', descend into the Atlantic, some 11 miles from the open sea. There is little doubt that Killary (Caol saile = the narrow sea inlet) is the finest fjord in Ireland (figure 27). With a depth of 13 fathoms over most of its length, a shallowing seawards and an entrance almost closed by islands, it bears the hallmarks of glacial overdeepening. But in no other Irish fjord are the valley walls so steep and so high, for here the bulk of Mweelrea rises from the sea in one enormous sweep to the summit ridge. Killary Harbour, slicing deeply into the upland tract, acts as the border between Galway and Mayo and is clearly a natural barrier between the mountainous country on its southern and northern shores.

12. The Connacht Uplands – Mayo

Mayo is a county of great geological diversity, with rocks ranging in age from the Lewisian gneisses of Erris, through a complex variety of Lower Palaeozoics, to the Carboniferous sediments of Clew Bay, Killala Bay and the eastern plains. Its topography, too, is varied, ranging from the quartzite and gritstone mountains of the western seaboard to the limestone Plains of Mayo and the Clew Bay drumlins. We are here concerned only with the uplands, which happen to lie along the western margins, creating a coastline as varied and as scenically spectacular as any in Ireland.

Murrisk

The short, stumpy peninsula of Murrisk, lying between Clew Bay and Killary Harbour, is a region of great scenic contrasts, for it not only contains Connacht's highest peak (Mweelrea) and one of Ireland's shapeliest mountains (Croagh Patrick), but also an intriguing coastline and some fine glaciated highlands. Its geology, too, exhibits important differences and in part these have been responsible for the scenic contrasts.

Along the southern margin lies Killary Harbour itself, eroded partly along an outcrop of less resistant slates and partly along a fault complex (the Killary Harbour faults), although the country hereabouts is dominated by the east–west trending Mweelrea Syncline which has affected a substantial thickness of Lower Palaeozoic rocks (figure 27). The Mweelrea Grits (between 5,000 and 10,000 feet thick) occupy the core of the syncline and, owing to their great resistance to erosion, they have survived to form a number of high mountain blocks, including the Partry Mountains and Mweelrea itself. At its western end the axis of the syncline is followed by the Owennaglogh river valley which drains the eastern slopes of the Mweelrea Mountains. The uppermost reaches of this lonely valley, hemmed in by steep, boulder-littered slopes, lead up to two isolated corrie lakes which crouch immediately beneath the summit of Mweelrea (2,668 feet). The coarse brown sandstones and conglomerates, the pebbles of which appear to have been derived from the erosion of older rocks in Connemara, form the cliffs above the valley sides but they are inter-bedded with layers of slates and volcanic rocks. Of the latter the tuffs appear as hard green and purple layers, with bright red patches of glassy, pumice-like material. At first it was thought that these harder layers were rhyolitic lavas interbedded with Ordovician sedimentary rocks, but although they are compact and lava-like in appearance they are in fact pyroclastic rocks (see glossary). The volcanic dust and the shards of volcanic glass were welded together into a coherent rock by their own residual heat immediately after deposition and are now known as welded tuffs or ignimbrites. The fact that they are interbedded with the current-bedded sediments of the Mweelrea Grits has suggested that at the time of their formation, in the Ordovician, explosive volcanoes were situated near to the contemporaneous shoreline. It has been further suggested that the eruptions which formed both the Mweelrea and the Sheefry tuffs must have been similar to the famous West Indian explosion of Mt Pelée in Martinique, in 1902. A Peléan type of eruption gives rise to a *nuée ardente*, a cloud of incandescent gas containing pulverized magma particles, which rolls rapidly down-slope before the products of the explosion settle on the sea floor. The pyroclastic rocks of Murrisk, how-ever, unlike those of more recent age in Antrim (chapter two), are the sole survivors of such a fiery episode, for there is no sign of Ordovician volcanic vents or fissures in the surface geology of Mayo. The Murrisk hills are the only mountains in Ireland where Ordovician vulcanicity has helped to create landforms of a stature comparable with those formed by Ordovician volcanic rocks in North Wales and the Lake District.

The deep north–south valley of the Bunndorragha river isolates the Mweelrea Mountains from the prominent mass of Bengorm (2,303 feet) farther east. It is aligned along another zone of faulting which has been picked out by denudational forces to form the deep trough now occupied by Doo Lough, cradled between the Sheefry Hills and the Mweelrea Mountains (figure 27).

The northern limb of the Mweelrea Syncline brings up an older series of rocks to the north of Bengorm and the Mweelrea Mountains. These rocks, known as the Glenummera Slates, are also of Ordovician age and occur as a steeply dipping narrow outcrop running parallel with the Mweelrea axis. Since the slates have proved less resistant to erosion than the grits, however, they have been etched out to form the Glenummera valley between Bengorm and the Sheefry Hills (figure 27).

The Sheefry Hills have been carved from the oldest Ordovician rocks of Murrisk, the Sheefry Grits, which, although of similar composition to the Mweelrea Grits (including the pyroclastic rocks), exhibit a pattern of tighter Caledonian folding, where dips are generally steep if not vertical. Like the Mweelrea Mountains the Sheefry Hills are fretted with corries, chiefly on their eastern and northern slopes, although it has been suggested that throughout the entire Ice Age all their highest summits, and those of Bengorm, stood as nunataks above the ice-sheets. One of the reasons behind such a claim is the presence of thick layers of frost-shattered debris on the summits themselves, indicative of lengthy periods of periglacial activity and of a possibility that they have never been over-ridden by the inland ice-sheets. F. M. Synge is of the opinion that the northwestern lowlands of Murrisk also were ice-free during the last major glacial episode despite the presence of ice-sheets in Clew Bay and the Connemara highlands.

The little town of Louisburgh is located near to an important geological boundary, for passing from east to west along the southern shores of Clew Bay is the Irish equivalent of the Highland Border Fracture Zone, which we last saw in counties Tyrone and Fermanagh (p. 55 and p. 86). Having been virtually lost for some 80 miles beneath the Carboniferous cover rocks of Leitrim, Sligo and eastern Mayo, this important zone skirts the northern slopes of Croagh Patrick, cutting off the Silurian quartzites, which form this prominent peak, from the coarse Dalradian greywackes, which appear intermittently as a narrow band between Westport and Louisburgh. Part of this Upper Dalradian group of rocks is known as the Westport Grits and has been extensively used as a building stone in the town from which they were named. Here, as everywhere else in the British Isles, the Dalradian rocks terminate southwards at the Highland Border Fracture Zone; so that, in a geological sense, Connemara remains an oddity, being the only location in the British Isles where Dalradian rocks come to the surface south of the Highland Border Fracture Zone. Another structural difference which distinguishes the geology of Connacht from that of central Scotland is the lack of a major topographical depression to the south of the fracture zone to coincide with the Midland Valley of Scotland. In its place the Lower Palaeozoic rocks of Murrisk and the Pre-Cambrian metasediments of Connemara survive to create a region of high relief.

Roonagh Quay at the north-western tip of Murrisk, besides being an embarkation port for a visit to Clare Island, is also a good point from which to view some of Connacht's westernmost islands. Far to the south-west the Dalradian rocks of Inishbofin rise as a series of low hills on the horizon. Nearer at hand the tough Ordovician rocks of Inishturk present high western cliffs to the Atlantic swell. But it is the prominent hump of Clare Island, three miles to the north-west, which constantly takes the eye. All these islands are virtually treeless owing to the climatic exposure.

Clare Island, for its small size (only six square miles), has a remarkably diversified geology and scenery. The oldest rocks are the dark sandstones and slates of Dalradian age, which occupy the triangular northern pro-montory, rising to a height of over 400 feet in the northern sea-cliffs. The youngest rocks are found in the easternmost promontory, beneath thick layers of till and peat. They consist of sandstones, shales and con-glomerates of Lower Carboniferous age and are lithologically similar to the rocks which occur along the coastal margins of Clew Bay farther east. Both of these rock series are cut off from the Silurian rocks, which occupy the remainder of the island, by a major fault zone which slices through the island in a west-north-west direction. Its character is so similar to the fault which flanks the southern shore of Clew Bay that most geologists would regard this as the westernmost extension of the Highland Border Fracture Zone, offset, together with the rest of Clare Island, some three miles to the north-west by a northerly extension of the Doo Lough–Maam tear-faults (figure 26). The Silurian rocks occupy more than half the island, and their grey flaggy sandstones, purple shales and greenish pebbly grits are responsible for the remarkable mountain of Croaghmore (1,520 feet). Its steep southern slopes coincide quite closely with the southerly dip of the rocks but its fantastic northern scarp face drops almost vertically to the sea from the very edge of the summit

From Clare Island the isolated mountain of Croagh Patrick looks quite majestic as it towers over the shores of Clew Bay. This dazzling quartzite pyramid reminds one of Errigal in Donegal, and although the make-up of the rock is similar, its age is different, for Croagh Patrick is built from Silurian quartzites which have been extensively contorted (figure 27). Its fame, as a centre of pilgrimage, is reflected by the gleaming white track which winds to the 2,510-foot summit, its sparkling stones constantly freshened by the feet of thousands of pilgrims who climb annually to the top. The view from its lofty peak is even more breathtaking than that from Errigal, for its base rises from the island-studded waters of Clew Bay, described by Thackeray as the most beautiful scenery in the world. The ever-changing colours of sea, land and sky, here mixed in a complex kaleidoscope and bathed in the ethereal Atlantic light, give to the view a quality unequalled in Ireland.

Clew Bay

Part of the uniqueness of the Clew Bay scenery must arise from the remarkable archipelago of islands which it possesses. Not only the number of islands but their pronounced whale-back form gives character to the bay, and it comes as no surprise to learn that they represent the partly submerged zone of a widespread drumlin swarm. Only Strangford Lough in county Down (chapter seven) exhibits a drowned drumlin landscape of comparable size, but we shall see that in the Mayo example the Atlantic waves have worked on the drumlins to produce landforms which are absent from the landlocked Strangford Lough. A further difference in the appearance of the two archipelagos is the widespread development at Strangford of the post-glacial raised beach. In Clew Bay this is feebly developed because of the limited post-glacial uplift which has occurred there.

Clew Bay and the Westport–Newport lowland, which lies immediately to the east, contain several hundred drumlins but of these over 80 comprise individual islands in the bay itself. As the full fetch of the Atlantic waves set to work on these unconsolidated hillocks of limestone till, so the westernmost drumlins were steadily worn back until they were completely destroyed. Today, the outermost drumlin islands exhibit steep seaward-facing cliffs, composed entirely of boulder clay, but much of the eroded material has been redeposited in the form of shingle spits, tombolos and forelands. Some of these spits, by virtue of the constant wave action, have succeeded in linking several of the westernmost drum-

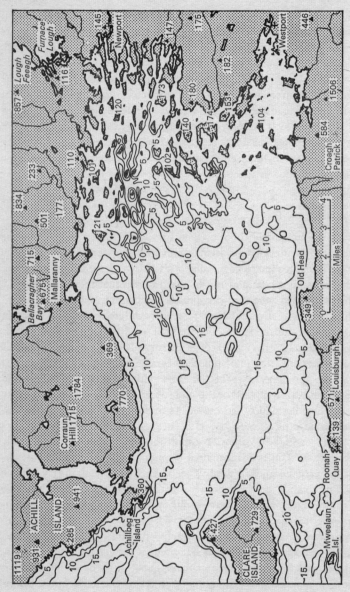

Fig. 28. The drumlin archipelago of Clew Bay (based on The Ordnance Survey).

lin islands to create a distinctive coastal pattern (figure 28). Since the formation of these western shingle barriers, the Atlantic waves have been unable to reach the drumlin islands in the inner recesses of the bay. Consequently, these inner drumlins do not exhibit the cliffing which characterizes their western neighbours. Many of the drumlin islands are farmed and some of them retain small settlements, but, in common with the depopulation of the Atlantic seaboard elsewhere in Ireland, most of the cottages are now derelict and thistles thrive in the former pastures.

At the south-east corner of the bay the picturesque town of Westport, huddled amidst its drumlin hillocks, is hidden away from the sea, despite its name. Although planned to be a major port for northern Connacht, the empty warehouses of Westport Quay testify to the failure of such an enterprise. Nevertheless, the planned town of 1780, with its interesting polygonal market place, its beautiful tree-lined Mall (reminiscent of an Amsterdam canal) and its fine Georgian mansion of Westport House, has a charm which is often missing from Irish towns.

The general structure of Clew Bay is that of a faulted syncline of Carboniferous rocks flanked by Old Red Sandstone and Dalradian meta-sediments to the north, east and south. Only in the centre of the basin do the limestones occur, although they are usually buried by a thick drift cover. Around the northern margins of the bay the northern limb of the syncline brings up the basal Carboniferous sandstones and conglomerates to form a narrow coastal outcrop between Mallaranny and Newport. On the whole, however, the Carboniferous sandstones have proved less resistant to denudation than their neighbouring rocks. Nowhere is this better illustrated than to the east of Newport, where the Carboniferous sediments occur as a narrow band between Clew Bay and Lough Conn. Here, the flanking masses of Old Red Sandstone create the Croaghmoyle hills (1,412 feet), overlooking Beltra Lough, and also contribute to the steep southern slopes of the Dalradian Nephin Beg range. Between these uplands the picturesque corridor of Glenhest, and its north-east extension of Glen Nephin, has been carved out along the less competent Carboniferous rocks (figure 29).

West of Mallaranny, the peninsula of Corraun has been almost isolated from the mainland by the incursions of the sea at Bellacragher Bay. This narrow defile between the high mountains carries the road we must follow on our journey to Achill Island, and its shelter from the searing oceanic

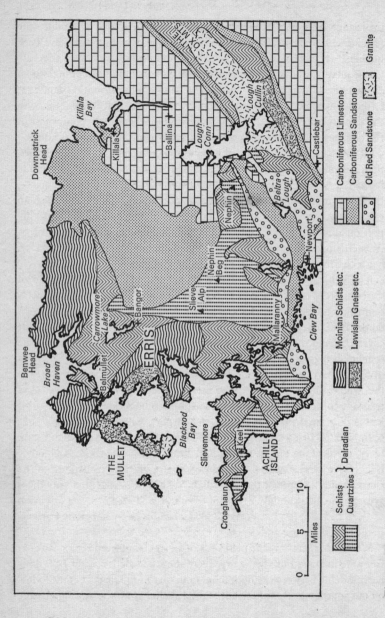

Fig. 29. *The geology of north Mayo (based on the Irish Geological Survey).*

Map labels:

Downpatrick Head
Killala Bay
Killala
Ballina
Lough Conn
Lough Cullin
OXMTS
Castlebar
Beltra Lough
Nephin
Newport
Nephin Beg
Clew Bay
Benwee Head
Broad Haven
Carrowmore Lake
Bangor
Slieve Alp
Mallaranny
Belmullet
ERRIS
THE MULLET
Blacksod Bay
Slievemore
Keel
ACHILL ISLAND
Croaghaun

Legend:

Dalradian:
Schists
Quartzites

Moinian Schists etc.
Lewisian Gneiss etc.

Carboniferous Limestone
Carboniferous Sandstone
Old Red Sandstone
Granite

Miles
0   5   10

1. *Fair Head, County Antrim. The escarpment of vertical columnar cliffs is formed from a sill of Tertiary dolerite which has been intruded into gently dipping Lower Carboniferous Limestones (buried beneath the screes). The upper beds of limestone have now been eroded, leaving the surface of the sill as a barren lake-strewn plateau.*

2. *The Giant's Causeway. The well-known hexagonal basalt columns of the main causeway are shown in the foreground. Beyond them the upper cliffs are composed of similar columns (seen forming the pinnacles on the skyline) of the Middle Basalts. The footpath is traceable below the upper cliffs out to the light-coloured band on the headland which marks the main Interbasaltic Bed.*

3. *Glenariff, County Antrim. The Upper and Lower Basalts, forming the bleak moorlands of the Antrim Plateau, have here been breached to reveal the underlying Mesozoic sedimentary rocks. Keuper Marls and Sandstones (Trias) form the valley floor whilst Cretaceous Chalk crops out below the basalt cliffs. Note the field patterns of the so-called 'ladder farms', and the Bann Lowlands in the distance.*

4. *The city of Armagh, showing its twin cathedrals, each located on neighbouring drumlins. Note how the street patterns have been influenced by the shape of these whale-backed hills.*

5. *Coalisland, County Tyrone. An area of despoiled industrial landscape in a rural setting. Opencast mining of brickclays, sands and gravels surrounds the brickworks, in a town where coal-mining is no longer important. (Compare plate 35).*

6. *The Sperrin Mountains, County Londonderry. This view, looking south-eastwards along the main ridge to Sawel Mountain, 2240 feet (with a black cloud-shadow on its summit), shows the dome-like shape of hills formed from Dalradian schists. Note the absence of corries and the incision of the Burn Dennet stream into the drift-filled valley east of Ballynamallaght.*

7. *The city of Londonderry and Lough Foyle. The ancient walled city can be seen on its hilltop in the centre of the picture to the left of the bridge. This overlooks the depression of the Bogside with its open spaces, sportsfields and gasworks, rising on the left to the newer housing estates of Creggan. The industrial complex of Maydown can be distinguished where the meandering river Foyle enters the lough. Note Magilligan Point (right) and Inishowen (left) which almost enclose the distant entrance to Lough Foyle.*

8. *Malin Head, County Donegal. The hedgeless striped fields pick out the raised beach succession between Ballyhillin village and the sea. The lowest raised beach (in the centre of the photograph) is of post-glacial age.*

9. *Errigal Mountain, County Donegal. This isolated 2466 feet cone of Dalradian quartzite forms a prominent landmark in north-west Donegal. Note the small peat cutting in the foreground.*

10. *The Cliffs of Slieve League, County Donegal. Here, at the Eagle's Nest, the almost vertical cliffs are carved from highly contorted Dalradian metasediments, mainly quartzites, and represent some of the highest sea cliffs in the British Isles.*

11. *Enniskillen, County Fermanagh. The town grew up at a crossing of the river Erne where an insular drumlin provided a site above the easily flooded marshlands of this region.*

12. *Carrickfergus Castle, County Antrim. This late-twelfth-century Anglo-Norman stronghold, built on a massive dyke of olivine dolerite, stands above the modern mudflats and the raised shorelines of the post-glacial marine transgression in Belfast Lough.*

13. *Strangford Lough, County Down. Partly submerged drumlins can be seen in the foreground; beyond them, in the centre of the lough, the low reefs, or 'pladdies', represent the remains of wave-eroded drumlins. The Ards Peninsula can be seen in the distance.*

14. *The Mountains of Mourne, County Down. Beyond the corrie-fretted granite peaks of Slieve Commedagh and Slieve Donard the coastal lowlands of the Kingdom of Mourne can be seen.*

15. *Carlingford Lough, County Louth. This narrow sea lough is cradled between the Carlingford Mountains of County Louth (right) and the Mountains of Mourne (left). Both mountain massifs are composed of igneous plutonic rocks although the low peninsula of the Kingdom of Mourne, beyond, is composed of Silurian and Carboniferous sedimentary rocks.*

16. *Georgian Dublin. The well-known ruby-coloured brick terraces of Dublin can be contrasted with the classical limestone façade and spire of St George's Church, Hardwicke Place.*

17. *Peat bogs in the Central Lowlands. Many of the raised bogs of the Irish Midlands have been extensively 'harvested' by mechanized cutting. The milled peat, cut from the large bogs in the foreground and middle distance, is utilized in Rhode power station, County Offaly, discernible in the distance.*

18. *An esker in County Meath. This sinuous ridge of sand and gravel near to Trim illustrates the way in which roads frequently follow the line of an esker. Note how the well-drained ridge, too steep for farming, is left under bracken, gorse and bramble.*

19. *Ben Bulbin, County Sligo. The cliffs are formed from the Dartry and Glencar limestones while the lower scree-covered slopes have been carved largely from the Ben Bulbin shales.*

20. *The Aran Isles, County Galway. The bare limestone pavements of Inisheer carry virtually no soil because of the soluble properties of the limestone and the scouring action of the Pleistocene ice sheets. Note the absence of trees in these windswept islands.*

21. *The Connemara coast, County Galway. This ice-scrubbed peninsula near Ballinaboy is composed of schists of the Connemara Dalradian Series. Note the small stony fields and how the settlement hugs the coastline.*

22. *Clifden and the Twelve Pins, Connemara. The town of Clifden is the best centre for exploring the quartzite peaks of the Twelve Pins, seen in the distance. A tract of Dalradian schists and crystalline limestones, with an intervening quartzite ridge, create the rolling foothills behind the town.*

23. *A thatched cottage, Achill Island, County Mayo. Note how the thatch is held in place by interwoven ropes, weighted by stones and pegged at the gable ends, in order to withstand the Atlantic gales.*

24. *A blanket bog in north Mayo. This view, near Ballycroy, shows part of the most extensive bog in Ireland. Lewisian gneiss is hidden beneath the peat but the quartzite peaks of the Nephin Beg range can be seen in the distance.*

25. *Shannon Airport, County Clare. This major international airport and its accompanying industrial estate contrast greatly with the rural scenery of the nearby Atlantic coastline (compare plates 21 and 27) and the neighbouring estuary of the Shannon.*

26. *A stone cottage in County Clare. Now used only as a cowshed, this former dwelling near Kilrush illustrates the use of Namurian flagstones for roofing purposes. Note the unusual half-hipped gable and the low chimneys built from the well-bedded flagstones of this region. (Compare plate 23).*

27. *The Cliffs of Moher, County Clare. These 600-foot sea cliffs are composed of flagstones, shales and sandstones of Upper Carboniferous (Namurian) age.*

28. *Mount Brandon, Dingle, County Kerry. The east face of this high mountain is gashed by a great chasm, now occupied by a series of paternoster lakes interconnected by waterfalls. The upper lakes are held on structural benches in the Dingle Beds but lower down this rocky staircase glacial overdeepening and morainic accumulations have assisted lake formation.*

29. *Killarney and its lakes. The valleys in these Old Red Sandstone mountains have been lowered by a glacier which moved north between the Eagle's Nest (left) and Torc Mountain (right) to reach the limestone plain at Killarney, seen in the far distance. The Upper Lake, with its ice-scrubbed shores and wooded islands, now occupies the overdeepened valley.*

30. *The Skellig Rocks, County Kerry. These remarkable, splintery sea stacks, lying some miles from the mainland (seen hazily beyond the Celtic cross), were carved from steeply dipping grits and flags of Old Red Sandstone age Note the characteristic corbelled roof and mortarless construction of the buildings (left) in the seventh-century monastic settlement of Skellig Michael and the Little Skellig stack beyond.*

31. *A landscape near Skibbereen, County Cork. This view, looking south-westwards along the axis of the eroded Clonakilty anticline towards Baltimore Harbour, Sherkin Island and Clear Island, gives an indication of the Armorican 'grain' of the rock structures in south Munster. The steeply dipping beds of Old Red Sandstone are picked out by the vegetation contrasts.*

32. *Kinsale and the Bandon river, County Cork. The drowned estuary of the Bandon river at Kinsale (right centre) is known as a ria. The rolling coastal plateau has been carved across strongly folded shales and grits (known as the Carboniferous Slates) whilst the distant mountains, on the borders of Kerry, are made of Old Red Sandstone.*

33. *The city of Cork. Located astride the braided channels of the river Lee, Cork is famous for its waterways and bridges, and also for the gleaming white Carboniferous Limestone of many of its buildings. Note the limestone spires of St Finbarr's Cathedral and the slate-hung façade of the nearby building (a common practice in southern Munster).*

34. *The Rock of Cashel, County Tipperary. This splendid group of grey limestone buildings, perched on a monoclinal fold of Carboniferous Limestone, is a famous landmark on the featureless plains of Tipperary.*

35. *The Leinster Coalfield, County Kilkenny. The conical spoil heap of this now defunct colliery, near Castlecomer, is an unusual feature in Ireland, where coal-mining has never been of great significance. Note the typically rural setting of the small Irish coalfields and the lack of industrial blight.*

36. *Shillelagh village, County Wicklow. This planned estate village, on the eastern flanks of the Leinster Chain, illustrates the use of local stone in the domestic architecture. Ordovician schists and Leinster Granite are combined in the walling but granite is used exclusively for corner stones, lintels and door jambs.*

37. *Gravel workings near Blessington, County Wicklow. Some of the worst spoliation of the Irish scene has resulted from gravel extraction in the extensive glacial drift deposits. Here, on the western flanks of the Wicklow Mountains, the end-moraine of the Midlandian ice sheet is being actively worked.*

38. *The Great Sugar Loaf, County Wicklow. This view, looking south across the prominent summit of Cambrian quartzite, shows the Vartry Plateau (right) and the coastal lowlands (left), carved largely from Cambrian sedimentary rocks. Note the glacial meltwater channel of Glencree in the foreground.*

winds has enabled the vegetation here to grow profusely. The most remarkable example is undoubtedly the Mediterranean Heath (*Erica mediterranea*), which at Mallaranny reaches its finest development in all Ireland. It is one of four heaths, found naturally in the Iberian peninsula of south-west Europe, which have spread to western Ireland, perhaps only in post-glacial times, without leaving any trace of their passage in southern Britain. Growing rampantly on the shores of Bellacragher Bay, this exotic heather reaches an incredible height of over six feet in the lee of the Corraun mountains.

Achill Island

To Dr Lloyd Praeger the charm of Achill lay in '. . . the broad undulations of the treeless, roadless moorland, the tall hills, the illimitable silver sea, the savage coastline, the booming waves, the singing wind, the smell of peat smoke and seaweed and wild thyme . . .' It is true that much of this romantic atmosphere remains, the type of atmosphere that makes many an urban dweller long for an escape to the Gaelic-speaking fringe of Atlantic Ireland. Nevertheless, Achill Island is changing, inevitably, as the Irish Tourist Board spreads its scenic fame throughout the world. The 'roadless moorland' now has miles of excellent tarmac to carry the sightseer around the 'Atlantic Drive' of the southern peninsula, or to the even more spectacular scenery of the western peninsula at Keem Bay. The 'savage coastline' has also been invaded by the ubiquitous caravan, whilst the villages have sprouted hotels, restaurants and gift shops. But the 'silver sea', 'the tall hills' and the climatic elements remain, so that off the beaten track Achill remains as hauntingly beautiful as ever.

The island is built almost entirely of highly folded and faulted Dalradian quartzites and schists, and the general rule that has pertained both in Donegal and in southern Connacht also applies here: that wherever quartzites appear the terrain is usually mountainous. Two magnificent peaks dominate the island, Slievemore (2,204 feet) in the north and Croaghaun (2,192 feet) in the west. The former, especially when viewed from Erris, has the majestic cone-shape of Croagh Patrick and Nephin, but whilst Croaghaun is more lumpy and squat it still creates a splendid western backdrop to the tiny white village of Dooagh which nestles at its feet. The westernmost extremity of Achill is formed from a steeply-dipping layer of schist, which creates an airy, knife-edged, pinnacle ridge, known as Achill Head, jutting far out into the Atlantic. Where geo-chemical activity has affected the mineral content of the rocks during metamorphism, small pockets of amethysts have been formed near the junction of the schists and the quartzites at Keem Bay. Here, where a limestone and a conglomerate mark the transition from the Achill Head schists to the Croaghaun–Slievemore quartzites, the lonely bay of Keem has been eroded into the steep coastal cliffs. Without doubt, the out-standing feature at the western end of the island is the north-west facing sea-cliff of Croaghaun, which plunges almost vertically from the summit cairn. This magnificent precipice, steeper than that of Slieve League in Donegal (p. 81) and higher than the cliffs of Clare Island or Mount Brandon (chapter fourteen), is regarded by some as the finest sea-cliff in western Europe. Unfortunately it can only be viewed from the sea or, with difficulty, from Achill Head. Despite its height, Slievemore has no major sea-cliffs, possibly due to its rather more sheltered position on the north coast, facing away from the direct attack of waves of maximum fetch. At the south-eastern corner of Keel Strand, however, the southern coast swings round once more to a north–south orientation, exposing a ridge of quartzite to the full force of Atlantic waves. Not surprisingly the sea has caused marked cliff recession here and has sculptured the hard quartzites into arches and stacks, so that the Menawn Cliffs and the Cathedral Rocks now form one of the best-known scenic attractions in Achill. The presence of the quartzite has also contributed indirectly to the superb beaches which characterize this part of the island, for weather-ing has broken down the rocks to form a fine straw-coloured sand.

Keel village, with its neatly whitewashed cottages, is the natural tourist centre of the island, and from here it is possible to visit the deserted village of Slievemore which straddles the foot of the mountain from which it takes its name. Looking so reminiscent of the well-known de-serted village street of St Kilda, off the Scottish coast, this old Achill village was abandoned in the nineteenth century, as the villagers moved down to the coast at Dooagh. Nevertheless, the old Slievemore cottages are noteworthy, insofar as they were used for the ancient custom of 'booleying' (see p. 110) as late as the 1930s. This almost certainly repre-sents the last occasion in the British Isles when the age-old tradition of transhumance was carried on. Two other cultural survivals in the Achill landscape are also worthy of note: the 'clachan' of ancient cottages in Old Dugort, and the hedgeless striped field pattern, related to the system of land-holding known as 'rundale', which can be seen at Ashleam on the Atlantic Drive. These three examples of settlement and land use were once widespread in Ireland but have survived longest in the hostile climate and terrain of the far west (plate 23).

When we turn to examine the glacial features of the Achill landscape a contrast is at once apparent between the western and eastern halves of the island. To the east of the Menawn–Bunacurry quartzite ridge the relief is generally lower and the terrain quite accidented, especially at Dooniver and the neighbouring island of Inishbiggle. Our experience of the steep drift slopes of the kame moraines, associated with the last glaciation in Ireland (the Midland General), immediately suggests to us that these hummocky glacial drifts in eastern Achill represent the western limits of this late ice-advance. West of the Menawn hills, however, a different landscape can be seen in the western promontory of the island. Its most striking features are the unbroken, smooth slopes of the mountains as they sweep down to the ocean fringe around Keel and Dooagh. The irregular kame topography of the last glaciation is missing and this has been taken as evidence to support the contention that western Achill lay outside the limits of the last glaciation, in common with the coasts of western Murrisk. By possessing such high elevations in such peripheral areas, Croaghaun and Slievemore appear to have survived as nunataks throughout all the advances of the inland ice-sheets. The significance of these mountain-top refuges in terms of surviving pre-glacial plant and animal life must not be overstressed, however, for they would have experienced a severe periglacial climate on the exposed summits. Furthermore, there are other glacial features on Croaghaun and Slievemore, which we have not yet examined but which are of considerable interest.

Most visitors to Achill Island will have noticed the large east-facing corrie, Acorrymore, which scars the slopes of Croaghaun, and will also have seen the corrie in a similar position on Slievemore, facing Old Dugort. But in order to view some of the most spectacular and intriguingly located corries in Connacht, one is forced to climb high over the northern shoulders of Croaghaun. Here, the intrepid rambler can view a collection of glacial phenomena unequalled in the British Isles. Lough Bunnafreeva West is perched behind its moraine on the very edge of the stupendous Croaghaun sea-cliff, and since cliff recession is slowly under-mining the moraine the lake level is gradually falling, as can be seen from the abandoned shoreline. Farther to the east, at lower elevations, three other corries occur, each with its jewel-like lake impounded behind the crescentic moraines. That of Lough Nakeeroge East is quite intriguing, for its moraine is being actively cliffed by the modern waves and it seems only a matter of time before the sea drains the corrie lake and breaks through into the corrie itself, the rock floor of which must lie below sea level. Dr A. Farrington has shown that, although inland ice-sheets never reached this far west during the Midland General glaciation, local glaciers existed in the Achill corries at that time (see figure 17).

North Mayo

The most desolate and least visited part of the Connacht Uplands occupies the north-western corner of Mayo, in the former barony of Erris, to the west of Ballina. Here, three broad scenic divisions can be distinguished and these correspond quite closely to the differences in the underlying geology (figure 29). Of these, only the first, that of the quartzite backbone of mountains, is true upland in the strictest sense, but the other two may be conveniently treated at this point, for they bear close affinities with the Connacht hill country. The second subdivision includes the coastal lands around Blacksod Bay and Broad Haven, together with the intriguing peninsula of the Mullet. These areas, regarded by many as the true Erris landscape, are underlain by the oldest rocks in Ireland, dating back to Lewisian and Moinian times. Finally, we can recognize the extensive plains of the Lough Conn–River Moy lowlands which lie to the east of the Nephin Beg quartzite range. Although these lowlands correspond almost exactly with the outcrop of the Lower Carboniferous sediments, they have not been described in chapter nine, owing to their geographical position and the fact that the eroded anticline of the Ox Mountains brings up older rocks to isolate the Ballina plains from the Central Lowlands of Ireland.

The outcrop of the Dalradian quartzites in Erris is roughly in the form of an inverted T with the horizontal axis running eastwards from Corraun Hill (1,715 feet) to the great conical peak of Nephin (2,646 feet), Con-nacht's second highest mountain (figure 29). The vertical component of the inverted T is the northward projecting ridge of massive quartzites which stretches from Nephin Beg (2,065 feet), through Slieve Car (2,369 feet) to Carraful Hill (890 feet) above Bangor. In the south-west, the Anaffrin (1,646 feet) and Glennamong (2,067 feet) quartzite ridge between Mallaranny and Nephin Beg falls steeply to the Ballycroy lowlands, where the Corraun tear-fault has brought the Lower Dalradian schists and lime-stones into contact with the tough quartzites of Upper Dalradian age which lie to the south of the fault. It has recently been claimed that the Corraun fault may be the south-western extension of the Leannan tear-fault of Donegal, itself regarded by some as the Irish equivalent of the Great Glen fault of Scotland. From whichever angle they are viewed these quartzite ridges dominate the whole of North Mayo, for their dark, heather-clad slopes, sharpened by a splendid suite of corries, rise to bare windswept tops. At the eastern end, as if standing sentinel over the approaches to Erris, is the inescapable pyramid of Nephin. Were it not for Croagh Patrick, some hundred feet lower, Nephin would stand supreme in Mayo as the shapeliest peak.

Like the highest peaks of Achill and Murrisk, the high summits of Nephin and the Nephin Beg range appear to have survived as nunataks throughout the ice age. Nevertheless, all the Erris lowlands bear traces of an older ice-sheet, so that the valleys between the quartzite peaks must have acted as avenues for ice-tongues on at least two occasions. During the Midland General glaciation, for example, the ice-sheet which occupied the Clew Bay lowlands pressed northwards through the cols at Achill Sound, Bellacragher Bay, Lough Feeagh and the Crumpaun River (west of Nephin). The westernmost ice tongue succeeded only in reaching eastern Achill and the mouth of the Owenduff river, north of Ballycroy, before its end moraine swung around the southern spurs of Slieve Alp, itself an outlier of the main quartzite ridge (figure 29). In the intervening hollow, near to Owenduff farm, glacial lake terraces skirt the hillsides at heights of between 400 and 500 feet, testifying to the former existence of an impounded pro-glacial lake at this site in the late Pleistocene. Judging by the freshness of the deeply-eroded gorge to the east of Slieve Alp, this must have been the channel through which the waters of the former lake found an exit to the ice-free lowlands farther north. To the east of the quartzite mountain ridge the Midland General ice-sheet failed to escape westwards from the Lough Conn–Moy river lowlands, thus leaving the entire north-western corner of Erris ice-free at this time (figure 17). The west-flowing Owenmore river, which breaks through the quartzite barrier at Bangor, now collects most of its headwaters from the Carboniferous basin to the east. Rather than regarding this as a superimposed stream, however, it appears more likely that its gorge, the Glenco Pass, now followed by the main Belmullet–Ballina road, was carved by meltwaters escaping from the eastern ice-sheet. Consequently, the eastward-draining streams on the dipslope of Carboniferous rocks now find it easier to double back westwards through the gorge than to cross the chaotic drift-choked terrain east of Bellacorick peat-fired power station. The alternative suggestion, of simple river-capture of the headwaters of the Deel and the Cloonaghmore drainage, seems a less likely explanation.

The Nephin Beg range rises from the largest blanket bog in Ireland, some 400 square miles in extent and equally divided between the areas to the east and west of the mountains. The most impressive tract is that to the north of Mallaranny, where the absence of settlement and the monotony of the treeless blanket bog inspired A.E. (George Russell) to write of the lonely road through the bogland leading to the lake at Carrowmore. And lonely it certainly is, possibly the least frequented region in all Ireland, for nowhere else is the featureless bog landscape so continuous and so trackless (plate 24). It hides a floor of highly contorted Pre-Cambrian rocks known as the Erris Complex, whose Lewisian gneisses and schists play virtually no part in the scenery. The nappes of the Erris Complex are generally equated with the so-called Iltay Nappe of the Grampians and north-west Ireland (see p. 59). The solid rocks are so obscured by peat that it was not until the 1960s that they were found to be amongst the oldest rocks i n the British Isles, equivalent in age to those which form the Outer Hebrides.

The coastlands around Blacksod Bay, especially those of the Mullet peninsula, are also reminiscent of the Outer Hebrides so far as their scenery is concerned. The curiously shaped peninsula of the Mullet, linked to the mainland by only a few yards of Dalradian schists, is a complex landform. Its northern sea-cliffs and hills are formed of quartzite and gneiss of Pre-Cambrian age, whilst the southern eminence of Termon Hill is formed from a late Caledonian granite. Between these two, the narrow-waisted peninsula consists of low rocky islands of schists and gneisses, linked together by remnants of glacial and periglacial drift and by tombolos of blown sand. The extremely high calcium carbonate content (over 80%) of the western beaches makes them comparable with the 'machair' of the Outer Hebrides; yet another interesting point of similarity.

The blown sand of the western coast covers about 15% of the total area of the Mullet and its margin has slowly migrated eastwards, except where judicious planting of bent grass (*arundo arenaria*) has stabilized the dunes. The only cultivated land is found in a narrow belt east of the dunes, sheltered from the battering winds and searing spray. Where the sand has blown on to the peaty clays behind the dunes, friable loamy soils support the tiny plots of potatoes and oats. But this narrow zone soon gives way eastwards to acid, ill-drained clays on the Blacksod Bay coast, generally unsuitable for cultivation and therefore given over to rough grazing and to the farm dwellings themselves. In response to the marked longitudinal zoning of the soil quality in the central part of the peninsula, the townland boundaries are arranged in narrow east–west bands in order to give an equitable share of the limited 'good land' to all. A great deal of the farming is at subsistence level and overgrazing on the 'machair' in the west is creating bare patches and problems of wind blow. Another problem now facing the occupants of the Mullet is that of fuel supply, for in the south the peat of Termon Hill (345 feet) has been entirely removed, leaving behind a stony wilderness of gleaming granite. The only remaining source of peat within the Mullet is on the northern hill land, an ironical situation for the people on the slopes of Termon Hill, who gaze eastwards across Blacksod Bay to the most prodigious peat bog in Ireland.

The wonderful range of sea-cliffs of north Mayo is virtually unknown to the tourist, and partly for this reason they are reputed to have been the home of the last breeding Golden Eagle in Ireland. Despite their inaccessibility, the north-facing cliffs, between Benwee Head and Downpatrick Head, are described by some writers as the most spectacular sea-cliff scenery in the whole of Ireland, even including Achill Island and the Cliffs of Moher (chapter thirteen). As we have come to expect, the highest cliffs occur where the well-jointed quartzites appear in the succession, and this is true between Broad Haven and Belderg where the grey, white and tan-coloured metasediments of Moinian age dominate the scenery. Benwee Head, with its natural arch, has one of the highest cliffs (over 800 feet), but it is also a magnificent viewpoint: southwards to the Mullet and Achill; eastwards to Sligo; northwards to Donegal, looking beyond the gigantic 300-foot sea-stacks known as the Stags of Broad Haven. The highest cliff occurs at Glinsk hill (1,002 feet), near Belderg, but undoubtedly the most remarkable feature here is the fearsome gash of Moista Sound. An igneous dyke has proved less resistant to wave attack than the surrounding quartzites, resulting in a narrow chasm, only a few yards wide, known as a geo. But, since the vertical flanking walls are 400 feet high and the gash 200 yards long, the spectacle of crashing storm waves in a confined space is awe-inspiring.

From Port Point eastwards, the Moinian quartzites are overlain unconformably by gently-dipping Carboniferous sandstones which form the coastal scenery all the way to Killala Bay. The most noteworthy feature is the prehistoric earthwork of Doonbristy at Downpatrick Head. Formerly a promontory fort, the Dun, perched on its vertical 150-foot cliffs of pale yellow sandstone, is now isolated from the headland by an 80-yard chasm, reputedly opened by a storm in 1393.

As we descend the road from Downpatrick Head to Killala, so we effectively leave the Connacht Uplands for the fertile meadows of the Moy lowlands. The Carboniferous basal sandstones are replaced by Carboniferous Limestones at Crossmolina, but they play little part in the scenery here for the drift cover is thick. The purple-brown bogs to the west of the town gradually give way to the bright green farmlands which lie between Lough Conn and Killala Bay. Here the drumlins and eskers provide better-drained soils, so that the region is among the best farming lands in Mayo. This increased prosperity is reflected in the thriving market town of Ballina, although the little town of Killala, with its crumbling warehouses and bishop's palace, beneath the round tower on the hill, was once the principal settlement on the bay which bears its name. At the back of the bay, almost closing the estuary of the Moy river, is the sinuous dune-covered ridge of Bartragh Island. It would appear that the wave-built ridge once grew steadily westwards from the Sligo shore, deflecting the tidal waters of the Moy westwards past the quays of Killala. It is claimed that in the fifteenth century the monks of Rosserk Abbey cut a channel across the eastern end of this lengthy sand spit, in order to trap the salmon on their course from east to west around the Irish coast before they reached the natural estuary of the Moy at Killala.

So the Moy now flows directly to the sea through the artificial cut and Killala has been left mouldering on its muddy backwater.

Lough Conn occupies a considerable area of the Ballina lowlands, formed, like its southerly neighbours of Corrib and Mask, at the junction of the old, hard rocks of the Connacht Uplands with the less resistant limestones of the plain. But, as if to demonstrate that lake formation is not simply a matter of differential rock resistance to denudation, the southern extension of Lough Conn breaks into the granite terrain of the Ox Mountains anticline (figure 29). Indeed, the adjacent Lough Cullin is enclosed entirely within the granite which has weathered down at this point to create sandy lakeside beaches. The granite at Pontoon has been so ice-scoured that it forms a bare, mammilated topography reminiscent of the Canadian Shield. To the south of Foxford, however, we are back into the seemingly endless plains of Central Ireland which stretch from here to the Shannon. These are the Plains of Mayo (Maigh Eo = the plain of the yew), far from the Connacht Uplands and devoid of their scenic charm, for here the land is featureless and uninteresting.

13. The Lands of the Lower Shannon

After the scenic glories of Galway and Mayo the lands of the Lower Shannon are something of an anticlimax, although their diversity of scenery is certainly more stimulating than the landscapes of the Central Lowlands. They are clearly very different from the landscapes of the Upper Shannon, whilst this is the only part of Ireland where the physically better-endowed lands of the south and east extend as far as the Atlantic coast. The unity which has been given to the estuarine country by the Shannon waterway has long been recognized, for this was the ancient Kingdom of Thomond and, since Limerick is the natural focus of the region, it became known to the twelfth-century Norman invaders as the Regnum Limricense.

The gentle folding of the Lower Shannon region has produced a series of east–west anticlines in the Palaeozoic rocks, where subsequent denudation has reduced the height of the upfolds by the gradual removal of the Carboniferous rocks. Thus the structural arches are now represented in many cases by isolated outcrops of older rocks, known as inliers, which protrude through the widespread Carboniferous cover. Where this cover was particularly thin, or where the denudation has been relatively fast, the Old Red Sandstone begins to appear. At first, this is only as narrow cigar-shaped outcrops, which mark the axes of the anticlines, as in the south of county Limerick (figure 30). Where denudation has proceeded further, however, a great deal of the underlying sandstone has itself been destroyed, along the crests of the upfolds, and in some places has been breached sufficiently to expose the older Silurian rocks at the core of the anticlines (figure 30). In east Clare, north-east Limerick and north Tipperary, the extensive areas of mountainland, on both banks of the Shannon, are composed largely of Silurian strata, but in all cases they are ringed by a hard rim of Old Red Sandstone which generally forms the

highest summits. In the synclines, where denudation has failed to penetrate completely through the Carboniferous strata, great thicknesses of
Carboniferous Limestone survive. These usually coincide with areas of
lowland, often choked with glacial drift, which stretch as broad corridors

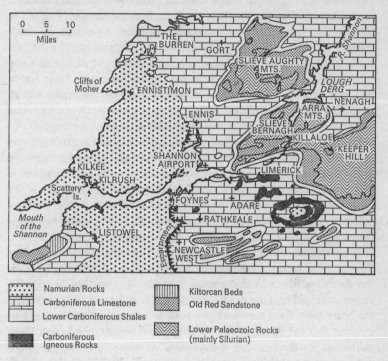

Fig. 30. *The geology of the Lower Shannon region (based on the Irish Geological
Survey).*

between the older, harder rocks of the mountain ridges. Finally, the
western tracts of Clare are built from Namurian shales and flagstones
which have weathered down to form a fairly acid and sterile soil which
supports only peat bog and barren rush-infested pastures.

Lough Derg and the Shannon

Where the Middle Shannon enters Lough Derg at Portumna, the scenery is little different from that of the Central Lowlands, for drift-covered Carboniferous Limestone is still dominant and the lake scene resembles that of Lough Ree. The scores of tiny islands in the northern half of the lake interject patches of dark green amongst the silver waters, for many of them carry thick groves of yew and juniper. Because of its calcareous rocks and its stony, damp shores, the northern fringes of Lough Derg exhibit some very rare plants, including the Willow-leaved Inula (*Inula Salicina*) which is widespread in continental Europe but totally absent elsewhere in the British Isles. As in most of the large Irish lakes, at least one of the islands contains remnants of early ecclesiastic settlement.

South of Scarriff Bay the scenery changes abruptly and any resemblance to Lough Ree rapidly disappears, for here the lake waters get narrower as the flanking hills close in from both east and west. The limestone is now replaced by shales and slates, so that the low, flat lake shores are superseded by steep wooded slopes rising to windswept heathery mountain tops. The acidity of the soils along the southern lake shores precludes the rich plant life which flourishes along the northern limestone fringes. It is interesting to recall that the eighteenth-century chronicler, Arthur Young, noted how the landowners at this southern extremity of Lough Derg dredged the rich shelly marl from the Shannon bed in order to improve the acidity of the slatey soils near Killaloe. A traveller approaching the latter town from the north, by road or lake, might be surprised to discover that the Shannon escapes from the mountain-girt Lough Derg at this point, through the narrow Killaloe gorge, ignoring the more obvious exit at Scarriff Bay, several miles to the north. The whole question of the evolution of this great river must now be examined in some detail in order to explain this apparent anomaly.

We have already seen, in an earlier chapter, how the Shannon, after leaving the Leitrim hills, flows lazily southwards across the great central plain of Ireland, with very little change of gradient. In its mid-course it has the apparent choice of turning west to Galway Bay or east towards Dublin, across the broad limestone lowlands. Instead, it meanders slowly on to Lough Derg where, inexplicably, it leaves the limestone and cuts deeply through the sandstone and slate hills at Killaloe before falling rapidly, more than one hundred feet, to sea level at Limerick. Having broken through this hard rock barrier it swings westwards into its fifty-mile-long estuary. Most writers have regarded the Shannon as a classic example of a superimposed river system, initiated many millions of years ago on a southward-tilted surface. The earliest geologists believed in a former cover of Upper Carboniferous rocks, which, they claimed, blanketed the whole of Ireland, except for the far north-west. Upon this layer of rocks a river system would have developed and as the Upper Carboniferous rocks were gradually destroyed, so the river system, which was responsible for their destruction, was etched into the underlying rocks, regardless of their structures. In the early part of the present century, J. R. Kilroe reconstructed a hypothetical summit-surface in central Ireland, at a height of almost 3,000 feet, in order to explain the anomalous course of the Shannon. A more recent writer, Dr A. Farrington, regards such a hypothesis as '... a remarkable essay in special pleading, (because) ... with over 2,000 feet of unknown strata to be eroded and fifty million years to do it in, the connection between the hypothetical post-Eocene surface and the present surface is so remote as to be meaningless.' In its place Dr Farrington proposes that the Lough Derg stretch of the Shannon should be looked at in terms of the present land surface and the local geological structures. Thus, he suggests that the Shannon originally flowed westwards through the limestone corridor at Scarriff Bay at a stage in Tertiary times when the Killaloe gap was not in existence. He believes that at the same time the narrow limestone wedge which divides the Arra Mountains from the Silvermine Mountains carried another west-flowing river (the forerunner of the present Killmastulla river) which then followed the Broadford gap through the Slieve Bernagh range (figure 31a). At this stage he regards the present Shannon estuary as being the outlet of the west-flowing Mulkear river which drained yet another limestone corridor to the east of Limerick in addition to the southern slopes of Slieve Felim (figure 31a). The stages of systematic river capture and lowering of cols in the slate and sandstone mountains, as suggested by Farrington, are traced in figure 31a–c, so that an alternative explanation to that of superimposed drainage can be presented.

The Killaloe gap, the most controversial landform in the foregoing discussion, is flanked by the Arra Mountains to the east and Slieve Bernagh to the west. The former, composed of highly folded Silurian

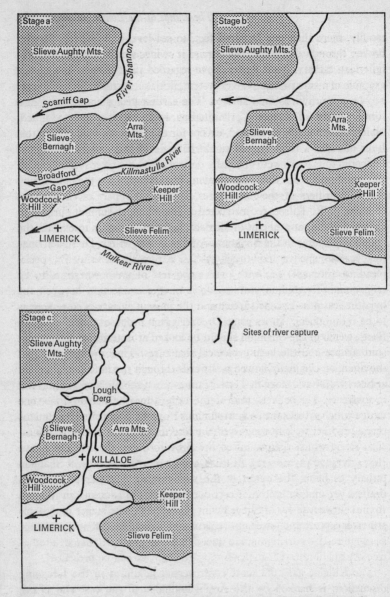

Fig. 31. *Stages in the evolution of the Lower Shannon (after A. Farrington).*
An alternative explanation to the hypothesis of superimposed drainage.

rocks, is most renowned for its slate quarries, which are still in production. Near Portroe a 400-foot band of grey slate has long been a source of some of Ireland's finest roofing material, much of which was formerly exported via the Shannon.

Slieve Bernagh (1,746 feet), although somewhat higher in elevation than the Arra Mountains, has a similar geological structure, for it is merely the western extension of the same eroded anticline. Here the intensely folded black shales have been sculptured into smooth dome-like summits clothed in dark heather, which contrast both in colour and in form with the geometric field patterns of the improved land which rises on all sides to the 1,000-foot contour.

In the Middle Ages both Slieve Bernagh and the neighbouring Slieve Aughty Mountains (1,312 feet) are known to have been heavily forested, forming part of the great Wood of Suidain. Only in the Cratloe Woods, at the south-western end of Slieve Bernagh, can remnants of this once famous forest still be seen. The forerunners of this beautiful oakwood are reputed to have been used in the construction of the hammer-beam roof in Westminster Hall, London and also in the Royal Palace, Amsterdam. The Cratloe Woods clothe the steep slopes of Woodcock Hill (1,010 feet), overlooking the city of Limerick, and between here and the Broadford Gap the more sharply pointed hills have been carved from a combination of Old Red Sandstone, Silurian conglomerates, and pink and white cherts of Ordovician age. The former slate quarries in the Slieve Bernagh Hills have now closed, whilst the former iron-working furnaces and forges of the region have also disappeared as the woodlands have been felled. The only mining activity carried on today in the vicinity of Lough Derg, apart from the Portroe slate quarries, is now confined to the limestone plain north of Slieve Aughty and west of Portumna. Here, at the village of Tynagh, the recent discovery of excellent deposits of lead, silver and zinc in the Carboniferous Limestone has led to a newly found prosperity for the region and an enormous opencast scar in the landscape.

The Limerick Lowlands

Soon after leaving the Killaloe weir the Shannon used to descend in a series of picturesque rapids before entering its tidal estuary at Limerick.

Today, however, the river is first impounded to form an artificial lake, above O'Briensbridge, and finally led ignominiously away through miles of concrete culverts to the great power station of Ardnacrusha. Thus the so-called Falls of Doonass, 300 yards wide and forty feet high, are but a shadow of their former splendour. Sufficient water is allowed to follow the natural river course to sustain the Shannon as a salmon river, but the voracious demands of the Ardnacrusha turbines have robbed the Lower Shannon of one of its most attractive spectacles, for a waterfall of this magnitude is unusual in the lower stretches of any major river. Since the Tarbert power station (producing 120 MW), lower down the estuary, is an oil-fired plant, Ardnacrusha (85 MW) is still the largest hydro-electric station on the Shannon. It is interesting to recall, furthermore, that for twenty years after its opening in 1929, Ardnacrusha supplied almost all of the country's power supply.

One mile below the junction of the Ardnacrusha tail-race with the natural waters of the Shannon, the city of Limerick stands at the tidal head of the estuary. Like Dublin, it was a Norse foundation, on an island at the last ford across the Shannon before the sea. Originally an Irish settlement, it was not long before the Norman settlers built their walled town on King John's Island, a drift-covered limestone platform surrounded by the Shannon and its backwater, the Abbey river. Present-day Limerick reflects the ensuing history in its urban fabric, for it is composed of three towns. The oldest is the English Town with its stone-built St Mary's cathedral and King John's Castle, the latter patched with bricks to fill the scars which date from the seventeenth-century sieges. English Town retains the narrow streets and irregular plan of a medieval town, although only fragments remain of the stone-built houses of the medieval merchants. To the south, across the Abbey river, Irish Town grew up, the two being walled and connected by a bridge in the fifteenth century. By Elizabethan times we read of '. . . Limerick's walls of marble blocks, and the stronger walls of the Irish Town, ten feet thick, and the houses for the most part of hewn blocks of black marble and built like castles' (D. Wolfe). No doubt the 'marble' referred to was the local description of the dark-coloured Upper Carboniferous Limestone which underlies the city. Most of the city walls were demolished in 1760 at about the time that the third phase of urban growth began – that of Newtown Pery. This geometrically planned expansion, westwards along the bank of the

Shannon, contains magnificent brick-faced terraces of classical Georgian design, comparable with many of the finest Dublin streets. It now forms the central business and shopping district, leaving the two older parts of the city untidy, deserted and decayed.

Stretching away south-eastwards from Limerick city is the eastern extension of the limestone Vale of Limerick, traversed by the road and rail links to Tipperary. This lowland corridor extends a narrow tract of first-rate farmland deep into the harsher physical environment which generally prevails along the western coast of Ireland. The rich farming landscape, with neatly trimmed hedges and mature hedgerow trees of sycamore and ash, gives an overall impression of efficiency and prosperity.

The bright green meadows of the vale are bounded to the north by the purple hills of Slieve Felim (1,524 feet) and Keeper Hill (2,279 feet). As in the case of the mountains around Lough Derg, these uplands are formed from eroded anticlines of Silurian and Old Red Sandstone rocks and likewise their highest summits occur not on the more friable Silurian shales and slates but on the tougher rim of Old Red Sandstone.

From a geological standpoint the most significant feature of the Limerick lowlands is '. . . the most compact and, for its size, one of the most varied and complete of all the Carboniferous volcanic districts of Britain [sic]' (A. Geikie). It occurs midway between the towns of Tipperary and Limerick, in the form of a synclinal basin structure, where rocks of two volcanic phases are interbedded with the Carboniferous sedimentary rocks which themselves form virtually a complete sequence from the Lower Limestone shales up to the Namurian shales and 'Millstone Grit' flags (figure 32). The volcanic activity, as in the Scottish Lowlands, appears to have been focused at a large number of small vents, leaving behind a wide variety of igneous rocks, including basalts, trachytes, tuffs, ashes and vent agglomerates. Among the Lower Volcanic Group the vent plugs of Derk Hill (782 feet) and Kilteely Hill (580 feet) are of striking appearance whilst the nearby Cromwell Hill (586 feet) is formed from a series of quartz–trachyte sills. The Upper Volcanic Group is best seen at Pallas Hill, to the west of Pallas Grean (New). The lavas now form the steep east-facing scarp of Knockseefin (743 feet), overlooking the prominent yellow-painted church of Nicker and the verdant pastures of the Mulkear river. The outcrop of the lavas and the sills in the synclinal structure is in the form of concentric ovals separated by layers of Carboniferous sedimentary rocks with gently inwardly inclined dip slopes (figure 32). Consequently the youngest Carboniferous rocks survive only in the centre of this basin-like structure, where the grey 'Millstone Grit' flags near Dromkeen have been extensively quarried in the past for the manufacture of paving slabs.

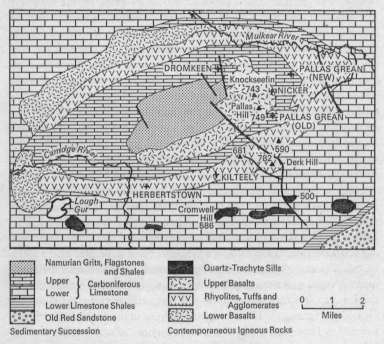

Fig. 32. *The Carboniferous volcanic rocks near Limerick.*

From the volcanic hills it is possible to look westwards across the remainder of the limestone Vale of Limerick, which is occupied, for the most part, by the drainage basins of the north-flowing Maigue and Deel rivers. But because of the drift cover one is conscious of the underlying geology in only a few instances: in the west where the impressive escarpment of Namurian shales and sandstones forms an abrupt termination to the lowlands (see below); and in the south where an intriguing group of sandstone ridges rises abruptly from the plain around Ballingarry. The latter represent three small denuded anticlinal crests which have exposed the Old Red Sandstone to form inliers within the Carboniferous Limestone succession (figure 30). Today they appear as darkly wooded 'islands' in the 'sea' of the fertile plain, their narrow east–west ridges broken only by the water gaps of the Deel and Maigue rivers which cross them at right angles. The way in which the drainage flows discordantly across the Armorican trend suggests that the rivers may have been superimposed on to the older rocks from a former cover of Upper Carboniferous rocks. The close proximity of the Namurian escarpment beyond Newcastle West lends support to such a hypothesis, for these Namurian rocks must have extended further eastwards at one time, judging by their outlier in the volcanic hills near Pallas (figure 30).

Lower downstream the Maigue river meanders through the attractive village of Adare (Ath dara = the ford of the oak) where the fine old oaks in the deer park and the quaintly thatched cottages are more in character with a Devonshire village than an Irish one. Some five miles farther down river an impressive ruin forms a prominent landmark for miles around. This is Carrigogunnel Castle, standing on its volcanic crag, overlooking the confluence of the Maigue with the Shannon estuary. The cliff face of the 100-foot eminence is built from layers of volcanic ash interbedded with columnar basalt, but the hill is also a good example of a 'crag-and-tail' formation. The southward orientation of the boulder clay tail, together with the alignment of the drumlins on both shores of the Shannon, demonstrates that the ice-sheets of the last glacial episode to affect these parts moved generally south-westwards across Clare to the Drumlin End-Moraine at Kilrush and Ballylongford (see p. 200).

South-West Clare

The landscape contrasts between the relatively fertile limestone vale of the east and the barren windswept shale and sandstone country of the west is a recurrent theme in any study of south-west Clare. In county Limerick, to the south of the Shannon, the junction of the Carboniferous Limestone with the overlying Namurian shales, flags and sandstones is marked by an impressive east-facing escarpment near Foynes. But as the junction is traced across the Shannon the scarp is less noticeable, although, to the south of Ennis, the western shore of the broad estuary of the Fergus river follows the line of weakness, where the Clare Shales mark the transition between the underlying limestone and the more sandy Namurian rocks further west.

The basin of the Fergus river is thickly blanketed with limestone till and carries the drumlin swarm of the Gort lowlands (p. 134) southwards past Ennis to the Shannon estuary. Wherever the drifts cover the porous limestone good farming land prevails, but occasional ridges of limestone, some 100–300 feet high, emerge above the drumlins and these are often given over to woodland. In 1776 Arthur Young described how the reclaimed 'sloblands', at the junction of the Fergus with the Shannon, yielded extraordinary crops when under tillage. But, were he able to view the coastal alluvial flats today, he would be astonished to see that they have yielded crops of concrete factories, roads and runways, for this is now the site of the great international airport of Shannon and its accompanying industrial estate (plate 25). But beyond the bustle of the airport Clare seems strangely empty, barren, windy and wild for, as the limestones disappear westwards beneath the Namurian scarp at Ennis, we pass into a different landscape as we travel into south-west Clare. Here, the Upper Carboniferous rocks occur in the form of a structural basin of Namurian sedimentary rocks which straddles the Shannon estuary. The lithology consists of some 1,500 to 3,000 feet of dark shales and siltstones with occasional sandstones, rarely more than 100 feet thick. The earliest geologists, having perceived thin seams of anthracite (two to eight inches thick) amidst the shales, classified the beds as Coal Measures, and such incorrect nomenclature persists even today on many geological maps. A later attempt to distinguish Yoredales and Millstone Grit within the succession is equally unsatisfactory and it is better to refer to the entire collection of rocks above the Carboniferous Limestone as Namurian.

The landscapes produced by the Namurian rocks are dreary and monotonous, with long undulating ridges rising from the plateaux to occasional flat-topped hills, the highest of which, Slievecallan, reaches only to a height of 1,274 feet. The acid soils, derived from the shaley till, are generally so waterlogged that they support extensive peat bogs between Ennis and the west coast, and at the best the pasturelands are wet and rushy. The stone walls, which were common on the limestones around Ennis, have now disappeared, replaced by hedgerows and occasional windswept trees. On the road to Kilrush some tillage appears, but only on the drumlins, for the remainder of the land use is permanent pasture or bog. As the thatched cottages and haycocks appear in the landscape one is obviously approaching Atlantic Ireland, and the increasing exposure ultimately banishes the trees from sight. Even the hawthorn hedges finally give up the unequal struggle against the elements, to be replaced first by gorse and then by flagstone walls. The Namurian flagstones are extensively used in the domestic architecture near the western coast, being liberally employed for roofing and walling the older cottages (plate 26), although the colour-washed houses of Kilrush have mainly slated roofs. West of Kilrush, as one crosses the end-moraine of the Midland General ice-sheet, trees, which were only occasionally seen as windbreaks around the houses, finally disappear, for there is no shelter from the salt spray on these featureless coastal plateaux.

The western peninsula of Loop Head, beyond Kilkee, is an entirely treeless landscape, where field boundaries are marked by earth banks in the absence of hedges and suitable flagstones, and where the thatched roofs of the cottages have to be securely roped to pegs set in the stone walls. But all is not desolation for, as in Pembrokeshire, the scenic glories are reserved until the very end of the excursion. The splendour of the landscape in south-west Clare is in its magnificent Atlantic coastline. Loop Head itself is a spectacular point from which to view the coastline of north Kerry, but nearer at hand the sheer-sided sea-stack, known as Dermot and Grania's Rock, attracts our gaze. The well-bedded shales and flagstones, whether they be folded or relatively undisturbed, lend themselves to sculpting by the ocean waves, and at the neighbouring Bridges of Ross the sea has created two remarkable arches through which the surf beats in on every Atlantic gale. Between Ross and Kilkee the cliffs get higher and more intricate in their design, with stacks, pinnacles, slabs and geos all well represented. A closer look at the bedding of some of the Namurian rocks exposed in these cliffs of western Clare will reveal that individual beds are strongly contorted or faulted without apparently interfering with some of the other beds which are devoid of such structures. The deformation, often in the form of recumbent folding and shearing, resembles miniature Alpine nappes, but is not due to orogenic forces but to a process known as slumping during deposition. It would appear that the sinking of the Namurian basin was faster than the infilling by sediments in mid-Carboniferous times, giving rise to unstable submarine slopes. Large volumes of sediment must therefore have collapsed downslope at intervals, ploughing up the surrounding sediments along the margins of the slump channels. Erosion by waves or currents would ultimately have planed-off the surface of the slump structure before normal deposition was renewed. Near to Goleen Bay another interesting group of phenomena, known as 'sand volcanoes', can be seen near to high-water mark. Up to 35 feet in diameter but only some 8 to 10 feet in height, these 'volcanoes' are nothing to do with igneous activity. They are thought to have been built by sediment-laden subaqueous water-spouts which arose as the slumped masses of material settled into position at the end of their slide.

From Donegal Point northwards the coastal cliffs get progressively lower in elevation and are replaced by a series of fine sandy bays and alternating rocky headlands all the way to Spanish Point. A well-ordered landscape of neat farm buildings and variously coloured cottages give an air of prosperity to this tract, which the seaweed-processing factory at Quilty and the turf-burning power station at Milltown Malbay do nothing to dispel. Beyond Spanish Point, however, the landscape begins to look more neglected as the plateau country of the interior, with its poorer soils, gets closer to the coast. One also passes back across the end-moraine of the last glaciation, so that it becomes common to see the rounded glacial boulders cleared from the fields and included within the stone walls. By the time Liscannor Bay is reached, however, the Doonagore flagstones have been used extensively not only in the field walling, but also in the roofing of many of the older buildings. They have been quarried on a large scale from the Doonagore quarry to the north of Liscannor, and so perfect is their bedding quality that they can be split into a great variety of thicknesses. In some cottages they have been used as door and window lintels and in others as massive roofing and flooring slabs. Outside, they have been used as forecourt paving and sometimes, set vertically on end, as stone fences.

It would be impossible to visit Lahinch or neighbouring Ennistimon without hearing stories of the nearby Cliffs of Moher, for these famous cliffs are to west Clare what the Giant's Causeway is to north Antrim. There is certainly no sense of disappointment with the Cliffs of Moher. Reaching heights of more than 600 feet and extending for five miles, these sea-cliffs come as a surprise to a tourist approaching from the landward side. A featureless plateau of rolling meadowland gives way abruptly to this awesome precipice. The sea-cliffs of Achill, Slieve League and Mount Brandon may be higher, but nowhere else in Ireland are the cliffs so vertical or so overhanging. From a base of shales, containing thin beds of sandstone and flagstone, the clearly stratified cliffs rise through hundreds of feet of flagstones to a thick yellow sandstone which forms a conspicuous ledge near the top of the cliff. Above this the uppermost 20–40 feet of the cliff is composed of the black Moher Shales (plate 27). Where they have weathered into a black muddy soil, these upper shales were mistakenly assigned to the Coal Measures by the earliest geologists. In all sorts of weather conditions, but especially in a westerly gale, the Cliffs of Moher are spectacular, easily justifying their reputation as one of the scenic highlights of Ireland.

The Mouth of the Shannon

The structural basin of Namurian rocks, which is responsible for so much of the uninspiring inland scenery of south-west Clare, extends southwards across the estuary into west Limerick and north Kerry. As in Clare the Namurian rocks are composed very largely of shales, flagstones and sandstones, which give to the low plateau country south of Foynes a barren aspect, with rushy pastures and bare heathery hills reminiscent of western Clare. In the valley of the tiny Oolagh river, to the north of Abbeyfeale, however, a small outcrop of true Coal Measures has brought a certain distinctiveness to the hamlet of Crataloe. The productive coal seams, which are generally buried by a thick layer of sandstone, are eight in number and occur in a complex east–west syncline on a ridge top. But since they occupy an area of less than two square miles and have only been sporadically worked, they have had an insignificant effect on the landscape and hardly justify the term Crataloe Coalfield.

The plateau country around this tiny coalfield declines in elevation westwards to the Carboniferous Limestone vale which extends southwestwards from Listowel to Ardfert, and the river Feale has cut a fairly deep gorge through the Namurian rocks on its journey westwards to the mouth of the Shannon. In the east, however, the Namurian flagstones and sandstones create a high east-facing escarpment, which rises to over 1,000 feet at Sugar Hill and Knockanimpaha overlooking Newcastle

West. Here, the main road to Tralee surmounts the scarp and at Barnagh Gap we can experience a most remarkable panoramic view over the Vale of Limerick. Immediately below us the escarpment drops steeply away as first the Foynes Shales (Lower Namurian) and then the Carboniferous Limestones replace the harder flagstones of the plateau. The lush grasslands of the Deel and Maigue river basins, neatly patterned with hedgerows and trees, are broken only by the darkly wooded Old Red Sandstone ridges near Ballingarry (p. 195). Away to the north the scarp retains its prominence past Ardagh and Shanagolden to the little port of Foynes on the Shannon estuary.

In a pre-war boat journey down the Shannon from Limerick to Foynes, the quality of the scenery so impressed the generally sardonic O'Faolain that he was moved to rhapsodize on the rural charm of this seemingly endless estuary. Today, however, the landscape has been invaded by industrial blight, created not only by the enormous cement factory utilizing the pure Carboniferous Limestone outcrop at Mangret, but also by the Shannon industrial estate on the north bank and by the oil tanks and harbour clutter at the rapidly expanding port of Foynes. Here, where the Namurian scarp overlooks the town and brings hard rock cliffs to the Shannon shore, deep water occurs at the narrowest section of the estuary. Accessibility to ocean shipping at all states of the tide has helped in the development of the port, which now handles the lead and zinc concentrates brought by rail some 45 miles from the Silvermine hills beyond Limerick.

The Shannon estuary between Foynes and Tarbert is narrow and deep where it cuts through the outcrop of the harder Namurian rocks, but by the time one reaches the vicinity of Scattery Island and Kilrush the waterway begins to widen and extensive sandbanks become exposed at low tide (figure 30). The amount of deposition which has taken place around the mouth of the Shannon would be normal in any major river, but in this case it may have been supplemented by the enormous amount of glacio-fluvial outwash left by the Pleistocene ice-sheets for subsequent waves and currents to fashion as they chose. For the opposing islands of Scattery and Carrig mark the end-moraine of the Drumlin Readvance stage of the last glaciation, thus leaving the promontories of Loop Head and of North Kerry unglaciated during the Midland General glaciation (figure 17).

14. The Southern Highlands – Kerry

In Kerry one can always sense the presence of the sea, partly because of its peninsular form and partly from the fact that its mountainous character provides the visitor with many vantage points from which to view its remarkable coastline. Kerry possesses some of Ireland's finest scenery, for here that impressive combination, high mountains mirrored in lakes, estuaries and bays of the sea, reaches its Irish zenith.

The mountainous nature of southern Ireland is indirectly a result of the Armorican folding which brought the formerly subjacent Old Red Sandstone alongside the less durable Carboniferous rocks in a series of tight east–west folds. A late period of Tertiary uplift in the south-west, together with a general eastward tilt, has meant that Kerry now possesses the highest land of all Ireland. Denudation by rivers and ice has lowered the Carboniferous Limestones and shales to levels well below the sandstone ridges, which now rise strikingly above the lowlands as bold mountain fronts. The relationship between geology and scenery is at its most simple in these southern highlands, for the Old Red Sandstone survives in the anticlines, which trend generally east–west in east Kerry and the Dingle peninsula but which, in the Iveragh peninsula and in west Cork, swing round into a north-east to south-west orientation. The intervening synclines contain the less resistant Carboniferous strata, which originally completely enveloped the Old Red Sandstone but which have subsequently been worn away from the upfolds, surviving only in some of the vales and valleys of the region. But the pattern of the folding which controls the major features of the relief and drainage is not quite as simple as we might have been led to suppose and the often-used analogy of the sheet of corrugated iron is not quite correct. Whilst it is true that the major upfolds correspond with all the main peninsulas and ranges, the individual mountains and valleys owe their form to more detailed structural characteristics (figure 33). Quite clearly the promontories of west Kerry and Cork mark the main anticlines whilst the bays represent the synclines. As we have already noted, however, Kerry has been uplifted to a greater extent than the areas farther east, with the result that the axes of the folds rise towards the west. Consequently, the synclinal valleys of east Cork and Waterford become attenuated as they are traced westwards, whilst the relatively narrow sandstone upfolds of the east gradually broaden and rise to the high mountain ranges of Kerry. Again, this general statement needs some qualification, for in detail the axes of the folds both rise and fall as they are traced across this Armorican tract, so that in places we can pick out elongated domes, known as periclines (similar to those of Ballingarry, p. 195), or boat-shaped synclines (which are better seen in county Cork), with folds pitching both eastwards and westwards.

Tralee and the Dingle Peninsula

From any vantage point at the eastern end of the Slieve Mish Mountains, which form the eastern end of the Dingle peninsula, the relationship between the geology and the topography is of text-book clarity. In the east the dark, rolling plateaux of Namurian shales and sandstones create a semi-circular line of 1,000-foot hills whose western slopes form a long curving escarpment overlooking Tralee in the north, Castleisland in the east, and Castlemaine in the south. Each of these towns sits squarely in the horseshoe-shaped lowland which marks the outcrop of the Carboniferous Limestone, the former astride the tiny River Lee and the latter two on the larger River Maine. As the limestone is traced seawards it passes below sea level to form the respective inlets of Tralee Bay in the north and Dingle Bay in the south. This curving lowland, its northern arm famed as the Vale of Tralee, demonstrates how erosion has lowered the less resistant limestones to a greater extent than the adjacent Namurian rocks and the Old Red Sandstone (figure 33). The latter crops out in the centre of a denuded anticlinal structure, where it builds the impressive range of the Slieve Mish Mountains (2,796 feet). Where their massive purple sandstones dip outwards to north, east and south, to pass beneath the Carboniferous rocks, they are ringed by a narrow outcrop of the yellowish Kiltorcan Beds, the youngest sandstones of the Old Red

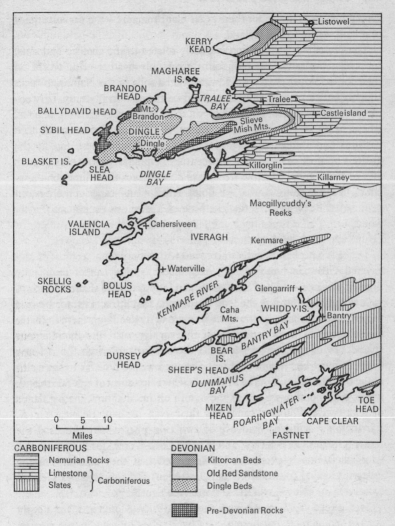

Fig. 33. *The peninsulas and rias of south-west Ireland (based on the Irish Geological Survey).*

succession, and famous for their fossil plant remains – the earliest legacy of a land vegetation in Ireland.

The present-day vegetation is closely related to the geology and soils, for whilst the sandstone mountains are totally heather-clad, except on their lowest slopes, so the acid, waterlogged soils of the Namurian rocks support only a poor, soggy pastureland on the eastern plateaux. Between the two, however, lies one of Kerry's most prosperous farming regions, where herds of the well-known Kerry black cattle thrive on the rich pastures and water-meadows of the limestone vale. Here too lie the greatest number of the nineteenth-century demesnes, so that small blocks of woodland and hedgerow trees have survived on these limestone lowlands, in direct contrast with the almost treeless landscapes of the western peninsulas. Records show that the Vale of Tralee was even more thickly wooded in Tudor times, with the famous oak, hazel and birch woods of Glanekinty choking the limestone valley as far north as Listowel.

Tralee is a neat and prosperous town, with some stately terraces of ivy-covered Georgian houses and a magnificent county hall of beautifully dressed blocks of Old Red Sandstone, carefully graded in shades of brown, yellow and red. But it is the land to the west that attracts us, for beyond the estuarine flatlands of the inner recesses of Tralee Bay, where Barnacle Geese graze in large numbers on the springy turf, the mountainous splendours of the Dingle peninsula thrust westwards into the Atlantic swell. It must be remembered that although we are now far to the south of the maximum limits of the Midland General ice-sheet of central Ireland, whose end-moraine we saw at the mouth of the Shannon, the highlands of south-west Munster generated their own ice-cap. Because Dr A. Farrington recognized evidence of two cold phases here, he used the terms 'Greater Cork–Kerry' and 'Lesser Cork–Kerry' for the earlier and later glaciations respectively. He suggested that they equate with the Eastern General (now known as Munsterian) and the Midland General (Midlandian) glaciations farther north (see figure 17).

The Slieve Mish range and the Stradbally Mountains are deeply scarred along their northern slopes by a series of magnificent corries, many of them containing moraine-impounded lakes. Both groups of mountains are composed of Old Red Sandstone which helps to build some of the summit tors and adds to the great spreads of clitters which mantle the upper slopes. The presence of this periglacial material has led some writers to suggest that, apart from its unquestionable corrie glaciation, the backbone of the Dingle peninsula was at no time overridden by external ice-sheets (figure 17). Lying, as it does, between the main ice centres of central Ireland and the Cork–Kerry Highlands, the Dingle peninsula contains summits high enough to have stood above the coalescing ice-sheets. But there is no mistaking the legacy left by the corrie and valley glaciers in these mountains, for large moraines sit astride most of the upland hollows.

The northern flanks of the Dingle Peninsula are also famous for their sandy beaches including the largest beach formation in Kerry. This is the remarkable tombolo of Castlegregory where a four-mile length of sand dunes has linked some of the limestone Magharee Islands (The Seven Hogs) with the mainland. In so doing a shallow lagoon, Lough Gill, has been impounded behind the landward end of the tombolo.

The Castlegregory peninsula is a splendid point from which to view the massive bulk of Brandon Mountain, at 3,127 feet the second highest mountain in Ireland. Built almost entirely of purple and brown Dingle Beds (the oldest Devonian rocks in Ireland), with great thicknesses of sandstones and conglomerates helping to create the towering precipices of its eastern flank, Brandon Mountain extends some six miles in a north–south direction. Its northern slopes fall steeply to the sea at Brandon Head, with the remarkable Sauce Creek and Beenaman cliffs vying with those of Achill Island and Slieve League as the highest sea-cliffs in Ireland. Between the summit of Brandon Mountain and that of its more dramatically shaped neighbour, Brandon Peak (2,764 feet), the mountain wall is split by a deep gash which runs obliquely across its face. An intriguing series of lakes occupies the glacial 'stairway' within the deep cleft, known as paternoster lakes from their likeness to a string of rosary beads (plate 28). Above Lough Cruttia the beetling crags overlook this ascending succession of ice-scoured rock basins, now water-filled and separated by bare rock-steps over which waterfalls cascade. The glacially grooved and polished rock slabs, bright pink because of their total lack of vegetation, appear so freshly glaciated that it seems as if the glacier had disappeared only yesterday. It needs little stretch of the imagination to visualize a steep, heavily-crevassed ice-fall in such a location, a phenomenon which must once have existed here some 12,000 years ago.

On the other side of the flat-floored, peat-filled valley of the Owenmore river, the road from Cloghane to Dingle town winds steeply up the slopes of Slievanea (2,026 feet) to the famous Conair Pass (1,354 feet) which carries one of the highest motorable roads in Ireland. Such a feat of engineering gives the less energetic tourist a unique opportunity to drive into a glacial corrie. The road climbs above the perfectly crescentic corrie moraine, with its impounded glacial lake a classic example of its type. A few minutes' scramble up the ice-smoothed rocks near the water-fall leads one back to an even more impressive lake, Lough Doon, embowered in a glacially-scooped rock-basin and encircled by a tremen-dous amphitheatre of purple cliffs. It has been stated that it was in this corrie that the first evidence of glaciation in Ireland was recognized and, to judge by its text-book appearance, this leaves no cause for surprise. The northward view from the Conair Pass is almost certainly one of the greatest in Ireland: the foreground corries, the moraine-littered slopes, the bleak, lake-studded valley floor, the frowning, cloud-capped cliffs of Mount Brandon and beyond them all the yellow dunes and glittering sea of Brandon Bay, with Kerry Head punctuating the hazy horizon. To the south, however, the landscape, though interesting, is not so impressive, for the green slopes leading down to the town of Dingle, on its natural harbour, lack the ice-plucked cliffs and glacial lakes of the north-facing slopes.

To the west of the little fishing port of Dingle coastal erosion has carved the western end of the peninsula into a fascinating succession of bays, headlands and islands. In addition to the Dingle Beds and the Old Red Sandstone an inlier of Silurian flags and slates helps to contribute to the coastal scenery between Dunquin and Smerwick Harbour. At Clogher Head the volcanic rocks, which are interbedded with the Silurian sedi-mentary rocks, are thought to be equivalent in age to those of Tortworth and the Mendips of southern England. To many people the real fascina-tion of the Dingle peninsula lies in the westernmost headlands and islands beyond Ventry, geographically isolated from the remainder of the region by the hump of Eagle Mountain (1,696 feet) with its solitary corrie.

To appreciate the area most fully one must approach it on the 'corniche' road around Slea Head, where J. M. Synge spoke of the 'severe glory' of the landscape and Professor R. A. S. Macalister listed the largest col-lection of prehistoric dwellings to be found anywhere in Ireland. Among the promontory forts, standing stones, souterrains and carved crosses, the beehive-shaped dwellings, known as clochauns, are the most interesting survivals, many of them still in use today as pigsties and outhouses. Almost forgotten skills in drystone building-construction reached their highest development in these treeless western peninsulas and islands of Kerry, where timber was in such short supply (plate 30). The tiny bee-hive chapel, known as the Oratory of Gallarus, built from local sandstone near to Smerwick Harbour, is possibly the finest example of this type of mortarless construction in western Europe.

So much has been written about the Blasket Isles, both by the islanders themselves and by numerous visitors, that it is unnecessary to do more than summarize their major characteristics. High ridges of purple sand-stone, similar to those of the mainland, have been isolated from the rest of the Dingle peninsula by marine encroachment. Atlantic waves have steadily whittled away at the rocks until they have produced the remark-able pinnacles, sea-stacks and precipitous cliffs which we see today, culminating in the distant Tearaght (602 feet) which rises like a cathedral tower above the ocean. Only the largest island, the Great Blasket (961 feet), retains its narrow ridge-like form, and only here was there sufficient grazing land to support a permanent population.

To the north of Dunquin the long sweeping hillslopes, patterned with stone walls, are suddenly broken by the grey castellated eminence of Minnaunmore Rock which interjects its serrated skyline near to Clogher Head. There seems little doubt that this ridge of Silurian schists represents a good example of a tor, occurring in a landscape which bears much evi-dence of periglacial solifluxion but little sign of former glacial activity. Many authorities believe that the amphitheatre of Dunquin, and possibly the Blaskets too, many of which carry tor-like landforms, were never over-ridden by ice at any time during the Quaternary.

Beyond the rocky promontory of Clogher Head, where the volcanics have withstood marine erosion to a greater degree than the surrounding rocks, the lowland around Ballyferriter has been carved from the less resistant Silurian flagstones and slates. To the south and east the moun-tains are made up of Dingle Beds, to the north the coastal hills of Bally-david Head and Sybil Head represent a linear outcrop of Old Red Sandstone (figure 33). The effects of marine encroachment are clearly demonstrated in this area, for where the sea has managed to break through the steeply dipping Old Red Sandstone ridge at the magnificent Three

Sisters cliffs it has quickly destroyed the Silurian rocks beyond, to create the beautiful sweep of Smerwick Harbour in the lowland vale. It needs very little stretch of the imagination to see that continued marine encroachment will ultimately inundate the vale, so isolating Sybil Head and Ballydavid Head into islands, in much the same way as the Blaskets were formerly created.

Killarney and its Mountains

The fame of Killarney depends on the unique qualities of its mountain and lake scenery, qualities which were so admirably assessed by Arthur Young as long ago as 1776: 'Upon the whole, Killarney, among the lakes that I have seen, can scarcely be said to have a rival. The extent of water in Loch Erne is much greater; the islands more numerous, and some scenes near Castle Caldwell of perhaps as great magnificence. The rocks at Keswick are more sublime, and other lakes may have circumstances in which they are superior; but when we consider the prodigious woods of Killarney; the immensity of the mountains; the uncommon beauty of the promontory of Mucross, and the isle of Innisfallen; the character of the islands; the singular circumstances of the arbutus, and the uncommon echoes, it will appear, upon the whole, to be in reality superior to all comparison.' All that remains is a need to explain the splendours of the landscape in terms of geology and landforms.

The most important factor appears to be the juxtaposition of the tougher Old Red Sandstone rocks with those of the more easily eroded Carboniferous Limestone along the line of the so-called Armorican Front. Wherever this geological situation exists in southern Ireland the contrasting resistance to denudation has produced a marked discrepancy in the ultimate levels of the sandstones and the limestones, as we have already noted. Nowhere is this more clearly seen than at Killarney where the mountains tower majestically above the limestone plain, but here two other important factors have also played a part. First, a considerable area of the mountainland near Lough Guitane is occupied by hard rhyolitic lavas and ashes of Old Red Sandstone age, which have helped to bolster the resistance of the sandstone country to denudation. Secondly, not far to the south-west of Lough Leane lay the centre of the Cork–Kerry ice-caps from which powerful glaciers must have moved northwards on two occasions (figure 35). Sufficient to say that they played no small role in the lowering of the limestone terrain between Torc Mountain and Killarney town, a zone now occupied by the lower lakes. It would be important to remember that, although Carboniferous Limestone was not involved, the scenic qualities of Derwentwater in the English Lake District owe much to the background of rugged scenery carved from the Borrowdale volcanic rocks, and also to the excavating prowess of the former glaciers. In place of the shapely outlines of Skiddaw, however, Killarney has the magnificence of Macgillycuddy's Reeks.

The Old Red Sandstone which forms the Reeks consists of layer upon layer of grits and slates, the lower formations being predominantly green in colour whilst the upper ones show every shade of red and purple. Similarly, the texture changes upwards, passing from coarsely-grained basal sandstones to thick bands of slate, often markedly purple in colour like those which give their character to the summit of Purple Mountain (2,739 feet). The slates have been produced by the effects of Armorican pressures on the argillaceous members of the Old Red Sandstone. But the main mass of the Reeks, including the highest summit in Ireland, Carrauntoohill (3,414 feet), is formed from the upper purple grits which strike generally from west to east. Although the general structure from which the mountains were carved is an anticlinorium, there is no wide zone of northerly dipping rocks along the northern slopes of the Reeks. In fact the main ridge of these high peaks is characterized by southerly dips, which led the Irish Geological Survey to infer the presence of an enormous thrust fault along the northern footslope bringing the lower beds of the Old Red Sandstone into contact with the Carboniferous Limestone of the plain (figure 34). This is now known as the Armorican Front, which can be traced eastwards through Mallow to the Irish Sea at Dungarvan and picked up again in Pembrokeshire where it forms the southern boundary of the coalfield.

In a sense the Reeks have been carved from a gigantic fault-line scarp although there is nothing of the simple scarp structure to be seen today. Glacial erosion has so fretted both the northern and southern slopes that it is difficult to piece together the geological structure. Above the cliffs and corries, however, the rugged ice-plucked topography changes rapidly into a turf-covered undulating summit ridge with no less than six peaks over-topping the 3,000-foot contour. The smoothness of its form, like that of neighbouring Mangerton and Purple Mountain, is thought to represent not the scouring effect of a glacial ice-sheet but the unconsumed relics of a pre-glacial upland surface which must have stood as a nunatak throughout the Ice Age. Nevertheless, there is little doubt that the numerous corries, with their basin lakes, bear the imprint of local mountain glaciers. One has only to follow the tourist path to the so-called Devil's Ladder, beneath the summit of Carrauntoohill, and to view the twin lake-filled hollows at the head of the Hag's Glen, to realize that this is the work

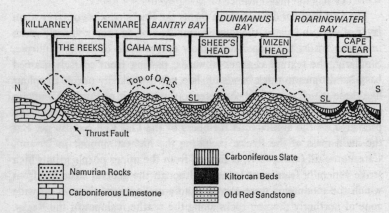

Fig. 34. *Geological section of the ria coastline of Kerry and Cork (based on the Irish Geological Survey).*

of glacial erosion. The same valley of the Gaddagh River includes the 'hanging' corrie of Lough Gouragh and the truncated spurs known as the Hag's Teeth, as if to demonstrate that Ireland's highest mountain is not lacking in the text-book examples of mountain glaciation. The enormous amphitheatre of purple cliffs which surrounds the hour-glass shapes of Loughs Coomloughra and Eagher, just to the west of Carrauntoohill, is an alternative route to the summit and in many ways is more wild and lonely.

The eastern end of the main ridge of the Reeks is abruptly terminated by the awesome valley known as the Gap of Dunloe. This great U-shaped gash, some 1,500 feet in depth, separating the Reeks from Purple Mountain, is famous to thousands of tourists who have traversed it on horseback en route from Kate Kearney's Cottage to the Head of the Gap. Few of them have stopped to consider that this deep glacial breach across the high watershed was the work not of the local mountain glaciers, for no corries feed directly into it, but of the major regional ice-sheet centred over Kenmare (figure 35). The ice would first have filled the pre-glacial

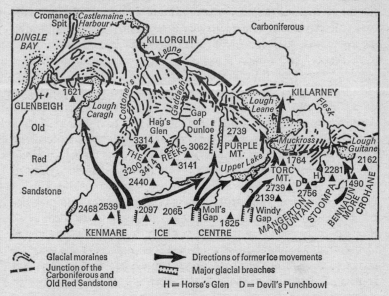

Fig. 35. *Killarney, showing the lakes, mountains and the major glacial features (after W. B. Wright and the Irish Geological Survey).*

valleys, most of which trend east–west following the strike of the region, but as it thickened the ice-sheet was forced to move outwards in all directions, lowering the pre-existing cols on the divides to considerable depths, in order to reach the northern plains around Killarney. We have already seen examples of what is known as 'glacial diffluence', or watershed breaching, in Donegal (chapter five), and the Gap of Dunloe is another striking reminder of the erosive powers of an ice-sheet. Moll's Gap and Windy Gap, respectively the routes of the modern and the old roads to Kenmare, form two other, less spectacular, examples of glacial breaches across major watersheds.

Before turning to the scenery of the famous lowland lakes of Killarney, it would be more convenient to complete our examination of the Killarney mountains by looking at the high domes of Mangerton (2,756 feet) and Stoompa (2,281 feet). The summit of Mangerton is a featureless, boggy plateau which curves eastwards around the precipitous lip of the Horse's Glen to the narrower summit ridge of Stoompa. Both the Horse's Glen and the perfect rock basin known as the Devil's Punch Bowl are glacially eroded features; the former carrying a series of paternoster lakes on successive rock steps in a deeply excavated valley; the latter a classic corrie lake at a height of 2,208 feet (figure 35). Its deeply incised, almost circular form, close to the summit of Mangerton Mountain, led many early travellers, including Arthur Young, to regard the Devil's Punch Bowl as the crater of 'an exhausted volcano'. It is easy to understand how the discovery of volcanic rocks within the Old Red Sandstone succession hereabouts led to such misinterpretation of the landforms, especially at a time when the effects of the Ice Age, with all its ramifications, had not been recognized in the British Isles. A similar confusion long remained over the equally crater-like corries of Llyn-y-gader and Llyn Cau on Wales's Cader Idris, while Arthur Young believed that the sandstone glacial erratics in the Killarney limestone country were tossed there by an eruption. Sufficient to say that, like Cader Idris, the mountains around Mangerton, including the sharply peaked Bennaunmore (1,490 feet), are craggy on account of their hard volcanic rocks, but their present form bears no real relation to that of the former volcano from which such materials were originally derived.

The summit of Mangerton is probably the best vantage point from which to view Killarney and its lakes, although most travellers will content themselves by alighting from their vehicles at the so-called Ladies' View on the Kenmare road (plate 29). But from any of these viewpoints one begins to understand the reasons for the remarkable quality of the Killarney scenery. It is the '. . . contrast between the low limestone lake trough with its green grass, red tillage, and filmy ferns, and the wild, heathery, purple hills, cliffs and jags, with their deep woods clambering to the sky' (Sean O'Faolain). In fact only Lough Leane and part of Muckross Lake occupy limestone country, while the Upper Lake and the so-called Long Range are nothing more than the flooded floor of a narrow, curving, glacially deepened trough, which breaches the main sandstone watershed between the Eagle's Nest and Torc Mountain (1,764 feet). Like the smaller Lough Guitane further east, the main lake of Killarney, Lough Leane, is partly dammed by large crescentic terminal moraines which skirt its northern shores (figure 35). But there is little doubt that the lake basin itself was excavated partly by solution and general lowering of the limestone floor by pre-glacial denudation, and partly by ice erosion at the junction of the Old Red Sandstone and the Carboniferous Limestone. Thus, whilst the Killarney shores and the north-eastern fringes of Muckross Lake are limestone fringed, the high sandstone peaks of Torc Mountain, Shehy Mountain (1,827 feet) and Tomies Mountain (2,415 feet) send steep, wooded spurs down to the southern and western lake shores (plate 29).

Along the limestone tracts of the shoreline impressive rock formations are found where the river Flesk enters Lough Leane to the east of Ross Island. Here, the limestone knolls, such as the Elephant Rock, which rise above the delta and the lake itself have been honeycombed by the lake waters into a series of remarkably shaped caves and pillars. The Colleen Bawn Caves of Muckross Lake are equally spectacular products of limestone solution. It has been suggested that the sculpting of the limestone into cavities along the modern lake shores is a result of wave action since there is no evidence of excavation beneath water level. It seems more likely that chemical solution of the limestone is greatest at this local watertable and that the waves may have helped indirectly by removing some of the weathered material. By no stretch of the imagination could waves have fashioned the extensive Colleen Bawn Caves; they may, instead, be a product of the period when glacial meltwaters coursed freely through this valley during the waning of the ice-sheets.

It would be impossible to leave Killarney without saying something of its remarkable vegetation, amply illustrated by the many-islanded Upper Lake which nestles amidst the luxuriant tangle of hillside woods. The woods around the Upper Lake appear to be quite natural, with the moss-draped oak trees ranging from 150 to 200 years in age. This wilderness of woodlands is a botanist's paradise for there are so few completely native oakwoods left in the British Isles. The 'strawberry tree' (*Arbutus unedo*) is another good reason why the Killarney woods are unique, for this Mediterranean tree reaches its finest development here, sometimes attaining heights of 30 feet, considerably greater than in its homeland.

The explanation seems to lie in the fact that its growth in south-west Ireland is unchecked by the dry Mediterranean summer!

The Iveragh Peninsula

South-west of the Killarney lakes and mountains the highland ridges extend seawards for some 30 miles to form a series of spectacular promontories and islands, known collectively as the Iveragh peninsula. Even if we exclude the Killarney mountains, more than 20 summits overtop the 2,000-foot contour, making this the most mountainous part of Ireland. When we add the eight 2,000-foot peaks of the more southerly Caha peninsula, which is mainly in County Cork, it is easy to see why the intervening Kenmare valley became the centre of the Cork–Kerry icesheets. So local was the last glaciation, however, that the western end of Iveragh remained ice-free in the Lesser Cork–Kerry (Midlandian) glaciation.

The geology of the Iveragh peninsula is relatively simple for its main structure is that of an anticlinorium of Old Red Sandstone grits and slates. It is bounded on the south by a narrow synclinal basin of Carboniferous rocks which have been worn down to form the Kenmare valley (figure 34). Only the eastern portion of this structure, between Kenmare town and Kilgarvan, remains above the sea, for the so-called Kenmare River, like Dingle Bay, Bantry Bay and Dunmanus Bay, is a classic example of a ria, or drowned valley, so characteristic of the coasts of the North Atlantic. Its floor descends gradually with a consistent seaward slope, unlike the glacially overdeepened fjords we have seen farther north which have a slope reversal and a submarine sill or threshold near their entrance.

To describe the scenery of the Iveragh peninsula we must follow for the most part the main T66 road which circles the peninsula from Killorglin to Kenmare, a route known to countless tourists as the Ring of Kerry. The limestone lowlands of Killarney, drained by the River Laune, descend westwards to pass beneath the waters of Dingle Bay near to Killorglin. Here the estuary of the Laune opens into an extensive landlocked bay, known as Castlemaine Harbour, which at low tide becomes a maze of sandbanks, mud flats and salt marshes. Its seaward margin is sheltered from the open Atlantic by the coastal foreland of Cromane, beyond which lie the magnificent dunes of Inch Spit. Cromane foreland owes little to marine action, for it is not a true shingle spit but a morainic mound tied to the mainland by a bog and a tombolo. We do not have to look far for the source of the morainic material, as a few miles to the south the mountain wall to the west of the Reeks is cleft by the deep glacial valley of Lough Caragh.

The detailed distribution of the end-moraines, relating to the ice-tongues which emerged on to the Killarney–Killorglin lowlands, have been recorded by W. B. Wright, whose early work on the glacial geology of Ireland remains second to none. He was able to demonstrate that the piedmont lobe of the Killarney glacier, joined by ice from the Gap of Dunloe, extended down the valley of the Laune to Killorglin, where it became confluent with the Cottoner's River glacier and the Lough Caragh glacier. The retreat stages of the latter can be clearly seen on the road from Killorglin to Glenbeigh, marked by a parallel series of crescentic moraines (figure 35). The innermost moraine encloses the beautiful Lough Caragh, flanked by its mountain sentinels of purple sandstone, whilst the outermost moraine, unrecognized by Wright, must be represented by the morainic mound beneath Cromane foreland.

Near the town of Cahersiveen the sea has managed to break through the high coastal ridge of sandstone at Doulus Head and Bray Head, thus isolating Valentia Island from the mainland. Armorican pressures have converted some of the island's finer-grained members of the Old Red Sandstone into green and reddish slates. The quarries of Glanleam once produced slates of immense size and great smoothness which were much in demand for the manufacture of billiard tables.

Back on the mainland a steep climb above Port Magee carries the coast road to a high col near Ballynahow, where excellent views may be obtained of most of the Kerry peninsulas. But it is the view to the west which holds the greatest fascination for lovers of dramatic scenery. Out across the turbulent seas of St Finan's Bay, some seven miles offshore and even more remote than the Blasket Isles, the grey, splintery outlines of the Skelligs can be seen. Only the Tearaght rocks of the Blaskets can approach the remarkable pinnacled form of this pair of rocky islets which rise sheer out of the Atlantic to heights of 714 feet and 440 feet respectively. Composed of grits and shales of Old Red Sandstone age, the jointing has been weathered to produce a series of fantastic spires and pinnacles, whitened with guano from the multitudes of sea-birds which nest there. It is almost unbelievable to learn that the Great Skellig (Skellig Michael) was settled by a group of seventh-century monks and that for one hundred years western Christianity, indeed western civilization, survived by clinging to such isolated refuges as this. Perched dizzily on ledges in the cliffs a number of drystone buildings, including beehive huts and corbelled chapels, are a legacy of this remarkable monastic settlement (plate 30).

The lanes around Ballinskellig's Bay are banked by thick fuchsia hedges which represent one of the most characteristic features of the Kerry scene but because of the salt spray and the exposure trees remain at a premium on these windswept headlands. Only where the mountains give protection from the prevailing winds do we find remnants of woodlands, as in some sheltered localities around the basin of Lough Currane, behind Waterville. The plan of this long, straggling tourist resort is determined by the curious configuration of the terrain, for it occupies a narrow isthmus between Lough Currane and the sea. The isthmus, like the Cromane foreland farther north, is built from a large end-moraine which sweeps around the western end of the lough. An excursion north-eastwards, up the valley of the Cummeragh river, reveals that even more spectacular crescentic moraines impound the mountain-girt lakes of Namona, Cloonaghlin and Derriana. The moraine enclosing Derriana Lough is particularly impressive for it can be traced without a break up both flanking ridges of this great rock basin. The southernmost arm of the moraine, which climbs the rocky arête between Derriana and Cloonaghlin, is so massive that it has succeeded in damming up a tiny marginal lake, Lough Mellinane, between the morainic *outer* slope and the mountain ridge – the only recorded example in Ireland. The ice-gouged valleys around Derriana and Cloonaghlin have incised their upper reaches deeply into the high mountain backbone of the Iveragh peninsula, each of their successive rock steps being occupied by a tiny lake in its ice-moulded basin, similar to those of the Horse's Glen at Killarney.

Back on the main road once more the tourist will stop only to admire the view from the celebrated Coomakista Pass before descending into the synclinal valley of Kenmare, most of which has been submerged beneath the ocean to form the ria known as the Kenmare River.

Thet own of Kenmare, as its name suggests (Ceann-mara = the head of the sea), was built at the first possible crossing point of the estuary.

Founded as an English colony in 1670 by Sir William Petty (an ancestor of the Shelbourne and Lansdowne families), it became famous for its ironworks which decimated much of the native woodland, although there was sufficient timber to feed the furnaces hereabouts until the middle of the eighteenth century. At one time timber was exported to Spain from the Kenmare and Killarney woodlands, but in the rugged terrain of Kerry transport to the coastal ports was considerably more expensive than the cost of felling. The valley of the Roughty river, between Kenmare and Kilgarvan, was also the scene of extensive copper and lead mining during the nineteenth century, although working has long ceased. It is interesting to recall that the Early Bronze Age settlers sought copper in these same lodes more than 4,000 years ago. The metalliferous ores, of which copper was by far the most important in these south-western peninsulas, were formed from mineral solutions which flowed under pressure along the joint and fault planes within the Old Red Sandstone and the Carboniferous rocks. The pressures were generated by the Armorican earth-movements which were quite intense in these parts, although there is a conspicuous lack of igneous activity.

One of the most interesting aspects of the Kenmare scenery is the effect which the former ice-sheets have had upon the landforms. W. B. Wright was able to assemble sufficient evidence to demonstrate that the approximate centre of the former ice-cap stood near the village of Templenoe. By a detailed study of the striations, grooves and roches moutonnées he was able to show that west of Dromore Castle ice-movement was down the Kenmare River, whilst at Kenmare itself the movement was up-valley. It has already been noted how the ice also moved northwards to breach the Killarney mountains, carrying Old Red Sandstone grits and volcanics out on to the Killarney plains as erratics. The limestone of the Kenmare valley too is strewn with large blocks of grit, some of which form conspicuous features at the old limestone quarries.

To the east of Kilgarvan, at a settlement called Morley's Bridge, Dr A. Farrington has drawn attention to an interesting example of river-capture. He believes that the pre-glacial drainage of the river Slaheny and the north-flowing headwaters of the Roughty formerly joined the Loo river, being carried thence to the north-flowing Flesk before emerging from the mountains at Killarney. Subsequent erosion by a strike stream cutting into the downfold of the Kenmare valley has led to the capture of the

Slaheny and Upper Roughty which now flow westwards to the Kenmare ria. The wind-gap at Morley's Bridge, near the so-called 'elbow of capture', was later utilized by meltwaters as an outflow from the impounded pro-glacial 'Lake Kenmare'. The latter is thought to have formed at an elevation of 320 feet during a down-wasting stage of the Kenmare ice-sheet, when the dead-ice mass lay west of Kenmare, thus impounding the waters of the normal drainage farther east. 'The shore-embankments and deltas of this lake are better developed and better preserved than those of any hitherto described glacial lake in the British Isles, with the exception perhaps of Glen Roy and Glen Spean, in Scotland' (W. B. Wright).

15. The Southern Highlands – Cork

The county of Cork is of such enormous extent that it displays as many as four quite distinct types of landscape: the western peninsulas, the southern coasts, the central valleys and the northern hills. The divisions are at once both topographical and geological for the landscape features owe virtually everything to the effects of the Armorican folding. This relationship of structure to scenery is even more clearly seen than in Kerry, for south of the Armorican Front the folds are more numerous and much more intense (figure 1). In the majority of cases the larger rivers are generally associated with the synclinal axes, flowing eastwards as a response to the overall west to east tectonic tilting. Only near to their estuaries do the rivers show a marked disregard for the structure and we shall examine this discordance later in the chapter.

Although the synclinal valleys of northern Cork have remnants of Carboniferous Limestone surviving at the centre of their downfolds, to the south of a line from Kenmare to Cork Harbour the Carboniferous rocks exhibit a change in facies so that the limestones are replaced by great thicknesses of sandstones, grits, slates and mudstones (figure 21). Nevertheless the latter are still depicted as part of the Carboniferous Limestone Series on the geological map of the back cover, since the fossil content of these rocks demonstrates that they are of Carboniferous age and are broadly equivalent to the Culm rocks of south-west England. Known generally as the 'Carboniferous Slates', these Culm rocks of southern Cork can be divided into the underlying Coomhola Grits and the overlying Ringabella argillaceous rocks (which include thin limestones). One of the major effects of the facies change can be seen where the arenaceous Coomhola Grits emerge on the flanks of the Old Red Sandstone for, despite their synclinal structure, the grits form high ground because of their great resistance to erosion. Near their type-site on the Coomhola river, which drains into the head of Bantry Bay, the grits rise eastwards to form the highest points of the Shehy Mountains (1,797 feet) of western Cork. Wherever the Coomhola Grits occur the topographic distinction between the synclinal valleys and anticlinal ridges is not so marked, for their resistance to denudation is almost equal to that of the Old Red Sandstone itself, with which they were originally confused. This is particularly true in southernmost Cork where the Old Red Sandstone uplands die away and their low ridges are virtually indistinguishable from those of the Carboniferous rocks.

There are two other instances in which the Armorican earth-movements have affected the landscapes of county Cork, albeit indirectly. The first of these concerns the compressive elements of the orogeny, for the intense pressures have resulted in the development of a marked cleavage and jointing within most of the affected rocks. This is best developed in the less competent argillaceous rocks, many of which have been converted into slates of great economic value, but is also seen in the limestones around Cork city. The second impact of the earth-movements was tot create a metalliferous zone in southern Ireland, of which the copper, manganese and barytes deposits of southern Cork form no small part. The results of their sporadic exploitation give a distinctiveness to a few isolated corners of the Cork landscape.

The Western Peninsulas

The backbone of the Caha Peninsula is made up of a tightly folded anti-clinorium of Old Red Sandstone which forms the summits of the Caha Mountains and of Slieve Miskish, their western extension. Its coastline, however, is not a simple one for the sandstones dip steeply to north and south from the antiform (often at angles of over 60°) to pass beneath the flanking Carboniferous rocks which often interject rocky promontories and islands into the waters of Kenmare River and Bantry Bay (figure 33). It is on these Carboniferous projections that much of the improved land and most of the settlement is found, as at Bear Island and the Kil-catherine promontory, for the more friable shales and slates produce not only a more tractable soil but also occupy the least elevated terrain. Elsewhere, on the sandstone coastline, the landscape is one of furzy heath and rocky knolls, empty fields and ruined cottages, with less than one-third of the peninsula under improved land. Although rising to more than 2,000 feet most of the higher summits of the Caha Mountains are featureless, peat-covered domes, with few intervening gaps except for the scenic Healy Pass with its remarkably engineered road. Much of their interest lies, therefore, in their glacial valleys, incised deeply into the mountainland. The largest of these (just in Kerry) is occupied by a long chain of interconnected paternoster lakes, the Cloonee Lakes, with the innermost ones occupying high corries. Glanmore Lake (below the Healy Pass), amidst its woodlands and purple rock cliffs, is reminiscent of Killarney, although its coniferous trees fail to produce the soft outlines which characterize the Killarney woods. But it is the austere waters of Glenbeg Lough which provide the most memorable mountain scenery, for here the lake is fed by a series of spectacular waterfalls which stripe the steep walls of the glacial trough with their silvery skeins.

Towards the western extremity of the peninsula the rural landscape is scarred by the abandoned workings of a mining enterprise. This is the well-known Allihies copper mine where copper-bearing quartz-lodes, up to 60 feet in width, slice through the Old Red Sandstone. Only the gaunt ruins of the mine buildings, the pock-marked surface and the roofless miners' cottages at the so-called 'Cornish village', survive today, although we are told that enormous quantities of copper remain at depth. Beyond the forlorn dereliction which surrounds Allihies the rocky ridge of Dursey Head snakes out into the Atlantic. The actual headland is formed by the wave-battered sandstone of Dursey Island, reminiscent in its form to the Great Blasket but separated from the mainland by a fearsome narrow gorge.

Some of the cliff-girt headlands between Dursey Head and Bear Island owe their particular prominence to the presence of volcanic rocks. Thus the steep slopes of Black Ball Head and some of the Bear Island cliffs are formed from bedded tuffs within the Carboniferous succession. Bear Island, formerly one of the most important British naval bases in Ireland (Lough Swilly and Cobh were the others), is now a relatively deserted place. But whilst Bear Island has been virtually abandoned by twentieth-century technology so the nearby Whiddy Island, farther up Bantry Bay, has been invaded. The waters of the Bay, famed in song and history, are today dotted with enormous oil-tankers coming to discharge their crude-oil at the Whiddy Island terminal. Like Milford Haven in

Pembrokeshire the presence of a deep water ria has been responsible for the location of such an industrial enterprise.

Next to Killarney and Connemara, Glengarriff, at the head of Bantry Bay, is one of the best-known scenic attractions in Ireland. Set in its south-facing valley amidst thick woodlands and circling mountains of Old Red Sandstone and Coomhola Grits, Glengarriff has been a tourist resort since early Victorian times. Thackeray saw it as the most delightful place in Ireland and inquired why tourists bothered to visit Switzerland and the Rhine when '. . . around the pretty inn of Glengarriff there is a country of the magnificence of which no pen can give an idea'.

A combination of the horizontal lines of the ocean and the vertical lines of the mountains has always appealed to lovers of the picturesque and at Glengarriff the sharp pyramid of the Sugar Loaf Mountain, 'almost too formal to be real', is everyone's idea of what a mountain ought to be. From the Sugar Loaf (1,887 feet) a magnificent panorama of the ria coastline of Cork and Kerry can be seen, with the summits of the Reeks and the Shehy Mountains terminating the inland view. The nearby Caha Mountains are scarred and pitted by glacial erosion, their purple rock hollows and valleys infilled with scores of tiny lakes, including the beautiful Barley Lake, which give to the area the character of a miniature Lake District. Nevertheless, despite the beauty of the lakes and hills, in the final analysis it is probably the woodland, so rare on these windswept Atlantic coasts, that gives distinction to Glengarriff.

Apart from its large central square and its splendid Georgian mansion the town of Bantry makes no lasting impression. It stands amongst a small drumlin swarm, the only one of significance in Munster, with drumlins helping to create some of the islands at the head of the bay and the high drift cliffs near the town itself (figure 17). In the mid-nineteenth century officers of the Geological Survey noted that the drumlins were '. . . clearly distinguishable from the hills of rock by their smooth regular forms and their green cultivated sides, while the rocky hills are rough, and dark with heather and gorse'. A subsequent study of the glacial geology by Dr A. Farrington has shown that the drumlins were moulded by the lower layers of the Lesser Cork–Kerry ice-sheet which, having crossed the Caha Mountains at Glengarriff, were deflected to the south-west and the north-east by the disposition of the Carboniferous-floored valley of Bantry Bay. Consequently, the majority of the drumlins have assumed an orientation parallel to the strike of the syncline, although it is suggested that the upper layers of the ice-sheet were able to continue south-eastwards across the intervening sandstone ridges to leave their moraines near Skibbereen. Unlike the Kenmare valley no evidence of an ice-impounded lake has been found at the head of Bantry Bay although meltwater channels, which breach the regional watershed at several places, were formed by marginal or sub-glacial drainage during Quaternary times. The main roads from Bantry to Dunmanway and Bantry to Macroom utilize such channels, the latter road following the celebrated Pass of Keimaneigh which leads from the Bantry Bay drainage system to the upper valley of the Lee. This narrow gorge, slicing through the Shehy Mountains for almost two miles, has vertical rock walls some 200 feet in height.

The bold, finger-like peninsula of Sheep's Head, with its ice-scrubbed spine of sandstone hills, divides the Carboniferous downfold of Bantry Bay from that of Dunmanus Bay to the south (figure 34). Except for its westernmost tip it is a simple anticlinal structure with the coastline following closely the geological boundary of the Old Red Sandstone and the Carboniferous.

Lying between Dunmanus Bay and Roaringwater Bay the peninsula which culminates in Mizen Head consists of a number of isolated hills and intervening valleys. Whilst the structure of Sheep's Head is so simple that of Mizen Head is complex for although its highest summit, Mount Gabriel (1,339 feet), is built of Old Red Sandstone, its northern hills, such as Mount Corin (946 feet), are composed of Coomhola Grits of Carboniferous age. Because of its lower elevation and its better soils the Mizen Head peninsula appears less barren than its more northerly neighbours, for over half its area is in crops and pasture. There are no glacial corries here and few signs of glacial erosion, it being noteworthy that ice-scrubbed landforms have become far less common as we have moved away from the Kenmare ice-centre.

Copper was formerly mined at Streek Head and Brow Head (near Crookhaven) where the ruined buildings defile some of the finest cliff scenery in the south-west. The mine shafts occur at the foot of the sea-cliffs and were driven down beneath the sea itself. By comparison the old copper workings at Ballycummisk (near Skull) and on the slopes of Mount Gabriel were far less hazardous. The hillsides around Mount Gabriel and Ballydehob are littered with abandoned workings, reminding us that during the nineteenth century the copper mines of west Cork were second only to Cornwall in terms of European production. The discovery of the Rhodesian fields, however, put an end to the exploitation of the 'Copper Belt' in Cork. In addition to copper, great quantities of barytes were once mined near the summit of Mount Gabriel but the world demand for this heavy white mineral has fluctuated considerably so that mining has been sporadic.

Mizen Head is often referred to as the 'Land's End of Ireland' since it is the most south-westerly point of the Irish mainland. But instead of the Cornish granite cliffs the magnificent cliffs of Mizen are composed of hundreds of feet of closely bedded sandstones and shales. The gently folded strata exhibit every shade of red and pink, and where the waves have cut deeply into both the joints and bedding-planes they have produced a fine collection of rose-coloured terraces, walls and buttresses. Farmers from all over west Cork used to take sand from the nearby Barley Cove beach because of its reputed agricultural value, but this ancient privilege has now been withdrawn, for tourism is now paramount in the economy of west Cork and Barley Cove has the only substantial beach for miles around.

The southernmost of the rias of south-west Munster is known as Roaringwater Bay, but its archipelago of islands and its tattered coastline make it a less clear-cut example than its northerly neighbours (figure 33). Its topographic confusion is largely the result of its structural complexity for between the major anticlines of Mizen Head and Cape Clear the bay has been carved from an intricate synclinorium. Thus, in addition to the various members of the Carboniferous Slates and the Old Red Sandstone, the Kiltorcan Beds of yellow sandstone also make an appearance, especially on the Lisheen peninsula and the nearby Inishbeg and Hare Island. Most of the smaller islands in the bay are now deserted and even the larger Long Island is losing its few surviving native Irish, their cottages being frequently sold to foreigners to serve as holiday homes.

The tiny port of Baltimore marks the southern tip of the mainland section of the 'peninsula' of Cape Clear. The inroads of the sea on this southernmost promontory have progressed even further than at Dursey Head, for the sandstone ridge has been breached at two places to produce the rocky and windswept eminences of Sherkin Island and Clear Island.

Even further out on its wave-swept pinnacle the famous Fastnet light-house marks the last unconsumed remnant of the slowly disintegrating peninsula. Cape Clear Island, because of its isolation, has retained its Irish language and folk-ways, and there are sufficient islanders remaining to give hope that it will remain a viable settlement.

The Southern Coast

The Fastnet rock is more than a turning-point for the well-known yacht race, it is the point at which the coast of Cork ceases to run across the grain of the land and begins to run parallel with it. From Cape Clear to Cork Harbour the southern coast is roughly aligned with the axes of the folding. This is not to say that the coast is a smooth one, for there are many notable headlands and bays, but it lacks the gigantic rias and peninsulas of the Atlantic coast. Because the coastline parallels the structural grain it can be regarded as an example of a 'Pacific-type' of coastline.

From Baltimore to east of Ross Carbery the coastline has been carved out of the southern limb of the Clonakilty anticline. But the remnants of Carboniferous Slate which survive on the two projecting promontories of Toe Head and Galley Head suggest that the Carboniferous rocks of another syncline lie not far off-shore. Along most of this southern coast the bays and estuaries run directly across the strike of the rocks but this may have been in part controlled by the presence of numerous north–south faults. One may have to invoke erosion along a fault to account for the odd phenomenon of Lough Hyne (near Baltimore) for no-one has yet been able to explain its genesis. This tiny, rectangular sea lough of incredible depth (24 fathoms) is connected with the open sea by a shallow channel over half a mile in length.

The deserted coastal landscapes around Skibbereen, a complex mix-ture of gorse and bracken, treeless rocky knolls, bogs and stone-walled fields (plate 31), have been described admirably by Somerville and Ross in their classic account of *Some Experiences of an Irish R.M.* It is note-worthy that many of the domestic buildings in these coastal villages of Castletownshend, Union Hall and Glandore are both walled and roofed in slate. The Madrenna slates from Leap and the dark blue Benduff roofing slates from Ross Carbery were once quarried on a large scale to supply most of southern Munster, leaving Benduff Castle surrounded by slate quarries and widespread spoil heaps. Nearby is the extensive manganese lode which runs from Glandore to Ross Carberry and also the barytes deposits of Duneen near Clonakilty but, like the slate quarrying, all mining activity has now ceased and mixed farming is the major source of employment.

Beyond Clonakilty Bay and the sandstone promontories of the Seven Heads the broad bay of Courtmacsherry has been carved from the ubiquitous Carboniferous Slates. The Old Red Sandstone dies away at the Seven Heads, not reappearing on the coast till Cork Harbour is reached (figure 36). In geological circles Howe Strand in Courtmacsherry Bay is famous as the type-site of the mid-Pleistocene raised beach, first recorded by W. B. Wright and H. B. Muff in 1904.

The eastern end of Courtmacsherry Bay is closed by the impressive Old Head of Kinsale, a bony finger of slates and grits projecting some three miles from the main coastline. The headland lighthouse stands on an outcrop of Coomhola Grits which, like the argillaceous rocks of the promontory, exhibit steep dips between 60° and 90°. Marine erosion, cutting along the east–west strike of the rocks to create an array of vertical cliffs, has almost succeeded in breaking through the isthmus at Holeopen Bay.

To the north of the Old Head lies Kinsale Harbour, regarded by many visitors as the scenic highlight of the southern coast. In reality the long twisting inlet is a ria, consisting of nothing more than the drowned estuary of the Bandon river where it breaks through the eastern end of the Clonakilty anticline (plate 32). The Bandon river is the first example to be encountered of the way in which the major southern rivers exhibit a marked disregard of geological structure in their lower reaches. We shall examine this problem more thoroughly later in the chapter; it is enough to note here that the Bandon, having followed an easterly course along a synclinal axis from Dunmanway to Innishannon, turns abruptly away from the Cloyne syncline to flow southwards across the topographical grain, in a direction structurally discordant with the Minane syncline and the Clonakilty anticline (figure 36).

Hidden from the open sea, on a sweeping meander in the estuary, stands the little town of Kinsale (Ceann saile = head of the tide), famous for its historic siege and battle of 1601. Kinsale is a delightful place, with

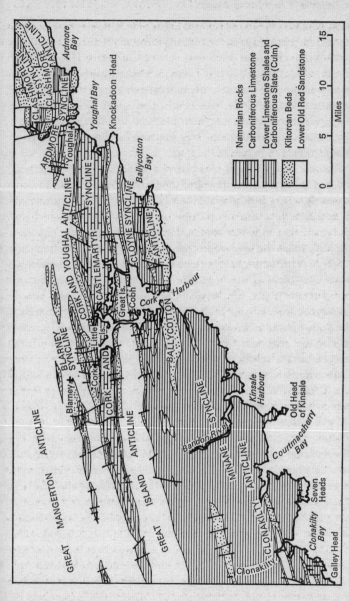

Fig. 36. The geology of southern Cork showing the effect of the tight Armorican folding (after J. K. Charlesworth and the Irish Geological Survey).

its narrow, winding streets, its stepped hillside lanes, its elegant Georgian terraces and its Flemish-gabled guildhall. When viewed from any of the surrounding hills the town is reminiscent of a Cornish or Devon fishing village, its tree-dotted slopes being criss-crossed with purple roofs and silvery-grey walls. The extensive use of local grey slate for wall-cladding is an attractive feature of the town, whilst the riot of pink valerian and the pastel colour-washed houses, both here and in its waterside suburb of Scilly, act as a perfect foil to the grey stonework and to the shimmering waters which seem to permeate the town.

For the next twenty miles, past Barry's Head, Robert's Head and Power Head the coast is composed of the Carboniferous Slates (usually the Coomhola Grits), but beyond Power Head the yellow Kiltorcan Beds appear again to form the sharp Ballycotton Point beyond which the coastline turns across the topographical grain once more.

At Roche's Point the sea has breached the east–west Ballycotton anticline of Kiltorcan sandstones to reach the less resistant Carboniferous Limestone and Slate of the neighbouring Cloyne syncline (figure 36). Working laterally along the strike, forces of denudation had already created a broad lowland vale in the limestone outcrop which the sea has now flooded to form the magnificent land-locked basin of Cork Harbour. Judging by the behaviour of the Bandon river, the narrow bottleneck entrance of Cork Harbour may represent the drowned estuary of the Owenboy river, whose upper reaches follow the Cloyne syncline eastwards to Crosshaven but which may well have swung round to breach the Ballycotton anticline at this point.

On the deep-water channel is the port of Cobh, dominated by its great Gothic-Revival cathedral which stands on a hillside above the town. The islands which lie in the harbour represent hill-tops which survived the general submergence, with their present landscapes demonstrating some of the ways in which the rural scene has changed during the twentieth century. Haulbowline Island has a steelworks, Spike Island a military camp, while the tiny tombolo island of Corkbeg houses part of the White-gate oil refinery. Cobh itself stands on a larger island, Great Island, which has given its name to another anticline of Old Red Sandstone that runs westwards from Knockadoon Head far into the interior of central Cork (figure 36). This steep sandstone ridge is broken only at two places, to the east and west of Cobh, by former river valleys now inundated by the sea at East Ferry and Passage West. To the north of the ridge the lime-stones of the Cork–Castlemartyr syncline have been lowered by erosion to form a broad vale reaching from Cork city to the sea at Youghal Bay. Into this lowland the marine submergence has infiltrated its waters to form the picturesque Lough Mahon, thereby isolating Great Island. The limestone vale between Cork city and Castlemartyr, rarely attaining the 100-foot contour, broadens eastwards to Youghal Bay and looks as if it ought to be the natural outlet of the river Lee into St George's Channel. Like the Bandon and the Owenboy, however, the Lee swings southwards, ignoring the Castlemartyr limestone corridor, preferring instead to follow a more difficult course through the sandstone ridge at Passage West and thence via Cork Harbour to the sea. The south-flowing Owennacurra river crosses the Castlemartyr syncline at Middleton and equally per-versely follows the East Ferry breach in the sandstone anticline to reach Cork Harbour (compare figure 36 with figure 38).

Cork City and the Southern Rivers

Cork, the third largest city in Ireland, is best viewed from the crest of Patrick's Hill, the steep sandstone ridge which rises to the north of the limestone valley of the Lee. From here one can appreciate its '. . . shim-mering panorama of smoke-webbed roofs, streets and rivers' that has been described so admirably by its native writers Sean O'Faolain, Frank O'Connor and Robert Gibbings. Unlike the Georgian red-brick of Dub-lin, Belfast and Limerick, the fabric of Cork is mainly a glittering white limestone, taken largely from the nearby quarries on Little Island, over-looking Lough Mahon. In a walk across the city from the gleaming white spires of St Finbarr's Cathedral, past the classical façades of the Court-house and St Mary's Church, one is constantly aware of elegant limestone buildings reflected in the burrowing waters of the Lee (plate 33). But the most fascinating architectural spectacle, perhaps, is the hilltop Italianate campanile of St Anne's Church with its famous bells of Shandon, for as if to demonstrate Cork's location astride a geological boundary its tower has two adjacent sides of limestone and two of sandstone. Several of the nineteenth-century buildings have a pleasing mixture of red sandstone and white limestone, but recent commercialism and industrialization is gradually changing the fabric and the face of the city, as exemplified by the massive Marina power station (120 MW) erected on the famous Quays in postwar years.

The Irish name for Cork is Corcach (= a marsh) which serves to remind us that the earliest settlement was on a marshy island in '. . . the spreading Lee, that like an Island fayre, encloseth Corke with his divided flood' (Spenser). The 'spreading Lee' formerly subdivided into several bifurcating channels, known as distributaries, as its waters reached the tidal limits of the estuary where, because its velocity was checked, a great volume of its alluvial sediment was deposited. When a river splits into this interlacing network of channels it is said to be braided, with such a process occurring not only near its mouth in anticipation of a delta but anywhere in its course where its velocity is checked by a sudden decrease of gradient. Ultimately, the majority of the Cork waterways were covered over to accommodate the spacious streets required by the eighteenth-century planners; Grand Parade, South Mall and Patrick Street appeared in this way. The latter's curving line demonstrates quite clearly the course of its underground river distributary.

In former years another example of river braiding could be seen up-stream in the Lee valley, in the region known as the Gearagh. Since the 1960s, however, this has been lost beneath the waters of a seventeen-mile lake, dammed to provide power for two modern hydro-electric stations. Thus, Ireland has lost a unique landscape and a singular landform which once saw the Lee running past '. . . a thousand wooded islets, under the overhanging fern-laden, moss-covered oaks; under the alders and hazels; through tangles of rushes, swaying tall weeds; through tortuous channels, trailing long grasses; an almost impenetrable jungle' (R. Gibbings). We know from the work of Dr Farrington that the braided section at the Gearagh resulted from the occurrence of a massive glacial moraine which crosses the river at Coolcour. Thus, during a retreat stage of the former Cork–Kerry ice-sheet, the Coolcour moraine acted as a dam for the glacial outwash carried by the swollen waters of the Lee when the ice-front stood at the so-called Lough Allua stage (figure 37). When the ice-sheet was even more extensive it left a series of older moraines across the valley as far downstream as Inishleena near to the confluence of the rivers Lee and Bride, but it is the massive moraine in the Bride valley, at the village of Killumney, which draws our attention for not only is it the biggest morainic accumulation in Cork but it also marks the eastern

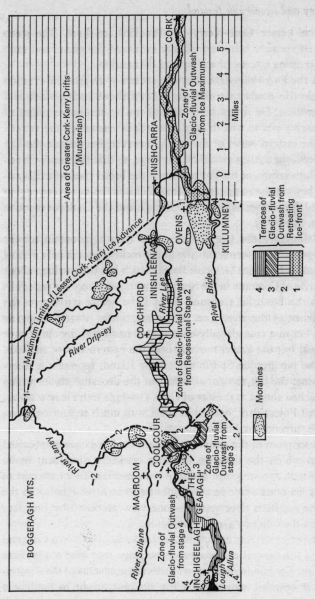

Fig. 37. *The valley of the River Lee, showing former ice-limits and glacial features (after A. Farrington).*
Note: *Much of the valley between Inchigeelagh and Inishcarra is now submerged beneath an artificial lake, constructed for hydro-electric purposes.*

limits of the Lesser Cork–Kerry (Midlandian) ice-sheet. The steep morainic hills are now being extensively excavated for gravel and sand extraction, creating a scene of widespread devastation.

Although the long valley-lake above Inishcarra is an artificial creation for hydro-electric needs that of Lough Allua above Inchigeelagh is a natural formation, for it has been ponded up by successive ridges of gravelly moraine whose well-drained sandy soils encourage the growth of gorse. The eastern outlet of the lough, however, lies outside the line of the former Lough Allua glacial retreat stage, so that the meadowlands of Inchigeelagh represent the flat terrace of the broad glacio-fluvial out-wash plain beyond the stationary ice-front. This is the same terrace that can be traced down-river as far as the Gearagh and the Coolcour moraine (terrace 4 in figure 37).

Above Ballingeary the Lee is little more than a mountain torrent 'cascading over natural weirs, sluicing under rocks', for it is only a short distance from its source at Gougane Barra. Much has been written about the great corrie of Coomroe in the Shehy Mountains, where the waterfalls plunge into the beautiful Gougane Barra Lake before starting on the lengthy journey as the river Lee. The romantically situated Gougane Barra Lake lies in a true glacially-eroded rock basin with its outlet over a bar of rock, but the gravel mounds near the eastern end of the lake, including the picturesque St Finbarr's Holy Island, represent a recessional moraine, the last recognizable halt of the decaying glacier which formerly reached almost to the city of Cork. Gougane Barra is now within a state-owned Forest Park, opened in 1966, with much replanting taking place on the surrounding Shehy Mountains.

In our description of the rivers of southern Cork we have emphasized the ways in which the drainage becomes markedly discordant in its relationship with the structure near the river mouths. In an attempt to explain this we must examine two opposing hypotheses relating to the origin of the southern river system – one view proposed by Professor A. A. Miller, the other by Dr A. Farrington.

One of the most striking aspects of the landscape of southern Cork and Waterford is the general accordance of the ridge tops over a wide area of the interior. For hundreds of square miles the sandstone of the Armorican ridges is bevelled across at a fairly uniform height to produce a classical erosion surface into which the river system is entrenched.

Professor Miller believed that the surface was composite, consisting of two platforms, one at a general height of 600–800 feet, the other between 200 and 400 feet. He called the upper surface the South Ireland Peneplane, which he saw as an uplifted platform of marine abrasion cut by the waves of a late-Tertiary sea and culminating at 800 feet in an old degraded 'cliff-line' against the southern slopes of the Boggeragh, Nagles, Knockmealdowns and Monavullagh Mountains. The lower surface, along the southern coastlands, he termed the Coastal Peneplane, formed by marine action at a later date. In both cases the spelling 'peneplane' was adopted instead of 'peneplain', since the latter is W. M. Davis's term for a surface of low relief produced by sub-aerial denudation whilst the former was suggested by D. W. Johnson to describe an uplifted surface of marine abrasion. Professor Miller reconstructed the former drainage pattern of southern Ireland to show that in his opinion the original consequent streams flowed southwards on the newly emerged sea-floor of the South Ireland Peneplane (figure 38). These rivers followed a direction consequent upon the slope of the uplifted sea-bed and may be termed extended consequents, as they extended their courses from the 'old land' to the new coastline some 20 to 30 miles to the south. But since the surface had been trimmed by waves across the east–west Armorican structures, Professor Miller believed that a trellis drainage pattern would develop by means of river capture. As a result, the subsequent streams, which could erode more easily along the strike of the rocks, became gradually more dominant at the expense of the consequents, eventually producing the predominantly longitudinal drainage pattern of to-day (figure 38).

Dr Farrington, whilst accepting the existence of the extensive surface between 600 and 800 feet (the South Ireland Peneplane), preferred to regard it as a Davisian peneplain produced by an essentially east-flowing river system. He demonstrated that the so-called South Ireland Peneplane slopes from west to east, not north to south, and that the degraded 800-foot 'cliff-line' is not supported by the field evidence. In the opinion of Dr Farrington the surface in question was developed on the Carboniferous Limestone (or on strata overlying the limestone), but owing to its poorer resistance to erosion the limestone surface has since disappeared so that the only peneplain remnants left are those on the Old Red Sandstone ridges. He suggests that although the Lee drainage is currently discordant with the structure this was not necessarily the case when it flowed at the level of the South Ireland Peneplane (i.e. approximately 700 feet) or at an earlier, higher level (figure 39). An examination of the reconstructed Armorican folds in figure 39 suggests that while at the

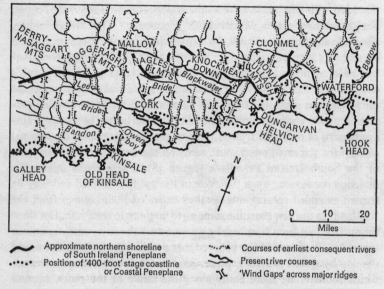

Fig. 38. *A hypothetical reconstruction of drainage evolution in south Munster. According to A. A. Miller, a former pattern of south-flowing consequent rivers on the South Ireland Peneplane has been replaced by the present structurally-adjusted subsequent river pattern. (Compare with figure 36.)*

present land surface only 40% of the section is occupied by Carboniferous rocks, at 700 feet this proportion increases to 60%, and at 1,300 feet to more than 90%. It is possible, therefore, that the river Lee was adjusted to structure when it flowed eastwards at higher levels but that as the limestone was destroyed it became gradually superimposed on to the formerly buried structures of the minor anticlines.

Northern Cork

To the north of the Lee valley a line of sandstone mountains blocks the northern horizon. The Boggeragh Mountains (2,118 feet) and the Nagles Mountains (1,406 feet) form a barrier between the prosperous farmlands of the Lee and those of its northern neighbour the river Blackwater which, like the Lee, follows an easterly course for much of its length. This line

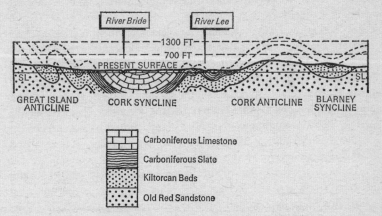

Fig. 39. *Geological section of the Bride and Lee valleys to the west of the city of Cork, to illustrate the decreasing exposure of Carboniferous Limestone during the lowering of the land surface (after A. Farrington).*

of mountains, their thickly forested slopes rising darkly above the valley of the Blackwater, represents an important geological boundary. We have again reached the Armorican Front, the northern limit of severe Armorican folding, running from Dingle Bay in the west to Dungarvan Harbour in the east. The general pressures from the south led to the formation of gigantic thrust-faults, between Killarney and Mallow, where Old Red Sandstone rocks have been pushed northwards on to the Carboniferous rocks. Although the mountain wall is not as high as that of the Reeks at Killarney the north Cork mountains exhibit steep northern slopes overlooking the Blackwater valley.

The Blackwater rises in the featureless boglands of east Kerry, where Namurian grits and shales build the low, heather-covered plateaux which overlook the Tralee lowlands. Near Kanturk the plateaux enclose a basin of productive Coal Measures of Ammanian age, occupying an area of more than a dozen square miles, and containing the most complete Coal Measure succession in Ireland. Like almost all the Irish coalfields, however, production was sporadic and has now ceased, largely because of difficulties of extraction. Owing to their close proximity to the Armorican Front the Kanturk coal seams have been severely folded and faulted, with many of the coals crushed and contorted and the strata left standing vertically.

On leaving the Namurian rocks the Blackwater turns eastwards along the northern slopes of the Boggeraghs before entering the narrow limestone strike vale at Mallow. Today Mallow is a prosperous little market town but hardly recognizable as the so-called 'Bath of Ireland' of Regency times. Once a notable spa based on the waters of a thermal spring, it has only a few buildings which still retain the Georgian character of the period. The surrounding countryside is largely given over to permanent grassland with cattle providing the basis of a thriving dairy industry. Sufficient trees survive in the well-ordered landscape to remind us that in Tudor times the extent of the forests in the valleys of these south Munster rivers was almost legendary. This is all part of the 'pleasant plain' described by Edmund Spenser, the renowned Elizabethan poet and writer who wrote his famous *Faerie Queene* at Kilcolman Castle near Buttevant. Between Mallow and Fermoy the Blackwater receives several important tributaries from the north and together these have lowered the limestone tract which lies between the encircling sandstone uplands of the Nagles, the Kilworth Mountains and the Ballyhoura Mountains.

A final word is necessary on the vagaries of the Blackwater river for like its neighbouring Lee this major river follows a course as puzzling as it is beautiful. From Mallow to Fermoy the Blackwater hugs the northern footslope of the Nagles, close to the junction of the Carboniferous and the Old Red Sandstone. At Fermoy it enters the eastward pitching Dungarvan syncline of Carboniferous rocks but rather than flowing along the structural axis of the downfold the valley has been carved along the northern limb where the Lower Carboniferous Shales overlie the Kiltorcan Beds. Thus the river does not occupy the centre of the limestone vale in its journey eastwards and in a few places it actually crosses on to the Kiltorcan Beds, suggesting that it may have been superimposed even in this supposedly 'structurally adjusted' stretch of its course. After a journey of some 70 miles, however, when it reaches Cappoquin, a mere ten miles from the sea at Dungarvan, the Blackwater leaves no doubt as to its superimposed origin for it swings abruptly southwards and cuts

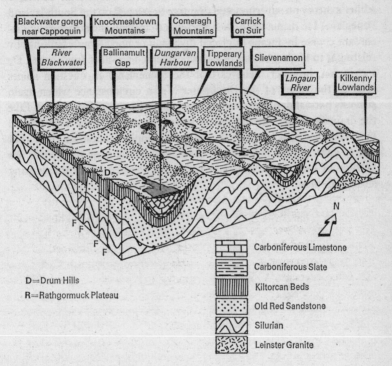

Fig. 40. *Central Waterford.*

through no less than four anticlinal sandstone ridges before reaching the sea at Youghal (figure 38). The sudden change of direction at Cappoquin and the virtually streamless limestone corridor between here and Dungarvan were among the many phenomena which prompted J. B. Jukes to write one of the earliest essays on river evolution as long ago as 1862 (figure 40). This classic paper described how the peculiarities of the drainage in southern Ireland, including the rivers of Waterford and

Wexford, could be attributed to superimposition from an initial surface at 2,000 feet, higher than the summits of the surrounding mountains.

It is important to remember that the anomalous course of the Blackwater between Cappoquin and Youghal, where it flows in beautiful wooded gorges through the sandstone hills, was the basis of Professor Miller's theory on superimposed drainage developed on the South Ireland Peneplane. He dismissed earlier attempts to explain the structurally discordant course by means of glacial diversion or north–south faulting, by relating it to his hypothesis of a newly emerged sea-floor (see above). Dr Farrington, however, believes that the 'peneplane' in question slopes towards the valley of the Blackwater '. . . a circumstance which again suggests normal drainage development under sub-aerial conditions'. Like the drainage of the Lee the stream pattern appears to have been created by a system which formerly flowed on a complete limestone cover, but due to lowering and stripping of the limestone the river Blackwater has become in part adjusted and in part superimposed on to the existing structural lines.

16. Waterford, Tipperary and Kilkenny

Although in a sense this region of Ireland is a transition zone between the Armorican structures of the south and the Caledonian structures of the east, its landscapes are unified by the presence of three major rivers, the Suir, Nore and Barrow. Known to the Irish as the 'three sisters', these lengthy waterways unite before reaching the sea in the wide estuary of Waterford Harbour. For the visitor travelling through the broad limestone vales, across the deep rivers and over the high ridges of older rocks, the landscape has close affinities with that of southern Munster described in the previous chapter. But the Carboniferous Limestone of the lowlands is more widespread, the hills rather more isolated, the coastline less dominant – in short we are passing progressively away from Armorican Ireland back into the landscapes of the Central Lowlands. The soils become gradually more fertile towards the north as we leave the acid drifts of the Old Red Sandstone for the limestone gravels of the Irish midlands. Thus the agriculture appears more prosperous and the countryside more orderly, except where the mountains of sandstone, slate and grit introduce patches of rough grazing and moorland into the rural scene.

Not only is there a change in landscape as we move from south to north, but also as we travel eastwards from Munster into Leinster, for here the meeting of the Armorican and Caledonian structures is the most important factor in any analysis of the scenery. The landscape of southeast Leinster will be described in chapter seventeen; here we need simply note that the uplands of the Leinster Chain, with their Caledonoid trend, culminate near the junction of the Nore and Barrow in the east of the region now under review. Nevertheless, although the older rocks of Wexford and Carlow disappear westwards beneath the Upper Palaeozoic strata, the buried 'Caledonian floor' (and especially the Leinster Granite) causes a change in the trend of the folding in Tipperary and Kilkenny (figure 1). In place of the typical east–west alignment of the Armorican south the trend swings round to north-east and south-west, though the folding is still of Armorican age. Thus the topography of the Coal Measures of Castlecomer and Slieve Ardagh have adopted this 'grain', as have the Silurian and Old Red Sandstone uplands of north Tipperary. It is not only in the uplands, however, that the contrasting structural elements can be seen, for in Waterford the lowlands too show the imprint of the Caledonian and Armorican earth-movements.

The Waterford Mountains and Coasts

The topographic contrasts between the mountains and the coastlands of Waterford are very largely a matter of structural differences. Whilst the highlands represent the unconsumed Armorican upfolds of Old Red Sandstone the coastal tract corresponds largely with an outcrop of Ordovician rocks, whose Caledonian folds have been bevelled across by a period of marine planation. But there are, in addition, two other geological elements which contribute to the Waterford scene: the limestone vales of Dungarvan and the Suir together with another Armorican structure that forms the plateau lands of Silurian rocks which flank Carrick-on-Suir. In combination all these contrasting rock types have given to Waterford a scenic heritage as varied in character as most of the larger Irish counties (figure 40).

In the south the rolling Drum Hills, carved largely from the Kiltorcan sandstones and Carboniferous 'Slates', represent the eastern termination of several Armorican folds. Their picturesque promontories of Ardmore Head, Mine Head and Helvick Head, between the limestone-floored bays of Youghal and Dungarvan, delineate the northernmost limit of Armorican folding along this coast, Helvick Head itself marking the line of the Armorican Front.

Across the Dungarvan lowland the high mountains of Waterford, carved from a massive anticlinorium of Old Red Sandstone, overlook the coastal plains and the beautiful valley of the Blackwater river. In the west the crest of the complex upfold corresponds with the oddly-named Knockmealdown Mountains, the highest summit of which culminates at a height of 2,609 feet. A road, climbing steadily northwards from Lismore past the well-known monastery of Mount Melleray, leads up to 'The Gap' at the crest of the ridge and on to a spectacular viewpoint on the famous 'Vee Road'. It is as well to pause at this spot, not only to appreciate the attractive corrie lake embowered in a veritable forest of rhododendrons, but also to contemplate the magnificent northern vista of the Mitchelstown limestone vale and the rearing peaks of the Galty Mountains beyond. But even more significant, this viewpoint will serve admirably to demonstrate an important geological principle for it is just possible to discern, some 25 miles away to the north-east, the misty outlines of the Slieve Ardagh Hills. Closer at hand the eminences of Slievenamon and the Galty Mountains frame this distant view across the limestone plain of Tipperary, and we shall see how both these nearby uplands have been fashioned from the same anticlinal axis of pre-Carboniferous rocks. Somewhat surprisingly, perhaps, we shall discover later in this chapter how Slieve Ardagh (and its neighbouring Castlecomer Plateau) are uplands which have been carved from synclinal structures, not from antiforms. Our lengthy excursions in southern Ireland will probably have given the impression that wherever upfolds occur they correspond with ridges of high relief and, conversely, that all downfolds are occupied by valleys or lowlands. In Armorican Ireland this certainly appears to be the case but the impression is an erroneous one for the majority of fold mountain ranges throughout the world exhibit a phenomenon known as 'inversion of relief'. Briefly, this implies that all the anticlinal arches, being most vulnerable to erosion because their joints are under tension, have ultimately been worn down to form areas of lowland or broad valleys. Conversely, the more resistant synclinal structures, with their joints closed by compression, are frequently left upstanding to form areas of high land, a good example of this being seen in Snowdonia, North Wales. For some reason the Armorican structures of south Ireland have not yet reached this stage of relief inversion, probably owing to the contrasting resistance offered by the Old Red Sandstone and the Carboniferous Limestone respectively, to forces of denudation.

The Comeragh and Monavullagh Mountains, which lie to the east of the Knockmealdowns, are also composed of Old Red Sandstone, where hundreds of feet of purple grits and brownish conglomerates and shales have been updomed into a gigantic arch. It will be seen in figure 40 how the eastern end of the arch has been worn away to reveal a core of Silurian rocks which, owing to their poorer resistance to denudation, have been worn down to form a rolling plateau. Known as the plateau of Rathgormuck, this oval-shaped exposure of dark grey slates and greenish grits has created a comparatively fertile tract of soils amidst the barren heathery hills of sandstone. Flanking this basin of farmlands the Old Red Sandstone has survived as a rim of low-wooded hills carved from a circle of inward-facing scarps (figure 40).

The eastern face of the flat-topped Comeragh Mountains (2,597 feet) has been severely quarried by a series of local corrie glaciers which have left behind a magnificent collection of cliffs, arêtes, rock-basin lakes and corrie moraines. The gigantic amphitheatre of Coumshingaun, thought by some to be the largest corrie in Ireland, is particularly notable for its precipices which rise 1,400 feet vertically above the lake to the highest summit, thereby exposing a considerable part of the Old Red Sandstone succession. Tors are very prominent on the intervening spurs and plateau top of the Comeraghs, suggesting that, in common with the other high mountain groups of northern Munster, these uplands may never have been over-ridden by the inland ice-sheets.

To the east of the Comeragh precipices and the Rathgormuck plateau the land surface descends gradually to a height of 200 feet at the coastal platform of Waterford. This distinctive coastal tract corresponds with the appearance of the Caledonian structures, for here the highly con-torted Ordovician rocks emerge from beneath the overlying Silurian and Devonian strata of the Armorican ridge and vale country.

Apart from the isolated exposure of Old Red Sandstone between Waterford Harbour and Tramore Bay, the south-facing section of the Waterford coast (east of Ballyvoyle Head) is composed entirely of Ordovician rocks. Among the sedimentary rocks, black shales and flagstones predominate over the impure limestone bands, while thick unfossiliferous slate beds and extensive sheets of volcanic rocks also occur. The volcanic series exhibit a bewildering variety of rocks, including tuffs, pillow lavas and keratophyres, all severely intruded by massive sills of dolerite, felsite and andesite. In this 15-mile stretch of coast the geology is very confused by the intrusive rocks and the innumerable volcanic necks, described by Sir Archibald Geikie as '. . . perhaps the most wonderful series of sections of volcanic vents within the British Islands'. Similar in age to the Ordovician volcanic rocks of the county Dublin coast (p. 125) the Waterford volcanics were probably formed in the same fiery episode when, from a chain of submarine vents, lavas were poured out and tuffs and agglomerates ejected. As they fell back on to the sea bed the volcanic materials eventually became interbedded with the normal Ordovician sediments. It has been suggested that a late phase of marine planation (possibly of Plio-Pleistocene age) ultimately bevelled this Ordovician complex which had been folded by Caledonian earth-movements and possibly by later pressures also. Thus the landscape we see today is one of a uniformly flat coastal plateau into which the streams have incised deeply, similar in many respects to the well-known coastal platform of Pembrokeshire which faces it across St George's Channel. The sea cliffs, however, are generally low and unremarkable in stature, but they alternate with pleasant sandy bays which attract a large number of visitors. In fact Tramore, with its enormous beach fronting a lengthy coastal spit, is the principal holiday resort in south-east Ireland. Not far away, beyond the sandstone cliffs of Swine's Head, lie the tiny ports of Dunmore East and Passage East, the colour-washed Georgian houses of the latter grouped attractively around the old market square overlooking Waterford Harbour.

The deep-water inlet known as Waterford Harbour is nothing more than the drowned estuary of the rivers Suir, Nore and Barrow, with the city of Waterford located five miles upstream on the Suir. Like many of the towns of the eastern coast Waterford was a Norse foundation at the lowest crossing point on the river, but only the circular Reginald's Tower survives from that early date. Although the city served as the major entry port for the Anglo-Norman invasion of Ireland the majority of its buildings date from the Georgian and early Victorian period. Bricks were rarely used but the local stone has been almost everywhere buried beneath layers of white- or cream-painted stucco. Behind its lengthy waterfront and bustling quays Waterford still retains the alleys and narrow streets of a bygone age.

Upstream from the city the swinging meanders of the river Suir crisscross the Devonian sandstone rim of hard rocks no less than three times as they leave the limestone-floored downfold below Carrick. Such disregard for structure suggests that the rivers of the region are superimposed from cover rocks which have been destroyed. Nevertheless, the curious course of the Suir above Clonmel, where it swings south to Newcastle, has suggested to several writers that, during an earlier stage of its history when the river flowed on a surface some 400 feet higher than at present, the entire drainage of the upper Suir probably flowed southwards across the eastern end of the Knockmealdowns to join the drainage on the South Ireland Peneplane. Its former course is now marked by the wide open valley of the Ballinamult Gap whose tiny stream was clearly incapable of carving such a major landform; here the Finisk river is an example of a misfit stream (figure 40).

The Hills and Vales of Tipperary

One of the most striking characteristics of the Tipperary scene is the way in which the landforms alternate between the slate and sandstone hill country and the intervening limestone vales, as one progresses from south to north. In contrast to the tight folding of the Armorican south, however, the more gentle flexures of Tipperary have allowed wider vales to develop in the limestone troughs, until the countryside finally opens out into the midland plain.

Significantly, the narrowest limestone vale, known as the Mitchelstown corridor, lies in the south nearest to the Armorican Front, squeezed in between the major upfolds of the Knockmealdowns and the Galty Mountains. The famous Mitchelstown caves, visited by a long list of illustrious travellers in the past 300 years, owe their enormous subterranean passages and galleries to the soluble properties of the Carboniferous Limestone. The older caves are now rarely visited, superseded by the New Caves, discovered in 1833 by quarrymen in their quest for the local mottled limestone, much in demand as 'marble' for decorative building work in nineteenth-century Ireland.

Near to Cahir, at the eastern end of the corridor, a significant geological discovery was made at Ballymacadam. Resting on the limestone surface amidst a small deposit of white pipeclay, still used as the basis of a local pottery industry, there are abundant organic remains including fossil pollen and some 'fossil wood'. Analysis has shown that the flora from which they were derived must have been Tertiary in age (possibly Oligocene), but that it was somewhat different from that of the Lough Neagh Clays and bore closer resemblances to the flora of the Eocene London Clay. The importance of the discovery is linked with its altitude of 250 feet, for the surface of the limestone must have been lowered by denudation to this level by early

Tertiary times before the formation of the clays. Such a proposal means that the earliest drainage of the Tipperary plains, by means of the Suir southwards through the Ballinamult Gap (500 feet), must have occurred at an even earlier date. It also suggests that the marked topographic distinction between the limestone vales on the one hand and the high sandstone mountains of Slievenamon and the Galties on the other must have existed for a considerable period of geological time, probably since Mesozoic times.

Like the plateau of Rathgormuck, to the south of Carrick-on-Suir, the anticlinal arch of Slievenamon has been breached at its eastern end to uncover the Silurian grits and slates. These have been worn down to a plateau some 600 feet in elevation, overlooked in the west by the steep-sided pyramid of Slievenamon itself where the Old Red Sandstone rises to an isolated summit (2,368 feet) (figure 40). The slate and gritstone plateau, drained by the Lingaun river, is bounded by a perimeter of low hills carved from the infacing scarps of Devonian sandstones, both the Old Red and the Kiltorcan sandstones. The Irish type-site of Kiltorcan lies nearby at Ballyhale, where the yellow sandstone quarries yielded the celebrated fossils of the very earliest plant remains and the first fresh-water mollusc.

As one traces the Slievenamon anticline westwards across the Suir valley the axis plunges in a westerly direction and the Devonian rocks disappear beneath the Carboniferous Limestone in the structural depression now followed by the Suir river as it meanders across the limestone plain. Westwards, however, the Devonian rocks reappear as the axis rises once again to form the anticlinal arch of the Galties. This narrow east–west mountain range, one of the few to top the 3,000-foot contour in Ireland, is built largely from Old Red Sandstone for, as we have seen so many times in southern Ireland, once the Devonian rocks are breached the underlying Silurian slates are generally lowered to a considerable extent. This is certainly true to the west of Galtymore (3,018 feet), where the centre of the anticline has been hollowed out to form the Ballylanders basin, before the anticlinal crest rises once more as the hard Old Red Sandstone of the Ballyhoura Mountains (1,703 feet) replaces the less resistant Silurian rocks of Ballylanders. In a sense, therefore, the great upfold of the Galties can be likened to an upturned boat with the keel representing the crest of the anticline. This relatively simple structure, however, has been complicated by denudation along the crest line so, to continue our analogy, the keel of the upturned boat has been broken through, revealing the interior – in this case the Silurian rocks.

From any angle the Galties are seen to rise majestically above the chequerboard of the fields which occupy the surrounding limestone plains. Their slopes sweep up to the summits from the Mitchelstown corridor without the intervention of foothills, the dark heathery moorland contrasting both in colour and in form with the miscellany of greens in the geometric pattern of farmlands below. These smooth southern slopes, however, give way to a steep northern face, pocked with deep corries and their accompanying moraine-impounded lakes. As in the case of the Dingle Mountains, the Knockmealdowns and Comeraghs, the long ridge of the Galties was too high to be over-ridden by the inland ice-sheets and, although it spawned its own little corrie glaciers, its summits are capped by tors built of massive conglomerate. Lying as they did, midway between the ice-sheets of Munster and the Irish midlands, the Galties and their north Munster neighbours were in the most favourable position in Ireland to remain as nunataks throughout the Ice Age. When Arthur Young visited their peat-covered summits in 1777 he repeated his earlier mistake at Killarney by interpreting the corrie lake below Galtymore's conical peak as occupying the crater of an extinct volcano.

The streams which drain the Galties' corries cascade steeply down the northern slopes into the beautiful Glen of Aherlow, once famed for its forest cover but now occupied by rich farmlands similar to those of Mitchelstown. Below the modern coniferous forestry plantations on the Galties' slopes the only trees surviving from the great Wood of Aherlow are found in the hedgerows, creating a scene reminiscent of the rich farmlands which skirt the mountainland of the Welsh border country. The prosperity of Aherlow presages the well-ordered farming landscape of the Golden Vale of Tipperary which lies just to the north, on the other side of the hump-backed ridge of Slievenamuck (1,216 feet). Whilst the Glen of Aherlow corresponds to a downfold in the Carboniferous Limestone the narrow, wooded ridge of Slievenamuck, as we might expect, is built from a linear exposure of Old Red Sandstone grits and conglomerates. But instead of dipping gently northwards to pass beneath the limestone the northern flanks of the sandstone have been thrust from the south until they *overlie* a small outlier of Namurian shales and mudstones which has survived above the limestone. The steep northern slope of Slievenamuck, overlooking Tipperary town, can therefore be regarded as a fault-scarp, whilst the good example of thrusting of older on to newer rocks has been taken by some geologists as a good reason for shifting the Armorican Front of thrusting and severe folding northwards to Tipperary (figure 1).

The Slievenamuck ridge was sufficiently elevated to act as a terminal barrier to the extensive Midlandian ice-sheet, which left its moraine (known as the Tipperary or South Ireland End Moraine) up to a height of 750 feet along the northern slopes of Slievenamuck. Where a gap occurred in this sandstone ridge the former ice limits can be traced as a morainic lobe into the Ballylanders basin. The hummocky kames of this glacial advance can also be seen sweeping across the eastern end of the Glen of Aherlow from Bansha to Caher, thus totally enclosing the narrow vale. It is no surprise to learn, therefore, that a pro-glacial lake was once impounded here between Slievenamuck and the Galties. A series of deltas was formed by meltwaters draining into the former lake, their heights corresponding closely with the elevation of the spillways and subglacial channels cut in solid rock along the northern slopes of the Galties. The deltas and channels now stand high and dry in the farming landscape of the glen for the lake was a transitory phenomenon. Examination has shown, however, that the lake level was lowered in three stages as the Midlandian ice-front melted down and fell back (550 feet; 400 feet; 295 feet).

The glacial sands and gravels in the vicinity of the South Ireland End Moraine have mixed with the calcareous tills to produce fertile, well-drained and easily worked soils near Tipperary town. Thus this broad limestone lowland is known as the Golden Vale, famous for the quality of its farming land rather than its scenery. In addition to the traditional cattle-rearing and dairying there are many acres of barley, wheat and sugar beet, much of which is produced for cattle feeding. The overall impression of the landscape, therefore, is one of highly organized mixed-farming with neat hedges and hedgerow trees surrounding the harlequin patchwork of various field crops.

Away to the east, across the valley of the Suir, the underlying limestone floor suddenly heaves itself above the ubiquitous glacial drifts where a small upfold has created a prominent, isolated knob of rock in the centre of the plain. This is the famous Rock of Cashel, capped by its 'hoary grey ruin', like an Irish Acropolis (plate 34). The clever use of local building stone, the subtle grouping of the chapel and cathedral about the round tower, have given to this ancient seat of Munster's kings an architectural quality rarely equalled in the Celtic world. The aesthetic appeal, coming largely from the sudden vertical intrusion into the horizontal line of the plain, can be compared with that emanating from the natural phenomena of Errigal, Croagh Patrick or Skellig Michael. One final bizarre but amusing legend is worth recording in the context of Cashel rock, for it is reputed to have been dropped there by the Devil who, having bitten a large piece from the ridge of the Devilsbit Mountain twenty miles to the north, spat it out. The gap in the mountain ridge is there for all to see, but the storytellers are not concerned with the processes of glacial breaching in the Irish uplands or bothered that the Devilsbit Mountain is made of Silurian grits whilst the Rock of Cashel is of Carboniferous Limestone.

Kilkenny and the Coalfields

To the east of the broad limestone vales of Tipperary the Slieve Ardagh Hills act as a watershed between the valleys of the Suir and the Nore. We have already seen how these hills represent a synclinal structure of Carboniferous rocks, left upstanding above the plain by virtue of their resistance to denudation during the lengthy erosional processes which led to this inversion of relief. In the elongated basin-shaped upland the steep out-facing scarps represent the outcrop of the Namurian flagstones which overlie the gently folded limestones. The upper part of the 300-foot north-west-facing scarp is built from the Bregaun Flagstones (equivalent to the Millstone Grit) which have been quarried both for export and the home market. They include some 'sand volcanoes', similar to those of western Clare (p. 198) and approximating in age to the Rough Rock of the Pennines. Of much greater importance, however, are the overlying Coal Measures which cover an area of 14 square miles in the centre of the structural basin. Discovered in the eighteenth century these Ammanian coal seams have been worked sporadically ever since, mainly around the tiny village of Coalbrook.

It was an eminent geologist, Charles Lyell, who, having visited the

Great Dismal Swamp of Florida in the nineteenth century, drew a parallel with the conditions there and the palaeo-environment of Coal Measure times. It was, of course, the decaying vegetable matter of these swamp forests which created the coal seams, but we must not assume that the Coal Measures are made up of one vast accumulation of coal. At various times the swamps were inundated by river-borne silts and sands so that the coal seams occur only intermittently amidst great thicknesses of shales, marls and sandstones. Periodically the sea overwhelmed the deltas to form the thin marine bands of fossiliferous shales and limestones. The oscillation of land and sea level in Upper Carboniferous times is reflected in the lithological succession where a rhythmic sequence known as a cyclothem has been recognized. The cyclic sedimentation of limestone (deeper sea), shale (shallower sea), sandstone (deltaic flat) and coal (swamp forest) may be repeated several times, although the cyclothem may be incomplete due to contemporaneous erosion. The causes of cyclic repetitions are not fully understood but the instability probably heralded the onset of the Armorican orogeny.

Beyond Kilkenny town, its attractive buildings sometimes faced with black 'Kilkenny Marble' (in reality a polished, shelly Carboniferous Limestone), the extensive upland of the Castlecomer Plateau forms the divide between the rivers Nore and Barrow. The plateau, covering an area of 150 square miles, is in reality both a structural and a topographical basin (figure 41). Its highest elevations are found on the Namurian grits and flags around the rim which forms a symmetrical out-facing scarp rising some 800 feet above the surrounding limestone lowlands. Like Slieve Ardagh its importance derives from the centrally disposed Coal Measures, the most extensive in Ireland, which here are 700 feet thick and include five workable seams. The seams are not greatly folded or crushed since the Armorican pressures failed to buckle the strata of the coalfields because of the underlying buried block of the stable Leinster Chain. Instead the stresses were taken up by major faulting which criss-crosses the basin.

The best seams (including the well-known Jarrow seam) produce a high-quality anthracite, and were formerly worked by normal shaft mining both in the eastern side of the coalfield near Bilboa and in the centre near Castlecomer. Today the collieries are closed, the conical pit mounds and winding-gear left standing forlornly amidst the farmlands (plate 35), replaced by extensive opencast working in the centre of the basin. Near here the Jarrow seam thickens locally to four feet, in what must have been a Coal Measure ox-bow meander, and it was this site that became famous for its remarkable collection of amphibian fossils (including seven new to science) discovered in the mid-nineteenth

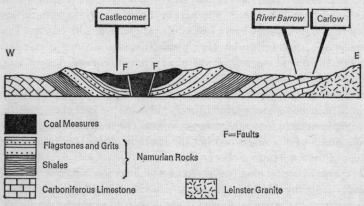

Fig. 41. *The Castlecomer coalfield.*

century. Between some of the coal seams bands of fireclay are found and these have given rise to a ceramic industry at the hamlet of Swan. The fireclays represent the mudflats of the Carboniferous swamp forest and they ultimately became the alkali-deficient 'seat-earths' for the coal seams themselves. Some of the Coal Measure sandstones from Castlecomer have been used as building stones and are especially notable at Kilkenny Cathedral and Jerpoint Abbey. Castlecomer town itself, planned by the colliery landowners, is a pleasant tree-lined market town, quite unlike the towns of the British coalfields. Even the little mining villages, such as Clogh, display a pastoral charm, for many of the miners' cottages are neatly thatched and whitewashed.

One of the earliest directors of the Geological Survey of Ireland, J. B. Jukes, believed that a cover of Coal Measures once blanketed most of the country. In his famous publication of 1862 he suggested that following the uplift of this Carboniferous-mantled surface the major Irish rivers were initiated and that these were responsible for the downwearing of the surface, so creating the present relief of Ireland. In so doing such rivers as the Suir, Nore and Barrow have destroyed most of the valuable Irish Coal Measures and have ultimately become superimposed onto the underlying older rocks.

17. South-East Leinster

This final corner of Ireland is a land of paradox – at once a region whose population is patriotically, culturally and economically quite Irish, but where the landforms, the scenery and some of the architecture are reminiscent time and time again of western Britain, and more especially of Wales. This is not surprising, perhaps, since the Welsh coastline lies but 60 miles away to the east, even though its geology is somewhat different in detail. The structural trends, however, are very similar on both shores of St George's Channel, being dominated by the well-known north-east to south-west alignment of the Caledonian folding. In Ireland the folding has produced a major anticlinorium within the Cambrian and Ordovician rocks of south Leinster and this has been invaded by an enormous granite batholith, the largest in the British Isles. Several periods of uplift have resulted in the unroofing of the granite by denudation and in most parts it forms the high ground of the so-called Leinster Chain of uplands, running from Dublin to Waterford.

The region is large enough to have its own scenic sub-divisions: in the west, county Carlow is a transition zone, straddling the junction of the Carboniferous rocks and the Leinster Granite; in the south, county Wexford, with some of the most fertile farming country in Ireland, has more than 90% of its land improved; in the east, the narrow coastal lowlands of Wicklow are crossed by rivers whose upper reaches drain the famous Glens of Wicklow. But overall it is the highlands of the Leinster Chain which dominate the scenery of south-east Leinster for one is conscious of their presence at almost every turn. From the isolated Brandon Hill (near New Ross) in the far south-west, through the massive Blackstairs and Wicklow Mountains of the centre, to the prominent outlines of the Dublin Mountains in the north-east, the rough moorlands of the Leinster Chain provide a scenic heritage beloved by generations of

Dubliners. The mountains form part of the highland 'rim' of Ireland, broken only in a few places such as Galway Bay, Dublin Bay, the Lagan Valley and Clew Bay. It is, however, noteworthy that the mountains which make up the 'rim' vary both in their elevation and in their degree of dissection. Thus, whilst the peaks of Donegal, Connacht and parts of Munster fail to reach 3,000 feet in height, of greater significance is the remarkable isolation of their summits, with very few areas exhibiting high, unbroken ranges of mountainland such as are found in Wales and Scotland. In the Wicklows, however, the mountains form a true massif where the 1,000-foot contour encloses an area of more than 200 square miles and where no high summits are isolated by extensive plains from their neighbours. In other words this is the part of Ireland most like the Welsh massif, less dissected and fragmented than the ragged landscapes of the Atlantic seaboard, a fact which Professor D. Linton attributed to the more effective denudational qualities of the Atlantic climatic elements. But it is probably true that, because the high Wicklow peaks are grouped together, their 3,000-foot summit does not appear to be as high nor as majestic as the lower but isolated peaks of Errigal, Nephin and Croagh Patrick.

Carlow and the Barrow Valley

From the eastern edge of the steep escarpment, which marks the outcrop of the Namurian gritstone perimeter of the Castlecomer coalfield, a fine prospect of county Carlow is revealed. As the scarp drops away beneath our feet so the road zig-zags down from the Upper Carboniferous rocks onto the Carboniferous Limestone floor which has here been picked out by the river Barrow to form a narrow corridor between the rushy pastures of the Namurian scarp and the relentless granite country of eastern Carlow (figure 41). This narrow limestone lowland, with its pattern of multi-coloured fields reflecting the mixed farming of the drift-filled Barrow valley, has long been an important routeway between the Central Plain of Ireland and the province of Munster. The ancient walled town of Carlow, on the edge of the Pale and at a bridgepoint on the Barrow, mirrors this strategic significance, its ruined Norman castle of light grey limestone built, like those of Ferns and Enniscorthy in nearby Wexford, with a rectangular keep and circular corner towers. Such an architectural style, uncommon in Ireland, reminds us of the Edwardian castles of Wales, and it is no surprise to learn that they were built by such men as William the Marshall of Pembrokeshire after the Anglo-Norman invasions of the twelfth and thirteenth centuries. Carlow's position astride an important geological boundary is reflected partly in the variety of building materials of this neighbourhood. Limestone is used extensively, although local granite often appears in the older buildings. The well-known brownish-grey Carlow flagstones have been freely incorporated both in the buildings and in the paving of villages and towns, having been brought from the Namurian scarp of the nearby coalfield. At the foot of this scarp the ruined Killeshin church utilizes a mixture of granite, flagstones, limestones and sandstones in its fabric, but the most remarkable use of stone, perhaps, is the dolmen at Brownes Hill near Carlow town, for its 100-ton capstone is a gigantic granite erratic block.

Although the river Barrow has kept closely to the limestone outcrop throughout its southerly journey across Kildare and Carlow, at Goresbridge it crosses on to the granite of the Leinster Chain. Its character immediately changes from that of a lazy, meandering river in a broad valley to one of a swift-flowing, steeply embanked river in a gorge-like valley. The 'goodly Barrow' described by Spenser has now left the rich farmlands and water-meadows of Carlow for the narrow, forested valley which carves its way through the granites of Brandon Hill (1,694 feet) and Blackstairs Mountains (2,610 feet). The river is now '... flowing thro' bold shores, in some places trees on the bank half obscure it, in others it opens in large reaches, the effect equally grand and beautiful' (A. Young). One of these open reaches is formed by the natural amphitheatre of the Graiguenamanagh basin whose isolated hill-girt character needs explanation. The pleasant little market town with quaint narrow streets has been built at the junction of the Ordovician slates and shales with the Leinster Granite. Where the granite has baked the shales by metamorphism an 'aureole' of mica schists has been formed and it is these which have succumbed more readily than the surrounding rocks to forces of denudation. The basin is filled with an attractive patchwork quilt of tiny fields, its mixed farming being more typical of the limestone plains of neighbouring Carlow and Tipperary. But its ruined Cistercian abbey is its most famous scenic contribution. Built by William the Marshall in 1204 on a picturesque loop of the Barrow, this splendid ruin is an exact replica of the more famous abbey of Strata Florida in Cardiganshire, South Wales.

Near New Ross the Barrow is joined by the Nore which, having left the limestone plains of Kilkenny, has followed an equally tortuous course through the Ordovician slates and shales around Inistioge. Like the Barrow the Nore has carved a gorge in this structurally discordant reach and Arthur Young has described how the river '. . . deep under the gloom of some fine woods, which hang down the sides of some steep hills . . . with cultivated fields . . . reaching almost the mountain tops: these are large and bold and give in general to the scene features of great magnificence'. It was the very boldness of the hills and the incision of the rivers Nore and Barrow across the Leinster Chain which prompted the geologist J. B. Jukes to write his famous 1862 paper 'On the formation of some river valleys in the south of Ireland'. In his opinion the anomalous drainage pattern, discordant with both the Caledonian and Armorican structural elements, could be explained only in terms of superimposition from cover rocks which have since all but disappeared from southern Ireland. Later authors substituted thick covers of Mesozoic rocks for Jukes's ubiquitous Coal Measure blanket, but we have already seen in the previous chapter (p. 244) how recent discoveries in Tipperary suggest that the present land-surface may not have been very much altered (except by ice) since early Tertiary times. Consequently, present-day opinion is tending to veer away from hypothetical high-level Mesozoic covers and simple concepts of superimposition, for it is now believed that river incision in southern Ireland may reflect the process known as antecedent drainage, whereby river down-cutting keeps pace with the long-term tectonic uplift of a region. Professor G. L. Davies reminds us of the difficulty of allowing the ancient consequent drainage of Ireland to persist through a late-Tertiary karstic phase and points to the work of Farrington on the Shannon as an attractive alternative to the general hypothesis of superimposition (figure 31).

Wexford – the Garden of Ireland

The county of Wexford takes its name from the large coastal lagoon where the river Slaney debouches into St George's Channel. Now known as Wexford Harbour, this was the Weis-fjord of the Norse invaders who were able to find shelter for their war galleys in the shallow bay whose shape and character clearly debar it from classification as a true fjord in the geomorphic sense. Apart from founding the settlement of Wexford, however, the Norse made little lasting impact on the scene and it was left to the Anglo-Norman invaders of the following centuries to turn this stretch of countryside into the so-called 'Normandy of Ireland'. They were responsible for the introduction of feudal land-management into Ireland and one must assume that since Wexford was the site of the first Norman landings the manorial field system was most firmly established here. Although the feudal fields have disappeared it is noteworthy that Wexford remains today the most English-looking rural landscape in Ireland. Typically English hedgerows and gardens, full of shrubs and flowers, surround the neat, thatched or slated cottages. But partly because of its good soils and partly due to the higher sunshine duration which Wexford enjoys the southern coastlands produce extensive crops of cereals, this area boasting the highest proportion of arable land in all Ireland. As if to emphasize the close affinity of these prosperous farmlands to the scenery of those on the similar calcareous glacial drifts of East Anglia, a forlorn but perfect windmill survives on the south coast at Tacumshin.

Wexford possesses the flattest coastline in Ireland because the deep glacial drifts have buried the solid rocks in all but a few important localities. The south coast, for example, has been sculptured by waves into an interesting succession of hard rock headlands alternating with long sweeping stretches of drift-backed shorelines (figure 42). Three important headlands break up the monotony of this low-lying drift coastline. In the west the long bony finger of Hook Head is carved from Carboniferous Limestone, its major claim to fame being the landing of the Earl of Pembroke (Strongbow) in 1170 prior to capturing Waterford '. . . by Hook or by Crook' (since the settlement of Crooke forms the other shore of Waterford Harbour). In the centre Forlorn Point, with its fishing port of Kilmore Quay, overlooks the Lewisian granite-gneiss of the neighbouring Saltee Islands which represent off-shore extensions of this oldest of the Irish Pre-Cambrian rocks. Their southern sea-cliffs and their springy grass hillocks, in summer ablaze with Sea-pink, Sea Campion, and Wild Hyacinth, support an enormous population of sea birds, one of the most important nature reserves in Ireland. The easternmost out-

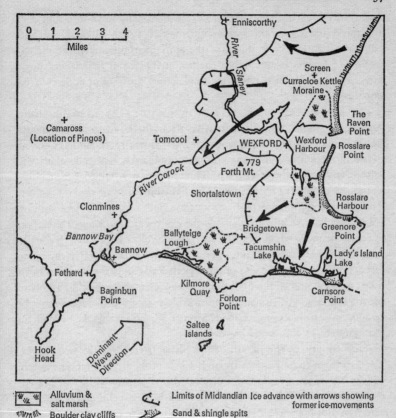

Fig. 42. *South Wexford, showing coastal features and the former ice-limits of the Midlandian (Midland General) Advance (after E. Colhoun and G. F. Mitchell).*

crop of hard rock is that of Carnsore Point, sometimes referred to as the 'cornerstone of Ireland'. This reddish porphyritic granite, of similar age to the Leinster Granite, has intruded the Lewisian gneiss, but neither of these rocks forms prominent sea-cliffs except on the Saltees. Between the three rocky headlands the ubiquitous glacial drifts have supplied abundant material for the waves to fashion into some of the largest coastal spits in Ireland. Longshore drift has extended the spits from east to west, although their gently curving shorelines face the dominant wave-direction (i.e. maximum fetch is from south-south-west between Hook Head and Carnsore Point). The building of the spits has impounded the coastal lagoons of Lady's Island Lake, Tacumshin Lake and Ballyteige Lough where the local drainage has failed to penetrate the lines of dune-covered shingle.

The sand-dunes are quite majestic in this part of Wexford, originally derived, no doubt, from the extensive glacio-fluvial deposits hereabouts (see below). The presence of so much fine-grained sediment has also led to the formation of numerous off-shore sandbanks, especially along the eastern coast of county Wexford. Thus the coast is famed for its shipwrecks, resulting in a string of modern lightships athwart the well-known Tuskar Rock lighthouse built on its tiny knob of granite. The shifting coastal sands were also responsible for destroying the ancient medieval town of Bannow which, except for the church, disappeared gradually beneath the encroaching dunes. To the north of Bannow Bay the name of Clonmines marks the site of an ancient lead- and silver-mining town based on local ores in the underlying Ordovician rocks. Not far away are the majestic tree-girt ruins of Tintern Abbey, founded in 1200 by monks brought over from its more famous Monmouthshire namesake by William the Marshall.

Wexford city, at the mouth of the Slaney river, was the first Anglo-Norman town to be built in Ireland. Little of its original fabric can still be seen for its town walls are incorporated very largely within the present buildings, most of whose stonework is now hidden behind grey stuccoed exteriors. But the ancient street-plan of tortuous streets and narrow alleys remains, hiding behind the dignified Georgian terraces of the quay, much in the manner of Waterford. Wexford Harbour, however, sheltered by the remarkable spits of Raven Point and Rosslare Point (figure 42) is too shallow to be of major commercial use, so that the cross-channel outport of Rosslare has usurped many of the harbour functions of Wexford itself. The city remains, therefore, essentially a cultural and market centre for the prosperous farming of the surrounding countryside. In order to explain one of the reasons for this prosperity one must look in some detail at the glacial history of the region, for much of its arable farming is based on the high quality of the local gravelly loams.

Taken as a whole the soils of Ireland suffer from two great drawbacks, so far as their farming potential is concerned: they are either extremely acid (partly from the non-calcareous bed-rock) or badly waterlogged (from the poor drainage and high rainfall) and usually have a combination of both. In some more favoured parts, however, one or other of these factors is not so marked and Wexford falls into this fortunate category. In addition to its extensive cover of calcareous till Wexford has an overlying shelly deposit of glacio-fluvial origin known as the 'manure gravels' which have been used by farmers to ameliorate the less tractable clay lands. Both these calcareous sediments were formed by the Midlandian ice-sheet which, having originated over central Ireland, moved off-shore and travelled southwards down the centre of the Irish Sea basin in conjunction with the allied Scottish and Welsh ice-sheets. We shall see how this late Pleistocene advance failed to over-ride the Wicklow Mountains, being forced by them to swing off-shore to the south of Dublin whereby the ice was able to incorporate much of the shelly sea bed of the temporarily waterless basin. In county Wexford, however, as the influence of the Wicklows decreased the Midlandian ice-sheet pressed on-shore to deposit its calcareous burden in a narrow coastal zone. Professor G. F. Mitchell believes that the ice crossed the Slaney river between Wexford city and Enniscorthy but failed to overcome the small eminence of Cambrian quartzites which make up Forth Mountain, overlooking the city. He has traced the ice-limits around the flanks of Forth Mountain from Tomcool south and east through Shortalstown to Carnsore Point (figure 42). At Tomcool the end-moraine divides the newer Midlandian unweathered shelly till on the eastern side from an older deeply weathered quartzite- and granite-littered till (probably Munsterian) on the western side. Associated with the latter till are landforms which are very rare in Ireland. Some ten miles west of Wexford city, at Camaross, a cluster of over 20 fossil pingos has been noted by Professor Mitchell. 'Pingo' is an Eskimo term, since modern pingos are found only in regions of permafrost, such as Greenland or Alaska. It is really a hydrolaccolith, with the up-doming of frozen ground being caused by water (instead of the analagous igneous rock in the true laccolith) which is trapped between layers of permafrost. This Pleistocene frost-mound would ultimately degrade and slump as the central ice core (the water body having frozen) melted out in post-glacial times. The resultant landform is a circular rampart, several feet across, sometimes filled by a pond. At Shortalstown the

Midlandian ice-sheet has ploughed up and contorted an organic layer of marine clays and sands which overlies the lower, deeply weathered grey till. Professor Mitchell and Dr Colhoun have been able to demonstrate that the fossil plants, pollen and shelly fauna of this horizon represent a true interglacial deposit, dating from the lengthy period of climatic amelioration which separated the Munsterian and Midlandian ice-advances. As such this clay may well be the only example of a Last Inter-glacial (English: Ipswichian) deposit so far discovered in Ireland, for all the other Irish interglacial sites are much older, belonging to the so-called Gort Interglacial (English: Hoxnian) (see p. 135). The fresh, hummocky, kame-kettle topography associated with the Midlandian ice-advance is well seen in the so-called Screen Hills or Curracloe kettle moraine to the east of the Wexford–Enniscorthy road, where solid rock is completely buried on the coast until Cahore Point is reached.

The old Anglo-Norman town of Enniscorthy, on the Slaney river, was long the centre of an important iron industry based on local ores and the extensive Coillaughtin oakwoods. Flourishing for almost 250 years, the Enniscorthy ironworks finally closed when the woods were exhausted in the early nineteenth century. Nevertheless the tradition of ironworking has been carried on in the region and Wexford today pro-duces most of Ireland's agricultural machinery.

The Wicklow Coastlands and Vales

To the north of Cahore Point, itself formed from Cambrian grits and shales, the Ordovician rocks reappear at the coast, having played no part in the coastal scenery since we left the Fethard headlands in southern Wexford. Apart from the quartzite outcrop of Forth Mountain (noted above) the Cambrian rocks contribute little to the Wexford landscape owing to their thick drift cover. As we approach the border of county Wicklow, however, scattered hills of igneous rock, incorporated in the Ordovician sedimentaries, break up the monotony of the coastal lowlands and the drabness of the seemingly endless boulder clay sea-cliffs of Wexford.

Nevertheless, to the north of Wicklow Head Cambrian rocks reappear along the coastal margin but, apart from the massive greywackes which form the sea-cliffs of Bray Head, the Cambrian slates have been eroded to form a low coastal plain, five miles wide and twenty miles long. Much of the actual shoreline is formed from a long dune-covered shingle ridge, followed by the railway from Greystones to Wicklow. Owing to severe coastal erosion in these parts the rail tracks have had to be relaid farther inland on more than one occasion. The planned Victorian elegance of Greystones, on its rocky promontory of Cambrian grits, contrasts with the more brash resort of Bray which has become a sort of Southend for the city dwellers of the neighbouring capital.

From Wicklow Head southwards the parallel ridges of Caledonian-folded Ordovician rocks run obliquely off-shore as the coastline crosses the structural trend at an acute angle. Thus the harder grits and volcanics frequently stand out as headlands whilst the slates and limestones have been eroded into bays now filled with glacial deposits and sand-dunes, such as those near Arklow. It is possible to distinguish two parallel bands of igneous rocks: the first appears near Wicklow town and can be traced as a series of lenses running south-westwards to form the peak of Croaghaun Kinsella (1,993 feet) before dying away in northern Wexford; the second is far more extensive for it starts with the dolerites of Arklow Head and extends as a series of andesites, trachytes, microgranites and even picrites and gabbros for some 80 miles south-westwards through central Wexford to the Waterford coast (see chapter sixteen). Apart from their effect on the topography of eastern Wicklow the real significance of the Ordovician and Caledonian igneous rocks in this region is their contribution to the formation of Ireland's most important metalliferous belt.

There are several ore-bodies associated with the emplacement of the massive Leinster Granite of Caledonian age and many of these lie in the Ordovician tract of country in county Wicklow. The most important are the complex copper and iron ores of Avoca and the lead and zinc ores of the Wicklow Glens. At Avoca the lodes extend conformably along the strike for over three miles and have been worked almost continuously since the eighteenth century. More than 3 million tons of copper ore have been processed since 1840 but the proved reserves are in excess of 22 million tons. Iron pyrites are an important subsidiary product of the Avoca mines. The effect of the workings on the landscape of the beautiful Vale of Avoca is a melancholy one, for the abandoned shafts and engine houses dot the hillsides. But it is the increasing size of the remorseless spoil-heaps which is proving the biggest eyesore in this beautiful valley, for the woodlands have to be cleared to accommodate the waste. The soft, pastoral scenery of this extremely attractive part of Wicklow is due in part to the splendid deciduous woodlands which infill the narrow valley and mantle the steep hillsides of the igneous rock outcrops. Where a subsidiary stream joins the Avoca valley at the Lion Bridge we are at the famous 'Meeting of the Waters', perpetuated in the poetry of Thomas Moore, and one is forced to wonder whether the sylvan charm will be destroyed more quickly by the rampant tourist clutter or by the large fertilizer industrial complex which is creeping insidiously up the Avoca river from Arklow. Between the two, at Woodenbridge, the Avoca is joined by the Aughrim, known as the 'Gold Mines River', for here on the wooded slopes of Croaghaun Kinsella the discovery of a gold nugget in 1796 led to a gold rush, repeated in 1935. The mother-lode has never been discovered but the great concentration of gold near the junction of the Cambrian and Ordovician rocks in Wicklow reminds us that the 'gold belt' of mid-Wales appears in a similar geological setting just across the Irish Sea. The widespread discovery of golden objects belonging to the Irish Bronze Age has led many people to believe that all the gold came from Wicklow, although modern analysis suggests that the gold of the ancient ornaments was not native.

If we follow the Avonmore river upstream past Rathdrum to Laragh, where the valley is cut deeply into the rolling dome-like hills, the scenery becomes reminiscent of an Exmoor landscape, with the thickly wooded combes of the lower, steeper slopes giving way upwards to the farmlands on the higher, gentler slopes of the hill-tops. From here it is but a short step through the oak and pine woods to one of the most-frequented tourist attractions of Ireland, the remarkable valley of Glendalough. Although we are now approaching the Leinster Chain, Glendalough is so different from the other Wicklow glens that it will be singled out at this point.

The deep glacial trough of Glendalough, set amidst attractive wooded mountains, was once the mecca for countless numbers of students from all over the western world who came to study at St Kevin's great monastic settlement during the several centuries of Ireland's 'golden age', prior to the Anglo-Norman invasions. A mixture of schists, slates and greenish calcareous sandstones was used to construct most of the now ruined buildings although some of the carved crosses are of Leinster Granite whilst the cathedral window is of imported oolitic limestone. Most of the ruins, described by Sir Walter Scott as '. . . the inexpressibly singular scene of Irish antiquities', are located on the flat top of an ancient delta now raised above the marshy fields at the confluence of two streams (figure 43). The delta and accompanying terrace (followed by the road along the north side of the valley) indicate that the former lake level in Glendalough was once 20 feet higher, impounded, perhaps, behind a terminal moraine now breached by the river. The name Glendalough (Irish = Gleann de locha) means valley of the two lakes, for post-glacial detritus, carried down by the Pollanass stream from a hanging valley, has formed a fan across the whole width of the glen, thus creating two lakes (figure 43). The small modern delta, at the head of the Upper Lake, is growing rapidly, possibly due to erosion by the river of old spoil-heaps from the mines farther upstream. Together with Glendasan and Glenmalure, Glendalough once formed the major source of Ireland's lead and zinc. The ores were formed in rectilinear fissure-veins, up to two miles long, both in the Leinster Granite and in its mica–schist aureole. Mining was mainly in the form of adits driven back into the steep valley walls but all activity has now ceased, leaving the abandoned workings scarring the hillsides. Nevertheless, it has been claimed by some that the ruined chimney and buildings of the Ballycorus lead works in county Dublin, using Wicklow lead for more than a century, add a certain charm to the neighbouring Dublin Mountains.

The Leinster Chain

The existence of the great plutonic mass of the Leinster Granite has influenced the scenery of south-east Leinster more than any other geological factor. Where the granite has been 'unroofed' it generally forms a rolling landscape of broad domed uplands (except in Carlow) which contrast in form with the more sharply peaked hills and the deeply incised valleys developed on the surrounding schists of the metamorphic aureole. This topographic contrast is often emphasized by the vegetation of the Wicklow Mountains for here the upper valleys (on the granite) are wide shallow corridors, dappled with mossy and rushy floors but completely treeless. As the valleys cross the boundary of the granite intrusion, however, the rivers often plunge into richly wooded but narrow glens which ultimately open out onto the coastlands or onto the Central Plain of

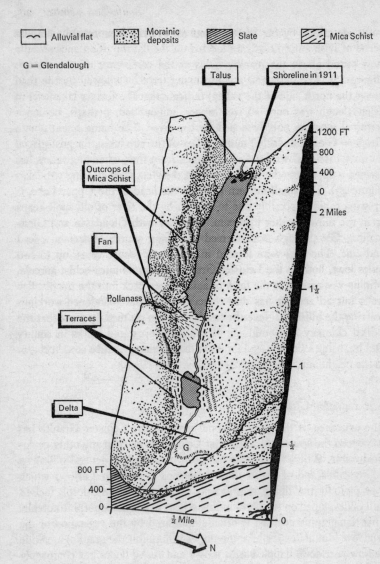

Legend:
- 〰 Alluvial flat
- ⣿ Morainic deposits
- ▨ Slate
- ▨ Mica Schist

G = Glendalough

Labels: Talus · Shoreline in 1911 · Outcrops of Mica Schist · Fan · Pollanass · Terraces · Delta · G

Elevations: 1200 FT · 800 · 400 · 0 · 2 Miles · 1½ · 1 · ½ · 800 FT · 400 · 0 · ½ Mile · 0

N

Fig. 43. *The Glendalough valley (after F. M. Synge)*.

Ireland. In the north-west the headwaters of the Liffey, the King's River and the Toor Brook exhibit this gradual constriction of the valley width as it leaves the granite, whilst in the north-east Glencree shows similar characteristics. But it is the narrow, steep-sided Glens of Wicklow farther south that have attracted most attention because of their picturesque beauty, and it is noteworthy that the waterfalls at the heads of the best-known (Glendalough, Glendasan and Glenmacnass) all occur approximately at the schist–granite junctions. Most people regard the incision of these ravines in the schists as evidence of the greater resistance of the granite to erosion and, since the surrounding Ordovician slates have generally been worn down to form lower foothills, the picture has grown up of the Leinster Chain being composed of a resistant granite mass surrounded by more easily eroded rocks. Dr Farrington has demonstrated, however, that, since Glenmalure has the same trough-form as its neighbours but fails to cross the schist–granite contact, then some process other than the reputed weakness of the schist is responsible for the form of the Wicklow Glens. He concludes, therefore, that on the whole the schist is more resistant to erosion than the granite and that ultimately the granite will be worn down to form a depression surrounded by a rim of mountains built of schist. The form of the Wicklow Glens, as one suspects, is very largely due to the work of glacial erosion but, paradoxically, it is the hardness of the schists which has led to them being trenched by the glaciers to a far greater depth than the granite. This is because the corries of the granite moorlands discharged their glaciers down existing pre-glacial valleys, causing great ice congestion where the valleys narrowed on crossing the schist exposure. As in the case of the Donegal fjords the constriction caused by the hard rocks led to glacial overdeepening.

The suggestion that in the course of time the Leinster Granite will be reduced to a depression or lowland flanked by schistose hills is partly borne out by the presence of the extensive Tullow lowland in county Carlow, where the granite rarely rises above 600 feet O.D. (figure 45). The Tullow region, with its well-ordered farmlands, rarely gives the impression that it is floored with reputedly intractable granite, except for the occasional granite-built church, but this is probably due to a veneer of calcareous drift carried by ice-sheets onto the granite from the limestones of the Barrow valley. Professor G. L. Davies expresses the view that the southern end of the Leinster Granite appears to have been unroofed by denudation much earlier than the granite farther north. Pebbles of Leinster Granite incorporated in the Old Red Sandstone of Kilkenny and Waterford lend support to such a hypothesis and a Devonian unroofing gives ample time for the reduction of granite in the area of the Tullow lowland. Surprisingly, however, in the Wicklows themselves fragments of the batholith's schist roof have survived to form the summit of Lugna-

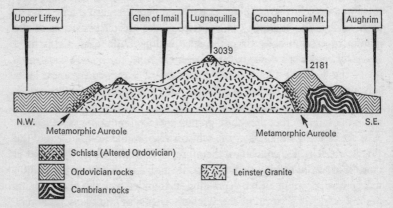

N.W.   Metamorphic Aureole   Metamorphic Aureole   S.E.

Schists (Altered Ordovician)

Ordovician rocks   Leinster Granite

Cambrian rocks

Fig. 44. *The Leinster Chain, showing the metamorphic aureole of the Leinster Granite and the remnants of the 'roof'.*

quillia (3,039 feet), Leinster's highest mountain, some 300 million years after the initial unroofing (figure 44). This has led to the conclusion that the Leinster Chain must have experienced a relatively recent period of uplift which has speeded up the process of unroofing by sub-aerial agencies after a lengthy geological time-span of slow denudation.

Between the isolated granite peaks of the Blackstairs Mountains and the more compact massif of the Wicklows the Tullow lowland is bounded on the east by a narrow line of uplands which corresponds everywhere with the outcrop of the schists (figure 45). Where the tributaries of the Slaney river cut through this belt of hard rocks they have carved deep gorges, more than two miles long, at Tinahely and Shillelagh. The hillsides in this attractive region are still sufficiently 'adorned with goodly woods' to enable us to reconstruct visions of the magnificent oakwoods which once allowed medieval Shillelagh to send timbers to roof not only

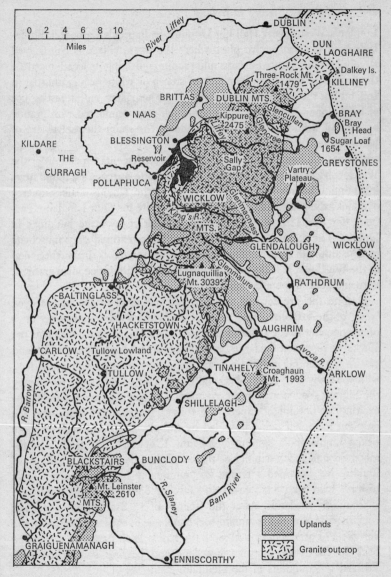

Fig. 45. *The Leinster Chain, showing relationship of the uplands to the outcrop of the Leinster Granite (after G. L. Davies and A. Farrington).*

London's Westminster Hall but Dublin's St Patrick's Cathedral. Shillelagh itself is an attractive place where the estate village is constructed
largely from a mixture of schist and granite, reflecting its location astride
the geological boundary. The lack of stucco or whitewash is unusual in
Ireland but the simple slate-roofed cottages here show an interesting use
of local stone – the schist and granite walls are reinforced with granite
lintels and window frames, whilst indoors the stairs themselves are of
bare granite slabs (plate 36).

Granite has been used extensively in the settlements which border the
Wicklow Mountains for Leinster's major granite quarries are found here,
including Glencree and Glencullen, while the famous Dalkey quarry
overlooks the coast. The latter supplied granite for Dun Laoghaire harbour, for the Thames Embankment and for many large buildings in
Dublin. The stone itself is generally a coarse-textured grey muscovite
granite although three varieties have been recognized at the northern end
of the Wicklows. It is the most alkaline of the British Caledonian granites,
with an excess of potash over soda.

Despite the presence of the scattered remnants of the undestroyed
'roof' of the batholith, the scenery of the Wicklow Mountains owes most
of its character to the Leinster Granite (figure 45). We have seen how the
Wicklows represent the largest area of continuous high ground in Ireland
and in the central massif there are only three passes below 2,000 feet,
with the Sally Gap (1,634 feet) and the Wicklow Gap (1,567 feet) being
the highest road passes in the country. The summits are generally un-
exciting, as one might expect in a rolling, peat-covered landscape, the
only rugged relief being provided by the glacial corries, such as those
below Lugnaquillia summit and below Kippure (2,475 feet). The re-
moteness and inaccessibility of these uplands, despite the proximity of
Dublin, has provided a refuge for 'mountainy men' throughout Irish
history, men who were ready to make predatory excursions into the
surrounding lowlands. After the 'rising' of 1798 a military road was
constructed along the mountain backbone, one of the last chapters in the
chronicle of attempts to overcome the native Irish partisans, stretching
back to the Anglo-Norman invasions and bearing comparison with
Edward I's conquests of the mountain fastnesses of Snowdonia, North
Wales. The military road enables one to drive to the attractive corries of
Lough Bray beneath the cliffs of Kippure and to see something of the

source of the former glaciers which helped to carve out the glacial troughs of the famous glens on the lower slopes.

As one might expect, the Wicklow Mountains were large enough to create their own local ice-caps during the Pleistocene, but careful research by Dr A. Farrington has shown that the relationship of the successive Wicklow glacial advances to those of the major Irish ice-sheets was not a simple one. We have seen that in Ireland, generally, there were two

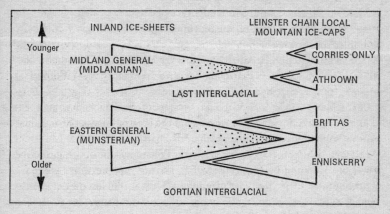

Fig. 46. *The relations of the invading inland ice-sheets and the local mountain ice-caps.*

main periods of glaciation following the Gort Interglacial (Hoxnian), known as the Eastern General (now Munsterian) and the Midland General (now Midlandian) respectively. In the region of the Wicklow Mountains, however, no less than six glacial phases have been recognized, demonstrating that the local ice-caps alternated with the invading Munsterian and Midlandian ice-sheets (figure 46). The stratigraphy of the drifts suggests that the local ice-cap did not advance simultaneously with the Munsterian and Midlandian climaxes but that the Wicklow glaciers expanded both before and after the major glacial maximum on both occasions. The Enniskerry drift is poorly exposed but is composed of a purely granitic boulder clay overlain by the Munsterian far-travelled drifts. At Brittas, on the north-western slopes of the mountains, another local glacial deposit (dominated by granite gravels) is seen to overlie the

Munsterian till and is itself buried beneath the hummocky limestone-bearing moraines of the Midlandian ice-sheet. Nevertheless, there is evidence in the higher valleys of the Wicklows to show that as the Midlandian ice-sheet was advancing from the north-west the local Athdown glaciation occupied the valleys, leaving extensive valley moraines and widespread outwash gravels in such places as the Vartry Plateau and the upper valley of the King's river (figure 45). This is the period when the Wicklow Glens received their final phase of overdeepening and their major morainic additions. Finally, as the Midlandian ice-sheets waned and virtually disappeared a short deterioration of climate saw the Wicklow corries reoccupied by tiny glaciers some 10,500 years ago, leaving behind small block moraines. Similar small moraines have been revealed from beneath the waters of Lough Nahanagan, a corrie lake near the Wicklow Gap, drained as part of a hydro-electric scheme.

At a lower level, on the western slopes of the Wicklows, an earlier water-supply and hydro-electric scheme has created the vast artificial lake of the Pollaphuca Reservoir which adds charm to the wooded hillslopes behind Blessington. The power station at Pollaphuca, however, has robbed the river Liffey of its former waterfall, leaving the streamless gorge as a sad reminder of its bygone splendours. This is the second occasion on which a lake has occupied the upper valley of the Liffey, for it has been shown that during the maximum of the Midlandian glaciation an enormous pro-glacial water body was impounded at a level of 930 feet against the western flanks of the Wicklows. The Midlandian terminal moraine near Blessington has become one of the most important Irish sources of sand and gravel, reducing the pleasant countryside to a scene reminiscent of a lunar landscape (plate 37). To the east of this moraine a magnificent series of varved clays, representing annual additions of mud to the lake-floor, was once revealed at the site of the pro-glacial 'Lake Blessington', where formerly the river Liffey could be seen cutting some remarkable meanders in the old lake bed. All are now drowned beneath the modern lake waters which burrow deeply into the inner recesses of the mountains.

If we journey eastwards from the lake, up through the remnants of an extensive Scots Pine forest, to the shoulders of Kippure (2,475 feet) with its prominent T.V. transmitter, it is possible to look back down the valley of the upper Liffey as it descends in a north-westerly direction. In pre-glacial times the Liffey must have continued northwards past Brittas, for an abandoned 'wind-gap' notches the horizon near Saggart Hill. At a later date, a tributary of the parallel stream of the King's river is thought to have captured the headstream of the Liffey, leaving the Brittas col deserted and leading all the drainage north-westwards through another col near Blessington. The final phase in the complex history of the Liffey drainage pattern appears to have been associated with the Ice Age for the Blessington col became blocked by drift, causing the drainage to be deflected southwards around the Midlandian ice-front to join the Slaney. Only in post-glacial times has the Liffey swung northwards again, flowing circuitously around the massive morainic accumulations near Naas before descending to the Dublin lowlands (figure 45).

On the eastern slopes of the Wicklows marginal drainage of Pleistocene age has also left its mark in the landscape. Here the meltwater torrents, flowing from the snow-capped summits, were likewise restrained by the edges of the lowland ice-sheets, causing them to cut spectacular rocky gorges in the margins of the Vartry Plateau as they sought to escape south-wards. The thickly forested ravines of the Devil's Glen, east of Round-wood, and the Glen of the Downs, above Greystones, are excellent examples of such glacial meltwater channels. The Vartry Plateau, now partly occupied by another reservoir for Dublin's water supply, has been described as an uplifted peneplain, carved in Tertiary times by the Vartry river in the less resistant Cambrian slates of this region. The plateau later acted as a receptacle for the morainic and glacio-fluvial debris of the Wicklow glaciers and its land-use pattern of heather–moor and sporadic farmland reflects the complex soil differences of this zone. The best farms occupy the floodplain of the Vartry river or the better-drained morainic mounds although cultivated land extends up to the upper limits of the peneplain at 1,000 feet in places. Above this farming land gorse and bracken predominate on the hillslopes although forestry plantations are creeping insidiously onto the Vartry Plateau from the Wicklow mountain-sides.

The northern end of the Vartry Plateau is dominated by the startlingly white cone of the Great Sugar Loaf (1,654 feet), a prominent landmark because of its sharp-peaked character rather than its absolute elevation (plate 38). Carved from a steeply dipping layer of massive Cambrian quartzite, this shapely peak and its less eminent neighbour the Little Sugar Loaf (1,123 feet) are more reminiscent of the Atlantic seaboard than of Ireland's eastern coastlands. But they will serve us well as a final viewpoint at the end of our tour of Irish scenery. The vista from the Sugar Loaf embraces most of the elements which we have described at length in the previous chapters. To the south, the scattered moorlands and farmlands, dotted with the typical slated or thatched white cottages; to the west, the schist and granite hills of the Wicklows crowned with deep peat-bogs and seamed with glacial troughs and corries. Eastwards the wooded gorge of the Glen of the Downs leads down to the coastal marshes and the precise Victorian villas of Greystones. Away to the north-west the rocky peaks of the Dublin Mountains are the final sentinels of the Leinster Chain beyond which lie the vast expanses of the drift-covered plains of the Irish midlands. Nearer at hand, amidst the beautiful oakwoods of Glencree, threaded by the highest waterfall in Ireland, there stands the mansion of Powerscourt with one of the finest formal gardens in Europe, epitomizing all that was best of Georgian elegance in Ireland. And finally our parting view, that to the north, for here, above the graceful sweep of Killiney Bay and the granite eminence of Dalkey Hill, we can glimpse the impact of modern urbanization on the Irish scene as the Dublin suburbs of pebble-dash and T.V. aerials sprawl into the age-old mountains.

Glossary of some Technical Terms

Note: A large number of the technical terms used refer to the 'periods' of geological time, e.g. Carboniferous. These are best understood by referring to figure 2.

Agglomerate: A rock of volcanic origin, composed of irregular blocks of various sizes, comprising solidified lava and fragments of the rocks through which the volcano has broken. Met with mostly in the pipes or necks of volcanoes.

Amphibolite: A metamorphic rock composed mainly of amphiboles, e.g. hornblende schist.

Anticline: An arch or upfold in the rocks, generally produced by the bending upwards of the beds under lateral pressure. Anticlines are structurally weak, and the upper part rapidly becomes worn away (see figure 40).

Anticlinorium: A system of folds which produce a complex arch or upfold.

Arenaceous: A term used to describe the sandstone group of sedimentary rocks.

Arête: A sharp mountain ridge, usually produced by the headward recession of two opposing corrie walls.

Argillaceous: A term used to describe the fine-grained group of sedimentary rocks, e.g. clays, shales, mudstones and marls.

Armorican: (see Hercynian).

Augite: A common mineral found in basic volcanic and plutonic rocks.

Aureole: The zone around an igneous mass within which metamorphic changes, mainly thermal effects, have been produced (see figure 44).

Barytes: A common mineral; barium sulphate ($BaSO_4$).

Basalt: A dark lava of basic composition, containing the minerals feldspar and augite, and sometimes olivine. Mostly crystalline but of fine grain.

Base-level: The lowest level to which a river system can lower a land-surface, usually the sea level of the time, but occasionally and temporarily a hard band of resistant rock.

Beds, bedding: Sedimentary rocks tend to break along planes parallel to that of their deposition, and thus form the beds or bedding of the rock. See also Joints.

Biotite: One of the mica group of minerals.

Boss: A large mass of igneous rock, intruded into and disrupting other rocks. Generally nearly circular in plan; often of coarse-grained rock such as granite.

Boulder clay: A deposit laid down under an ice-sheet. Frequently a mixture of clay with boulders, but may contain very little of either, and therefore preferably called till. May be tens of feet thick and spread over hundreds of square miles.

Breccia: A composite rock consisting of angular fragments of older rocks cemented together with various minerals such as lime.

Caldera: A very large crater formed by the coalescence of smaller craters or by the collapse of surface rocks into a large underground magma chamber.

Caledonian: The mountain-building period which dates from Middle Ordovician to Middle Devonian times.

Cauldron subsidence: A process whereby a cylindrical portion of the crust is thought to founder, allowing magma to well up around the sides to fill the resulting cavity (see figure 14). This is often associated with the structure known as a Ring-complex where magma infills the ring cavity as a dyke or pours out at the surface as a lava (see figure 15). Cone sheets are also ring structures.

Chert: A hard, flint-like rock, originally a sand, in which the sand grains have been cemented together by the deposition of silica from solution.

Cirque (Corrie or Cwm): An amphitheatre or armchair-shaped hollow, usually excavated on a mountainside; the slopes are precipitous, the floor nearly level. Due to glacial erosion. In Britain they are commonest on north-east facing slopes, especially in Wales and the Lake District.

Cleavage: A term used to describe a plane of breakage in a mineral and also the re-orientation of mineral particles within a rock due to intense deformation. It represents a partial recrystallization of a fine-grained rock without necessarily destroying the traces of bedding (e.g. slate), although further pressure may produce a foliated rock (e.g. schist) with all traces of bedding destroyed.

Clitters: A residue of rock waste, frequently including some large blocks, on a gentle slope after denudation has reduced the original surface. Common on the granite moors of Devon and Cornwall, frequently near tors.

Cone sheets: (see Cauldron subsidence).

Confluence: Junction of two streams, or of a tributary to a main river.

Conglomerate: a rock which consists of an aggregate of pebbles or boulders in a matrix of finer material: a pudding stone. Formed by rapid streams and powerful currents.

Consequent (or dip) streams: A stream which flows in the direction of the dip of the rocks on which it was initiated; the direction of the stream is a 'consequence' of the original inclination of the surface.

Corrie: (see Cirque).

Cuesta: A landform consisting of an inclined surface parallel to the dip of the bedding planes (dip slope), and an escarpment steeply inclined in the opposite direction.

Cyclothem: A rhythmic sequence of sedimentation, repeated several times, which illustrates a slow spasmodic subsidence. Often found in the Coal Measures.

Denudation: The combined action of weathering, erosion and transportation, to reduce or dissect the existing land-surface.

Dip: The tilt of a bed of rock along its direction of steepest inclination, measured in degrees from the horizontal; also the direction of this dip.

Dip slope: The long, gentle slope of an escarpment, following in general the dip of the rocks.

Dolerite: A dark-coloured igneous rock, basic in composition and resembling a basalt, but composed of rather larger crystals. Generally occurs in a small intrusion such as a dyke or a sill, where it crystallized from a molten state.

Doline: A small closed depression in limestone country, formed by the roof collapse of an underground cavity.

Dolomite: Sometimes known as Magnesian Limestone; composed of the double carbonate of magnesium and calcium: $(Ca, Mg)CO_3$.

Drumlin: A low whale-backed ridge of glacial boulder clay, thought to have been fashioned beneath an ice-sheet. The long axis of the ridge is generally parallel with the direction of former ice-movement.

Dyke: A sheet-like body of igneous rocks which cuts discordantly through the structures of the bed rock. They occasionally occur as dyke swarms.

Erratic: A rock which has been transported by ice a great distance from its source, and has been left stranded when the ice melted.

Escarpment: A unit of scarp and dip slope. Cuesta is an alternative name.

Esker: A long, sinuous ridge of sand and gravel, formed by a sub-glacial stream, but after melting of the ice-sheet left unrelated to the surrounding topography.

Eucrite: A type of gabbro.

Fault: A dislocation in the rocks, where one side has moved relatively to the other. Many fault planes are nearly vertical, others inclined at small angles. Faults have been produced by a variety of causes: some are due to intense lateral pressure, others to differential uplift or to tension (see figure 10).

Fault-scarp: A scarp arising along the line of a fault, caused by the differing resistance of the rocks on either side of the fault, the more resistant rock being eroded more slowly, and hence standing up.

Feldspar: A mineral group comprising various complex silicates of alumina and potassium, sodium and/or calcium. Abundant constituent of most igneous rocks.

Felsite: A fine-grained intrusive igneous rock.

Ferruginous: Containing iron in some form, usually as an oxide; descriptive of rock.

Flagstone: A rock that splits readily into slabs suitable for flagging (as in pavement construction).

Flint: A siliceous rock, grey or black; composed of very minutely crystalline silica. Occurs mostly as nodules in the Chalk.

Freestone: A quarrying term to describe a stone easily quarried and which can be dressed or cut in any direction into blocks of any size.

Gabbro: A coarsely crystalline rock of plutonic origin (see Plutonic). It differs from granite insofar as its constituent minerals are more basic than acid.

Gneiss: A metamorphic rock, crystalline and coarse-grained, somewhat resembling a granite but showing a more or less banded arrangement of its constituents.

Granite: An igneous rock, composed of crystals of quartz, feldspar and mica, of coarse grain. Results from the slow cooling of a large molten mass.

Granophyre: An igneous rock of medium-sized grain in which the quartz and feldspar crystals are intergrown.

Greywacke: A type of sandstone in which the angular particles are poorly sorted.

Grike: A cleft in the bare limestone pavements of karst scenery.

Grit: A rock much like a sandstone, composed mainly of grains of quartz. The grains are either more angular or larger than those in sandstone.

Gypsum: A mineral, commonly formed under arid climatic conditions with strong evaporation. Also known as alabaster ($CaSO_4 2H_2O$).

Head: A mixture of clayey material and frost-shattered stones, formed in an earlier periglacial climate, and which under these conditions moved down quite gentle slopes, thereby causing some rounding off of slopes and cliffs.

Hercynian: The mountain-building period of Permian times.

Horst: An upthrown block of rocks between two parallel faults.

Igneous rock: A rock formed by the consolidation of molten material. The characters of the rock depend mainly on the composition of this material, and on the conditions under which it cooled. Material ejected as lava generally cools quickly, material intruded in small masses less quickly, and material in large masses very slowly: the quickly cooled material may be glassy or very finely crystalline (e.g. basalt); the slowly cooled material is coarsely crystalline (e.g. granite). Thus most igneous rocks are crystalline.

Incised meander: Part of an old meander which has become deepened by river incision due to uplift of the land or a fall of sea level.

Inlier: A mass of older stratified rocks showing through the surrounding newer strata.

Ironstone: A sedimentary rock characterized by its ferrous carbonate content. Common in the Lower Jurassic and Coal Measures.

Isostatic: Describing the concept of Isostasy, whereby the earth's crust is maintained in a state of near equilibrium. The weight of a continental ice-sheet may cause a temporary downsag, but this will recover when the ice melts. Such vertical crustal movements will result in regional tilting of raised shorelines formed in glacial or early post-glacial times.

Joints: Divisional planes which traverse rocks perpendicular to the plane of their deposition, cutting them in different but regular directions and allowing their separation into blocks. They are due to movements which have affected the rocks, and to shrinkage or contraction on consolidation. See also Beds, bedding.

Kame: A steep-sided ridge or conical hill of stratified sands and gravels formed by meltwaters marginal to a down-wasting ice-sheet.

Karst: Irregular limestone topography characterized by underground drainage; a streamless, fretted surface of bare rock which is honeycombed with tunnels; created by solution of the limestone by ground water.

Kettle-hole: A depression in glacial drift, often enclosed, made by the melting out of a formerly buried mass of ice and the subsequent collapse of the overlying drift.

Keratophyre: A fine-grained volcanic rock rich in sodium, potassium and feldspar.

Laterite: A residual deposit formed by deep chemical weathering under tropical conditions. It is composed of hydrated iron oxide although aluminous laterites and ferruginous bauxites are common (see p. 36).

Limestone: A sedimentary rock consisting mainly or almost entirely of calcium or magnesium carbonate, derived from the shells and fragments of former organisms, and deposited originally in water.

Lopolith: A saucer-shaped igneous intrusion which is concave upwards, its shape often controlled by the existing folding (see figure 16).

Magma: A molten fluid generated at great depth below the surface and thought to be the source of igneous rocks.

Marl: A calcareous clay. Marlstone.

Meltwater channel: A deep gorge or valley, now frequently streamless, which was carved out by glacial meltwaters below or marginal to an ice-sheet. (See Overflow channel.)

Metamorphic rock: A rock which may originally have been either igneous (metadolerite) or sedimentary (metasediment) but which has undergone such changes since the time of its formation that its character has been considerably altered: in extreme cases it may be difficult to ascertain its original nature. Heat and pressure are the chief agencies of metamorphism. The commonest rocks of this class are gneiss and schist. Metamorphosed.

Mica: A mineral group comprising complex silicates of iron, magnesium, alumina and alkalis. Several different types can be recognized. Mica can be split into exceedingly thin, flexible plates. An important constituent of granite and other igneous rocks, and of some sedimentary rocks.

Mineral: A constituent of a rock, either an element or a compound of definite chemical composition. Mineral as used here has not the same meaning as the 'Mineral Kingdom', which principally includes rocks. Rocks are aggregates of one or more minerals and usually occur in large masses or extend over wide areas.

Montmorillonite: A clay mineral, similar to Fuller's Earth, remarkable for its capacity to take up or lose water.

Moraine: An accumulation of gravel and blocky material deposited at the margins of an ice-body.

Muscovite: One of the mica group of minerals.

Nappe: An overturned fold in which the axial plane is horizontal.

Nunatak: An area of high land or an isolated peak which protrudes above an ice-sheet; it often exhibits widespread periglacial phenomena.

Olivine: An olive-green mineral common in basic igneous rocks.

Oolite, oolitic: A limestone of marine origin, composed of more or less spherical grains, each with concentric layers of calcium carbonate, usually formed in shallow water; probably the grains are of chemical origin.

Outcrop: The area where a particular rock appears on the surface. The rock may continue beyond its outcrop, concealed at depth beneath the surface.

Outlier: A mass of newer stratified rocks detached from their main outcrop by subsequent denudation and separated from it by an area of older rocks.

Overflow channel (or Spillway): A deep gorge or valley carved out by the overflow of a pro-glacial lake at the margin of an ice-sheet. These channels are generally streamless.

Peneplain: A land-surface of low-relief, worn down by prolonged weathering and river erosion. An extensive peneplain needs for its formation a considerable time during which sea level remains practically stationary. (See also Peneplane, p. 233).

Peridotite: A class of ultrabasic rocks consisting mainly of olivine.

Periglacial: A term used to describe those of the cold climate processes and landforms which result from frost action. This term covers frost-shattering, frost-heaving and solifluxion. It is usually most severe at ice-sheet margins.

Permafrost: Permanently frozen ground.

Pillow lava: Lava extruded under water to form pillow-like masses.

Plagioclase: A series of sodium/calcium feldspars.

Platform: An erosion surface produced by marine agencies. Also Peneplane.

Plutonic: A term referring to rocks of igneous origin formed at great depth, by consolidation from magma; the rocks are generally coarse-grained.

Polje: A large depression in a limestone karst region, probably formed by sub-aerial agencies.

Pro-glacial lake: A lake impounded by ice-sheets against an area of higher unglaciated ground. The lake disappears either by overflow through the lowest gap in the watershed or by melting of the ice-sheet.

Pyroclastic: A term used to describe rocks formed from the fragmental ejected products of a volcanic explosion.

Quartz: One of the commonest minerals in the earth's crust. Composed of silica (oxide of silicon). A constituent of granite and sandstones. Crystals are hexagonal prisms terminated by pyramids.

Quartzite: A highly siliceous sandstone. A rock composed mainly of quartz. Breaks with rather a smooth fracture. Usually very tough.

Rejuvenated stream: A stream which has received added power to cut vertically into its bed, usually owing to the uplift of the land.

Regolith: The loose, incoherent mantle of rock fragments, soil, etc. which rests upon the solid bedrock.

Residual: An isolated hill which stands above the surrounding country because it has resisted erosion to a greater degree. It is the remnant of an older surface which has been almost totally destroyed by the action of streams or marine agencies. Such a hill rising from a sub-aerial peneplain is known as a monadnock.

Ria: A long, narrow inlet of the sea, caused by subsidence of the land or rise in the sea level. It is generally regarded as a drowned river valley which deepens gradually seawards.

Rift valley: A valley which has been formed by the sinking of land between two roughly parallel normal faults.

Ring-complex: (see Cauldron subsidence).

Roche moutonnée: An asymetrical rock outcrop owing its distinctive shape to glacial smoothing. The smoother slopes face the direction of former ice advance whilst the steeper ice-plucked slope is on the lee side.

Rock: The geologist does not necessarily confine this term to hard, resistant rocks; he may refer to anything from poorly consolidated sands, gravels and clays to massive, hard stone beds as 'rock'.

Sandstone: A sedimentary rock composed mainly of sand grains, chiefly grains of quartz, cemented together by some material such as calcium carbonate.

Schist: A metamorphosed rock characterized by the parallel alignment of its constituent minerals.

Serpentine: A clearly banded rock of varying colours produced by metamorphic hydrothermal action on ultrabasic rocks.

Sill: An intrusive sheet of igneous rock, more or less following the bedding of the rocks it invades, but occasionally changing its position among the beds (e.g. the Fair Head Sill).

Silt: A very fine-grained sediment with particles between $\frac{1}{16}$ and $\frac{1}{256}$ mm. in diameter.

Slate: An argillaceous or clay rock which breaks along planes (cleavage) produced by pressure. The cleavage planes may coincide with the original bedding or may obliterate it almost completely. Metamorphic.

Solifluxion: The process of slow flowage of the surface rock waste downslope when saturated with ground water, frequently under a periglacial climate.

Spit: A point of land, generally composed of sand or shingle, which projects from the shore of a water body, frequently at a river mouth or bay entrance.

Stack: A mass or pinnacle of rock left isolated by retreat of coastal cliffs.

Stratum, plural strata: A layer or layers of rock, usually referring to bedded sedimentary rocks.

Strike: The direction of a horizontal line on a dipping stratum; level-course of the miner. The strike is at right angles to the dip. The strike direction is generally the trend of the outcrop of the stratum.

Subsequent (or Strike) stream: A stream tributary to a consequent stream or originally so, following the strike direction. Generally along the outcrop of a less resistant bed.

Superimposed drainage: A drainage system that has been established on underlying rocks, independently of their structure, from a cover rock which may have disappeared entirely.

Swallet: A funnel-shaped depression in the surface of a pervious rock (usually limestone) linking with a subterranean stream passage developed by solution.

Syncline: A trough-like fold in the rocks generally resulting from lateral pressure. In some cases (e.g. south-west Ireland, figure 34) the surface reflects the structure, but owing to the wearing of the rocks on either side many synclines ultimately stand out as hills or mountains (e.g. figure 41).

Tectonic: An adjective used to describe structural phenomena as opposed to stratigraphic phenomena.

Till: (see Boulder clay.)

Tombolo: A sand or shingle bar connecting an island with the mainland.

Tor: A castle-like rock pile which crowns summits of certain well-jointed rock landscapes, or occasionally occurs at the crest of valley slopes; frequently found in granite but can occur in other well-jointed rocks; its origin is uncertain, with deep-surface weathering, normal sub-aerial weathering or periglacial processes all being suggested by various writers.

Transgression: An advance of the sea over a former land area, due to a change of relative land and sea level.

Tufa: Material deposited by calcareous springs; usually white or yellowish. Sometimes soft, sometimes hard enough to form a building stone.

Tuff: A rock composed of the fine-grain material ('ash') ejected by volcanoes. Often arranged in beds or layers which have accumulated under water.

Unconformity: The relation of rocks in which a sedimentary rock or group of rocks rests on a worn surface of other rocks (sedimentary, igneous or metamorphic). Frequently the plane of unconformity separates rocks of vastly different ages and the rocks beneath the unconformity are of more complex structure than those above (see figures 7 and 40). Unconformably, unconformable.

Watershed: The divide between the drainage basins of two rivers (in English usage). American usage defines watershed as the whole of a river catchment basin.

Water table: The level below which the rocks are saturated by groundwater. If the water table intersects the surface a spring will result.

Weathering: The general result of atmospheric action on the exposed parts of rocks. Rain, frost, wind and changes of temperatures tend generally to help in the disintegration of the surface rocks. This is known as mechanical weathering. Chemical weathering is a sub-surface rotting, generally by groundwater.

On Maps and Books

Despite the numerous sketch maps of geology and landforms included in the present volume the reader may wish to seek further information from published geological and topographical maps.

Amongst the publications of the Republic of Ireland (produced by the Ordnance Survey, Dublin) are two useful series of topographical maps at the scale of 1 inch and ½ inch to the mile respectively. Both series show contours but only four sheets of the current 1-inch series are coloured – covering Dublin, Cork, Killarney and the Wicklows, as special Tourist District maps. Nevertheless, all the Irish Ordnance Survey maps at the ½-inch scale are coloured and these cover the whole of the Republic of Ireland.

The most up-to-date geological map of Ireland is published by the Geological Survey of Ireland at a scale of 1 inch to 12 miles. Subsequent slight amendments to this 1962 edition can be abstracted from a smaller-scale geological map of the British Isles published by the Institute of Geological Sciences, London (the current, fifth edition was published in 1969 at the scale of 1:1,584,000).

Northern Ireland publishes its own topographical and geological maps through the offices of the Ordnance Survey and the Geological Survey in Belfast. Of the topographical maps both the 1-inch (third series) and ½-inch (second series) sheets are coloured and contoured. Only a few sheets of the 1-inch geological series (solid and drift editions) have so far been published by the Geological Survey of Northern Ireland, covering North Antrim, Dungannon, Belfast and Carrickfergus.

Readers wishing to become more familiar with the general principles of geology or with more specific aspects of the geology of Ireland may find the following books of interest:

H. H. Read and Janet Watson, *Beginning Geology*, Macmillan, 1971.
A. Holmes, *Elements of Physical Geology*, Nelson, 1969.
J. K. Charlesworth, *The Geology of Ireland: An Introduction*, Oliver & Boyd, 1966.

J. K. Charlesworth, *The Historical Geology of Ireland*, Oliver & Boyd, 1963.

Some interesting aerial views of Irish scenery are contained in:

D. D. C. Pochin Mould, *Ireland from the Air*, David & Charles, 1973.

Index

More about Penguins and Pelicans

Penguinews, which appears every month, contains details of all the new books issued by Penguins as they are published. From time to time it is supplemented by *Penguins in Print*, which is a complete list of all titles available. (There are some five thousand of these.)

A specimen copy of *Penguinews* will be sent to you free on request. For a year's issues (including the complete lists) please send 50p if you live in the British Isles, or 75p if you live elsewhere. Just write to Dept EP, Penguin Books Ltd, Harmondsworth, Middlesex, enclosing a cheque or postal order, and your name will be added to the mailing list.

In the U.S.A.: For a complete list of books available from Penguin in the United States write to Dept CS, Penguin Books Inc., 7110 Ambassador Road, Baltimore, Maryland 21207.

In Canada: For a complete list of books available from Penguin in Canada write to Penguin Books Canada Ltd, 41 Steelcase Road West, Markham, Ontario.

Geology and Scenery in England and Wales

A. E. Trueman

New edition completely revised by J. B. Whittow and J. R. Hardy

Why the country looks as it does interests the motorist and the holiday-maker as much as geological structure concerns the student. This Pelican explains very simply why some districts are wooded and others cultivated; why rivers often take the long way round to the sea; why hills may be jagged or rounded; why features like Wenlock Edge or the Chilterns run from north-east to south-west, and a thousand other cases where the landscape of England and Wales is decided by the underlying strata, or the superficial deposits.

Geology and its allied sciences have not stood still since Sir Arthur Trueman's study established itself as a little classic many years ago. For this new edition the whole book has been thoroughly revised, to take account of recent findings, by Drs Whittow and Hardy of Reading University. They have completely rewritten several sections, replaced the drawings with appropriate photographs and added many new text figures and maps.

Much, however, of Sir Arthur's delightful text still stands in a book which makes an anti-clockwise tour of the country from the Cotswold Stone Belt and the Chalklands to the granite cliffs and moors of Cornwall and Devon, describing each region in fascinating detail.